Facing up to Jesus in the Gospels and Paul

Gerald O'Collins, SJ

Connor Court Publishing

Copyright © Gerald O'Collins SJ

ALL RIGHTS RESERVED. This book contains material protected under International and Federal Copyright Laws and Treaties. Any unauthorised reprint or use of this material is prohibited. No part of this book may be reproduced or transmitted in any form or by any means, electronic or mechanical, including photocopying, recording, or by any information storage and retrieval system without express written permission from the publisher.

ISBN: 9781922815835

Cover design by Maria Giordano

Front Cover Photo: The Homeless Christ, Wikipedia Commons.

Printed in Australia

Contents

Preface	v
Acknowledgments	xiii

Gospels

1) Being made "perfect" according to Matthew 5 and 19	3
2) "Many are called but few are chosen" (Matthew 22:14)	11
3) The Child as the Face of God (Mark 9:36–37)	25
4) The Fearful Silence of Three Women (Mark 16:1–8)	37
5) The Virginal Conception and its Meanings	49
6) Believing as Verbal in John's Gospel	63
7) Translating John 21:14 and its Significance	83

Pauline Correspondence

8) Does Philippians 2:6–11 present Christ as a Superior Angel?	101
9) Revisiting Angel Christology in Philippians 2:6–11	113
10) Collaborators of the Apostles and Vatican Reform	125
11) The Faith of Jesus (Hebrews 12:2a)	145
12) Translating Hebrews	159

Jesus Questions

13) Jesus between Poetry and Philosophy	181
14) The Freedom of Easter Faith	195
15) A Cumulative Approach to the Resurrection	215
Epilogue	241
Index of Names	243
Biblical Index	249

Preface

With God any time is the right time. Confessed as God's "unrepeatable and unimprovable revealer," Jesus challenges us all the time to attend closely to what he does, what he teaches, and what he has become through birth, life, crucifixion, resurrection, and sending of the Holy Spirit.

Can we find and promote deep significance in his being conceived through the power of the Holy Spirit? How do we expound and negotiate his call to a life of perfection? Did his words about "few being chosen" indicate a well-populated hell? What does Paul's language intend about the crucified Christ "being highly exalted" (Phil 2:9)? Can we elucidate the facts and forces involved in accepting Jesus' resurrection?

We open with seven chapters prompted by the Gospels. Chapter 1 examines an issue from Matthew. Usually translated "perfect," *teleios* appears in Matthew's Gospel—twice in an exhortation (in the Sermon on the Mount, 5:48) to imitate our heavenly Father's boundless love, and once in an invitation to a rich young man (19:21) to divest himself of his great wealth and join the disciples in following Jesus. What are the grounds and difficulties for Christians who embrace this *imitatio Dei* and *imitatio Christi*?

The second chapter takes up a warning that closes Matthew's version of the great banquet ("many are called but few are chosen," Matt 22:1–14). Does this indicate that the population of hell exceeds, even far exceeds, that of heaven? Matthew sets out an allegorizing account of a royal banquet to come at the end. The second set of guests stand for members of the Church, warned in serious, apocalyptic terms to produce good works, which are worthy of their calling and which will be recognized in the final judgment. Taken with similar passages in Matthew, the warning of Jesus about the king's banquet invites an appropriate response. It does not offer information, still less precise information, about the final state of all Christians and other human beings.

Joel Marcus in his outstanding commentary on Mark offers numerous illuminating comments on what he calls "the parable of the child" (Mark 9:36–37). This parable, like others, makes Jesus vividly present and so reveals God. Chapter 3 shows how Marcus could have recognized more clearly the call to recognize in vulnerable, little children the disclosed presence of God who has sent his Son into the world. The face of even insignificant children—or perhaps especially of insignificant children?—brings us the face of God. The mystery of God is reflected in the mystery of the child.

Chapter 4 aims at reinstating an older interpretation (offered, e.g., by R. H. Lightfoot) of the astonishment, fear, and silent flight with which three women initially responded to the message they heard from the angel in Jesus' open and empty tomb. It was an appropriate reaction to the revelation of the resurrection. The chapter rejects the theory of an unexpected failure on the part of female disciples. Throughout Mark's Gospel they have proved exemplary in their following of Jesus, right through to being present at his crucifixion. Mary Magdalene and her two companions remained temporarily silent until they could deliver their message to the appropriate persons, Peter and his companions.

Chapter 5 ("The Virginal Conception and its Meanings") takes up Jeffrey Archer's *the Gospel according to Judas*. Judas dismisses the virginal conception of Jesus as no more than another example of "Greek myths that tell of gods in heaven who produce offspring following a union with women of this earth." To attribute such a view to a first-century Jew like Judas seems strange, since the earliest evidence shows Jewish critics of the Christian movement rejecting the virginal conception as a case of illegitimacy—a very different explanation. Such Greek myths do not in any case provide plausible sources for the two accounts of the virginal conception (Matt 1:18–25; Luke 1:26–38). Yet such historical debate is insufficient. One should illustrate the religious significance and theological importance of the virginal conception within the whole story of Jesus: for instance, the role of his conception in revealing the Trinity at work for human salvation.

Chapter 6 investigates why in John's Gospel the verb *pisteuein* (to believe) occurs nearly one hundred times whereas the corresponding noun *pistis* (faith) never appears. Those who comment on this feature of John are often content to contrast briefly the action-oriented nature of the verb *pisteuein* with the disposition or even possession suggested by the noun *pistis*. More remains to be said. What do experts in Greek syntax observe about the different force of nouns and verbs? Why does John employ such nouns as "life," "glory," "light," and "love (*agapē*)" and not simply the corresponding verbs? These nouns point to the unconditional, absolute Life, Glory, Light, and Love which the incarnate Son of God displays and in which believers can participate. For John, Christ should be called abounding Life but not abounding Faith. Believing is the appropriate, ongoing relationship of disciples to Christ himself, not a divine attribute of his in which they can share.

Chapter 7 examines two verbs in John 21:14, which are, from the viewpoint of syntax, in the passive voice. Do we face here a divine passive—the action of God in raising and revealing the dead Jesus, even if this action is not explicitly stated as such? Or is this passive voice to be understood as a case of middle voice? Jesus inasmuch as he is divine performs the action (resurrection) and "receives" the results of his action, the new risen life in which he appears. By ignoring the possibilities of middle voice, some translations miss the significance of ending John's Gospel by proclaiming the active involvement of Jesus (as divine) in his own resurrection from the dead and final appearance to the disciples.

With Chapter 8 we move to Pauline correspondence, with "Pauline" in a traditional sense including the Letter to the Hebrews. Paul Holloway, in the light of Jewish apocalypticism, has detected an angel Christology in a hymnic passage of Paul's Philippians (2:6–11). At the end of the last century, James Dunn had read there an Adam Christology, a view accepted now, at least in part, by some scholars. The new thesis of an angelic Christ proposes that he changed himself into human form, and was highly elevated after his crucifixion to bear the divine Name and share the divine throne. But we do not find in the passage itself the language of angels and thrones which this thesis requires. Paul has not developed elsewhere any Angel Christology that would support Holloway's proposal. Philippians 2:10–11 applies to Christ the classic language of Second Isaiah about the adoration of the one, true God, and not the language of some principal angel.

Chapter 9 continues the debate with Holloway, in the light of the reply he published in the *Expository Times* for April 2022: "Ideology and Exegesis: A Response to Gerald O'Collins." My response to Holloway is published here for the first time.

Chapter 10 takes up Massimo Faggioli's search for early traditions that could be retrieved and supply a theological, Christ-centered vision for reforming the Vatican Curia, the present collaborators of the Bishop of Rome. The New Testament yields scarce information about Peter's "co-workers." The seven certainly authentic letters of Paul, however, show such apostolic collaborators functioning with Paul on mission, and doing so in a variety of ways that prefigure the tasks of the modern Curia. The diocese of Rome is founded on the martyrdom of Peter *and Paul*. The Christian men and women who collaborated with Paul provide, not so much markers for administrative changes, but rather an inspiring vision for a biblically based, Christ-oriented reform of the Vatican Curia.

Chapter 11 shows how a large majority of English *translators* of Hebrews 12:2a have introduced "our" when they identify the subject of "faith" mentioned in the Greek text. *Commentators* on Hebrews have, however, overwhelmingly understood the faith in question to be the faith exercised by Jesus himself and, only secondarily, our faith in him. Many contemporary translators have simply followed their predecessors rather than consulted the commentators.

Chapter 12 examines four passages in Hebrews to illustrate further questions facing translators of that important text on Christ and his priesthood. In the twentieth century translations of the Bible into English proliferated and the flood continues. To exemplify issues that translators meet, this article takes up four passages from the Letter to the Hebrews, comparing and contrasting three classical translations (by Tyndale, Douay and the King James Version) and three modern versions (the Revised English Bible, the New Revised Standard Version and the Revised New Jerusalem Bible). Defects show up (e.g., a tendency to wordiness that borders on paraphrase) along with masterly translations, such as the Revised English Bible's rendering of Hebrews 12:2a, "our eyes fixed on Jesus, the pioneer and perfector of faith."

With Chapter 13 we move to the third part of this book and two major questions about Jesus. First, may we compare him with philosophers and/or poets? Do they help us to understand better the language of his preaching?

Chapter 14 enters the long-standing debate about the appearances of the risen Christ and the discovery of his empty tomb. Some critics dismiss the appearances as hallucinations and/or the merely subjective experiences of those who have been bereaved. But a reasonable case can be made for the historical reliability of the appearances and that discovery. Nevertheless, believing in the living Christ is not simply the conclusion of a rational argument. It remains the freedom of a faith that enters into a loving commitment to Jesus our risen Redeemer.

When considering the resurrection of Jesus Christ, Thomas Aquinas proposed a "cumulative" approach.[1] As Chapter 15 explains, "cumulative" expresses the tasks that face those who explore faith in Jesus risen from the dead. They deal with issues of at least three major kinds: philosophical; biblical/historical; and theological/spiritual. These areas overlap, notably over the nature of God and what is involved in acknowledging God's action in raising Jesus from the dead. This chapter engages in a mapping operation, and details major philosophical, historical/biblical, and theological issues to be faced.

The epilogue will draw together the fifteen chapters around the figure of Jesus Christ, recalled, glorified, and praised by all the 27 books of the New Testament.

This book is dedicated to Guy Bennett-Hunter and his colleagues who publish *The Expository Times*. My warm thanks go out to them and others who in various ways helped towards producing this collection: Alexei Bodrov, Brendan Byrne, Brian Davies, Hans-

---

[1] *Summa theologiae*, Ia.q.55.6 ad 1; see also *Summa contra gentiles*, III.ch. 38.

Georg Gadamer, Robin Gill, Niels Gregersen, Paul Hoy, Dorothy Lee, Patrick McMurray, Declan Marmion, Terrence Merrigan, Philip Moller, Antonio Spadaro, Brendan Walsh, Jared Wicks, Ronald Witherup, the staff at the Dalton McCaughey Library (Melbourne), and audiences who heard as lectures a few of these chapters.

My special thanks go to Manfred Cain for checking so carefully the proofs. My special thanks go also to Michael Gilchrist for his patient and professional preparation of the book's layout.

Gerald O'Collins, SJ, AC
Jesuit Theological College, Parkville, Australia.

Acknowledgements

While recognizing that some texts which fed into this book have been altered and extended, I wish to thank the journals in which they originally appeared:

Chapter 1 ("Being made perfect (*teleios*) according to Matthew 5 and 19," *Theology*, 2021); chapter 2 ("'Many are called but few are chosen,' (Matthew 22:14)," *Expository Times*, 2021); chapter 3 ("The Child as the Face of God," *Irish Theological Quarterly*, 2023); chapter 4 ("The Fearful Silence of Three Women (Mark 16:1–8)," *New Blackfriars*, 2021); chapter 5 ("The Virginal Conception and its Meanings," *New Blackfriars*, 2008); chapter 6 ("Believing as Verbal in John's Gospel," *Expository Times*, 2023); chapter 7 ("Translating John 21:14 and its Significance," *Expository Times*, 2021); chapter 8 ("Does Philippians 2:6–11 present Christ as a Superior Angel?," *Expository Times*, 2022); chapter 10 ("Collaborators of the Apostles and Vatican Reform," *Irish Theological Quarterly*, 2017); chapter 11 ("The Faith of Jesus," *Expository Times*, 2023); and chapter 13 ("Jesus between Poetry and Philosophy," *New Blackfriars*, 1976).

Chapters 9 and 12 have not been previously published anywhere.

For permission to republish the chapters (1, 2, 3, 6, 7, 8, 10, 11) that began as articles in the *Theology*, *Expository Times*, and the *Irish Theological Quarterly*, I also want also to thank Sage Publications. For chapters 4, 5, and 13, I thank John Wiley & Sons for articles that appeared in *New Blackfriars*.

For two chapters previously published as chapters in books, I express my thanks to St Andrew's Biblical Theological Institute, Moscow (for chapter 14, "The Freedom of Easter Faith") and Peeters Publishers, Leuven (for chapter 15, "A Cumulative Approach to the Resurrection").

My gratitude also goes out to Manfred Cain for his unfailing help, as well as to Regis College (University of Toronto) for the permission to reproduce the Homeless Jesus by Timothy Schmalz.

G. O'C.

The Four Gospels

1

BEING MADE PERFECT (*TELEIOS*)

ACCORDING TO MATTHEW 5 AND 19

Usually translated "perfect," *teleios* appears in Matthew's Gospel—twice in an exhortation in the Sermon on the Mount to imitate our heavenly Father's boundless love (*imitatio Dei*), and once in an invitation to a rich young man to divest himself of his great wealth and join the disciples in following Jesus (*imitatio Christi*). This article explores the grounds and difficulties for Christians who wish to embrace this *imitatio Dei* and *imitatio Christi*.

Mark Laynesmith has already tackled issues raised by the use of *teleios* (usually translated "perfect") in the Gospel of Matthew.[1] However, there is more to discuss. Unlike the other three canonical gospels, Matthew uses on two occasions the adjective *teleios* to describe the ideal attitude and behavior of Christians as being complete and boundless in love.[2] First, in the Sermon on the Mount delivered to his disciples (Matt 5:1–2), Jesus concludes an exhortation to practise an unbounded love also directed towards one's

---

[1] M. Laynesmith, "Difficult Texts: Matthew 5:48—are Christians to be 'perfect'?," *Theology* 124 (2021), 117–19.
[2] See Walter Baur, Frederick William Danker, William F. Arndt, and F. Wilbur Gingrich, "*Teleios*," *A Greek-English Lexicon of the New Testament and Other Early Christian Literature*, 3rd edn (Chicago: University of Chicago Press, 2000), 995–96; Gerhard Dellling, "*Teleios*," *The Theological Dictionary of the New Testament* (Grand Rapids: Eerdmans, 1972), vol. 8, 67–78.

enemies: 'Be *perfect*, therefore, as your [plural] heavenly Father is *perfect*' (Matt 5:48). Second, when a rich, young man who has kept the commandments including the general precept of "loving your neighbor as yourself [singular]," asks, "what do I still lack?," Jesus puts to him a demanding invitation: "if you wish to be *perfect*, go sell your possessions, and give the money to the poor, and you will have treasure in heaven; then, come, follow me" (Matt 19:18–21).

Here I have cited the 1989 NRSV, which in all three occurrences in Matthew translates *teleios* as "perfect." It lines up with other versions that follow William Tyndale (d. 1536) in choosing "perfect" for Matthew 5:48 (twice) and 19:21: Douai (NT, 1582), King James Bible (1611), RSV (1946), JB (1966), NAB (1970), NIV (1973), and the ESV (2001). Tyndale himself had fallen into line with the Vulgate, which in both Matthew 5 and 19 rendered *teleios* as *perfectus*.

So far I have found only one major English translation that broke with this tradition: the NEB (NT, 1961). It translated Matthew 5:48 as "there must be no limit to your goodness, as your heavenly Father's goodness knows no bounds." and Matthew 19:21 as "if you wish to go the whole way." A revision of the NEB, the REB of 1989, keeps its translation of the first passage (unlimited or boundless goodness), but reverts to the traditional rendering by rendering the second passage as "if you wish to be perfect." Have the NEB and the REB, in the case of Matthew 5:48, gone beyond what the texts *say* to what they understand them to *mean*? In any case what does *teleios* convey in these two Matthean passages?

The Sermon on the Mount

The first occurrences of *teleios* come in a section of the Sermon on the Mount that elaborates "the better righteousness" (Matt 5:20). Redefining the neighbors whom we should love to include our enemies, Christ states: "Be perfect, therefore, as your heavenly Father is perfect" (Matt 5:48). This call to love one's enemy sharply contrasts with the contemporary teaching from the Dead Sea Scrolls, where "the sons of light" are to "hate" all "the sons of darkness" (1QS 1.10–11). Being "perfect in all that has been revealed of the law" (1QS 8.1–2) or "walking in the way of perfection" (CD 2.15; 1QS 8.18, 21; 1QSa 1.28) does not require loving one's enemies and praying for them. A number of observations can help us grasp the meaning of *teleios* in Matthew.

First, like other scholars, W. D. Davies and Dale C. Allison suggest that Matthew has changed an original *oiktirmōn* (merciful) (Luke 6:36) to *teleios* (perfect), as well as introducing "heavenly" to describe "your Father."[3] Pharisees and, even more, the community of the Dead Sea Scrolls, had highlighted the call to holiness (Lev 11:44, 45; 19:2; 20:7), and understood it to entail separation from all things unclean. Jesus himself seems to have elevated merciful love above holiness (e.g., Matt 12:7) or at least to have redefined the practice of holiness as the exercise of such merciful love.

Second, "nowhere in the OT or in the Dead Sea Scrolls is God called *tāmim* or *teleios*."[4] Nevertheless, the people of God are summoned to "remain completely loyal (*teleios* LXX) to the Lord your God" (Deut 18:13). They are to be "holy (*hagios* LXX), for I the Lord your God am holy" (Lev 19:2). They are to embrace holiness because God chose them and delivered them from captivity: "I am the Lord who brought you up from Egypt, to be your God" (Lev 11:45). At least explicitly, as we shall see below, the motivation proposed for unlimited love in the Sermon on the Mount differs.

---

[3] W. D. Davies and D. C. Allison, *Matthew*, vol. 1 (London: T. & T. Clark, 1988), 563.
[4] Ibid. In the NT only Matt 5:48 names God as "*teleios*."

Third, "Matthew assumes but never says that Jesus is perfect,"[5] unlike Hebrews 5:9 which speaks of Jesus "being made perfect (*teleiōtheis*)" (see Heb 2:10). At the start, Matthew presents Jesus as "God with us," the one "who will save his people from their sins" (Matt 1:21, 23). After overcoming the temptations of the devil (Matt 4:1–11), Jesus enunciated the nine beatitudes, self-descriptions that sum up the perfection of his life (Matt 5:3–12). But the issue of Jesus being himself perfect belongs rather to his meeting with the rich young man (see below).

Fourth, "the motivation for being perfect in love is grounded in the Father's perfect love, in his giving without measure."[6] Ulrich Luz speaks of a correspondence between an extreme demand (made on human beings) and the extreme love exercised by God: "the extreme demand to love one's enemy corresponds to God's extreme love towards sinners and outcasts."[7] This extreme love makes God *the* role model displaying unlimited goodness.

Fifth, Matthew emphasizes "God's deeds, not his nature. God gives good gifts to the just and to the unjust, and this from love of both."[8] In the words of the Sermon on the Mount, "your heavenly Father makes his sun rise on the evil and on the good and sends rain on the righteous and on the unrighteous" (Matt 5:45, NRSV). This is to draw conclusions about the character of God from the benevolent, creative and re-creative divine power, which is disclosed in the natural world and showers gifts even upon sinners. Such knowledge of God's disinterested love, derived from the *creatio continua*, underpins an *imitatio Dei*, and is available to everybody. The *imitatio Christi*, which will emerge in the second passage we consider (Matt

---

[5] Davies and Allison, *Matthew*, vol. 1, 563.
[6] Ibid.
[7] Ulrich Luz, *Matthew*, vol. 1 (Augsburg: Fortress, 1989), 287.
[8] Davies and Allison, *Matthew*, vol. 1, 563.

19:18–21), obviously implies some knowledge of Christ.

Unlike Matthew 5:45, the OT *imitatio Dei* was based on the exodus from Egypt and the Sinai covenant (Lev 19:2). Yet any distinction between knowledge of God through events of (religious) history and through events of nature should not be pushed too far. The supreme religious events of Christ's crucifixion and resurrection were accompanied in Matthew's story by natural phenomena. Darkness over the whole land and an earthquake (Matt 27:45; 51–54) accompanied the crucifixion; a "great earthquake" accompanied the resurrection (Matt 28:2).

Moreover, the passage in the Sermon on the Mount inculcating love for one's enemies, while calling on its hearers to be "perfect as your heavenly Father is perfect," opens with the voice of Christ speaking with divine authority: "I say to you" (Matt 5:44). It is obedience to him as loving, sovereign Lord that is at stake; in the words of Davies and Allison, this is "the overriding factor."[9] Imitating God in his perfect love means accepting the supreme authority of Jesus and imitating his love. Introducing the prayer of forgiveness from the passion story of Luke 23:34, Irenaeus expounds in terms of Christ the call to be perfect in love: "the Word of God who said to us, 'Love your enemies and pray for those that hate you,' himself did the very same thing upon the cross" (*Adversus haereses* 3.18.5).

Sixth, both occurrences of "perfect" in Matthew follow lists of specific commandments (5:21–48 and 19:16–21).[10] In both cases, being perfect presupposes and goes beyond observing the basic commandments that are expected to guide and govern human behavior.

The (explicit) *imitatio Dei* in the first occurrence of *teleios* ap-

---

[9] Ibid., 565.
[10] Ibid., 563.

peals to the disciples of Jesus in general. In the case of the second occurrence, a specific appeal is made to a particular individual, a rich young man who is not a disciple but comes to consult Jesus; in this case, as we shall see, an *Imitatio Christi* is implied.

The Call to a Rich Young Man

Matthew reworks Mark 10:17–31, changing, for instance, the rich man into a rich, young man and adding the idea of perfection. The young man professes to have fully observed the commandments, including the broad injunction about "loving one's neighbor as yourself" associated with the decalogue. He has taken a quantitative approach in keeping the entire law. Nevertheless, he approaches Jesus, because he seems to have felt what Jesus states as "lacking one thing" (Mark 10:21; Luke 18:22). Matthew modifies these words to "if you wish to be perfect" (Matt 19:21), echoing the earlier language addressed to the community of disciples about being "perfect as your heavenly Father is perfect."

Here the full invitation to a particular person about the way of perfection assumes a thoroughly specific and personal ("follow me") form: "go sell, your possessions and give the money to the poor, and you will have treasure in heaven; then, come, follow me." In this call story, Jesus "demands not alms but everything," a "whole-hearted obedience to" himself.[11] He is the answer to the question about the way to eternal life (Matt 19:16). The gift of such life is offered here and now through following the person of Jesus Christ, and does not allow for a delayed response.

But the rich young man, at least for the time being, fails to obey. "Unable to relinquish familiar security for the uncertainties of dis-

---

[11] Davies and Allison, *Matthew*, vol. 3, 46, 48.

cipleship," he "refuses to give up goods for the sake of Jesus"[12] and goes away. Jesus himself recognizes how difficult it is for rich people to enter the kingdom of heaven (Matt 19:23–24). But God can make "all things possible" (Matt 19:26). Peter and the other disciples for whom Peter speaks see themselves in pointed contrast to the rich young man: "we have left all things and followed you" (Matt 19:27).

Those Called to Perfection

The Sermon on the Mount calls on the indefinite number of those who are already disciples of Jesus to "be perfect as your heavenly Father is perfect." That perfection involves loving one's enemies and praying for them. The invitation in Matthew 19, however, goes out to a particular individual who is not yet a disciple but is described as young and rich. He is called to embrace a perfection that entails (a) divesting himself of his wealth, (b) passing the proceeds on to poor people (without any suggestion that they have been his enemies and are now to be loved effectively by his generous gift), and (c) becoming one of Jesus' wandering followers.

Given that the various invitations embedded in the Sermon on the Mount are addressed to a wide group of disciples, we are not informed about the *success* of those invitations. How many disciples imitated their heavenly Father by adopting the attitude and behavior of loving and praying for everyone, even their enemies? In the case of the rich young man, we know that he turned down the invitation to perfection by refusing to accept its terms—giving away his great wealth and following the homeless Jesus.

The *difficulty* of being 'perfect as your heavenly Father is perfect' (in the matter of loving one's enemies) is not explicitly noted. In the case of the rich, young man, Jesus himself dwells upon the central

---

[12] Ibid., 46, 49.

difficulty, that of renouncing one's wealth in the cause of the divine kingdom (Matt 19:23–24). The parable of the marriage feast would show Jesus to be aware of other excuses that stand in the way of people accepting the call of the kingdom (Matt 22:1–14; see more clearly Luke 14:15–24).

The call to an *imitatio Dei* who is perfect is expressly stated in Matthew 5:48. The episode concerning the rich, young man in Matthew 19:16–30 involves an *imitatio Christi* through following Jesus, also presented as a perfect role model. We have cited verses which support agreeing with Davies and Allison that Matthew assumes that Jesus is perfect. To these passages in Matthew we can add such items as Jesus' appeal "come to me and rest" (Matt 11:25–30). In a self-description found at the heart of this appeal, Jesus calls himself "meek and humble of heart" (Matt 11:29), echoing and expanding the third beatitude (Matt 5:3). Following him entails following someone who lives out the beatitudes, which constitute, in the light of Jesus' example, the completeness of Christian life.

I remain grateful to Mark Laynesmith. He expounded difficulties found in translating the general call of Matthew 5:48 and touched on its particular counterpart in 19:16–30. That prompted me into exploring further Matthew's contribution on the two related invitations to be *teleios* or unconditionally complete in our imitation of God and our imitation of Christ.

2

"Many are called but few are chosen" (Matt 22:14)

A Well Populated Hell?

Matthew's parable of the royal wedding banquet evokes Jesus' practice of table fellowship with sinners and his promise of a final heavenly feast for the redeemed in the coming kingdom (Matt 9:11–12; 26:29). It leaves readers with various questions and challenges—above all, the meaning of an apocalyptic warning not found in Luke's version, nor in the version provided by the apocryphal Gospel of Thomas (n. 64) but only in Matthew's Gospel: "many are called but few are chosen" (Matt 22:14).[1]

Matthew's parable ends with a general warning about not missing out on the final festival of God's kingdom. But does it do so in more specific terms—as a prediction of prospects for salvation?

In his book *Will Many be Saved?*, Ralph Martin uses the language of salvation rather than that of called and chosen. Yet "saved" can and should be understood as involving being "called" and "cho-

---

[1] Setting out various "elements of Jewish apocalyptic discourse" to be found in Matthew, David H. Wenzel explains that such discourse "is often characterized by a focus on the end of the age with elusive symbolism, double meaning, and *tones of finality*" ("The Gospel of Matthew and Apocalyptic Discourse," *The Expository Times* 132 (2020), 159–70, at 260; emphasis mine). Whatever we say about the meaning of Matt 22:14, the verse carries "tones of finality."

sen." Martin aims at expounding relevant teaching from the Second Vatican Council (1962–65), as well as at evaluating the "salvation optimism" of Karl Rahner and Hans Urs von Balthasar. The teaching of Vatican II leads him to engage with Paul rather than Matthew.

Martin takes up our verse ("many are invited but few are chosen") when he notes how several Greek Fathers of the Church (Irenaeus, Basil, Cyril of Jerusalem, and John Chrysostom) interpreted Matthew 22:14 to mean that "the majority will refuse to avail themselves of the gifts of salvation and be lost." Such an interpretation of the closing message of Matthew's parable anticipates that hell will be well populated and, in fact, will have a larger population than heaven.[2]

How does Matthew's longer parable (Matt 22:1–14) relate to Luke's similar, but certainly not identical, parable of the great banquet (Luke 14:15–24)? Luke speaks simply of a "great dinner" which "someone" organizes, and not, specifically, of a wedding banquet for the son of a king.[3] This specification made by Matthew, incidentally, inevitably suggests Jesus as the bridegroom presiding at the final banquet of heaven.[4]

In Luke's version only one slave brings the king's invitation to the

---

[2] R. Martin, *Will Many be Saved? What Vatican II Actually Teaches and its Implications for the New Evangelization* (Grand Rapids: Eerdmans, 2012), 237. His reference to these Greek Fathers corrects the claim that Augustine was *the first* to "give hell a larger population than heaven" (W. D. Davies and Dale C. Allison, *Matthew*, vol. 3 (Edinburgh: T. & T. Clark, 1997), 207, fn. 75). Apropos of Martin's interpretation of Vatican II, see Peter De Mey, "Revisiting the Redaction History of *Lumen Gentium* 16–17 in Response to a Recent Debate in Catholic Theology of Interreligious Dialogue," in P. De May et al. (eds), *Answerable for Our Beliefs: Reflections on Theology and Contemporary Culture Offered to Terrence Merrigan* (Leuven: Peeters, 2022), 347–90, at 347–49, 388–90.

[3] As Davies and Allison point out, in Matthew's version of the parable only the king speaks (Matt 22:4, 8–9, 11–13); this "underlines his authority" (*Matthew*, vol. 3, 194).

[4] Craig A. Evans, *Matthew* (New York: Cambridge University Press, 2012), 417: the identification of Jesus with the bridegroom "probably started with Jesus himself."

group of guests originally envisaged. Only one slave (the same one) is subsequently despatched to invite people off the streets, and he is sent out twice to fill up the number of those attending the banquet (Luke 14:21–23). In Matthew's version different groups of slaves communicate the invitation both to the original invitees and to the substitute group. The latter group accepts the invitation and at once makes up the number of guests required; there is no need for a slave to go out a second time to have a sufficient number of guests, as in Luke's version. That version of the parable introduces several motives for the original invitees declining the king's invitation (the purchase of land, the purchase of five yoke of oxen, and recent entry into marriage) which find nothing equivalent in Matthew's version. Likewise, Luke includes no killing of the king's slaves (Matt 22:6) and no destruction of the murderers' city (Matt 22:7), an item which obviously recalls the Roman destruction of Jerusalem.

Luke's account does not introduce the detail of someone being found unworthy to attend the wedding banquet and the king ordering him to be arrested and flung into "the outer darkness where there will be weeping and gnashing of teeth" (Matt 22:13).[5] Nor does Luke end with Matthew's sombre, apocalyptic warning about many being called and few being chosen, even if, in Luke's account, the man offering a great dinner insists at the end that "none of those who were [originally] invited will taste my dinner" (Luke 14:24). He hardly needs to say this, since all members of that group had already made their excuses for not coming for the dinner anyway

---

[5] Matthew's account of what happened to the first set of invitees ends with mass punishment (Matt 22:7), whereas the story of the second set ends with an inappropriately dressed guest being severely punished. Davies and Allison raise the question: "why is the man's punishment so out of proportion to his offence?" (*Matthew*, vol. 3, 196, fn. 19). If we follow Matthew's way of viewing the story allegorically, the man is punished for lacking the wedding garment of good works (see Luz, below).

(Luke 14:18–20).[6]

Should the warning incorporated by Matthew be softened down to what Ben F. Meyer proposed: "Many (= All) are Called but Few (= Not All) are Chosen"?[7] Or should its severity be maintained: "all are invited but only a few will be saved"?[8] It is that closing warning and its interpretation which this chapter explores.

The Setting for Many Called and Few Chosen

The parable in Matthew contrasts a series of invitations to the king's wedding feast. It pictures two follow-up invitations to a group of people who had originally received an advance invitation. When they received the first follow-up invitation, the invitees, we are told, "did not want to come." They not only refused the honour of sharing in a royal wedding feast but they also withdrew a "previous or presumptive promise" of attendance.[9] The king then sent other slaves who, in his name, were to stress what awaited the invitees: "behold, I have prepared my meal, my oxen and fatted animals have been killed, and everything is ready. Come to the feast." This invitation represents an advance, as Luz comments: "now the king has his guests told in concrete terms about the culinary joys of the marriage feast for which in truly royal generosity he has slaughtered numerous steers and other animals. This generosity is a sharp contrast with the rudeness or indifference of the invitees, who with no

---

[6] On Luke's version of the parable, see François Bovon, *Luke*, vol. 2, trans. Donald S. Deer (Philadelphia: Fortress Press, 2013), 362–79.

[7] *New Testament Studies* 36 (1990), 89–97.

[8] Ulrich Luz, *Matthew*, vol. 3, trans. James E. Crouch (Minneapolis: Fortress, 2005), 57. On the same page, fn. 77, Luz notes a similar warning in 2 Esdras: "many have been created, but few shall be saved" (8:3). Evans introduces the same reference, notes that there are further parallels in Jewish literature of late antiquity, and supplies one such parallel: "there are more who perish than will be saved" (2 Esdras 9:15) (*Matthew*, 379).

[9] Davies and Allison, *Matthew*, vol. 3, 199.

apology at all continue to pursue farming or business activities."[10]

That generosity contrasts even more with some others among the invitees. They laid hands on the king's slaves, abused them, and killed them. Naturally infuriated, the king sent his troops, destroyed the murderers, and burned their city.

The first set of invitations ended, unexpectedly, in total failure and even catastrophe. It is strange that not a single one of the originally invited guests agreed to come (Matt 22:1–7). Davies and Allison speak of a "most paradoxical vision: all the expected guests are absent and only unexpected guests are present." They add: "one is reminded of 8:11–12, where the sons of the kingdom lose their places at the messianic banquet and have them taken by people from afar."[11]

This first part of the parable in Matthew has often been understood to allegorize the negative reaction of Israel to the prophets, to Jesus himself, to the apostles and other Christian missionaries,[12] with the people off the streets in the second part representing Gentiles. As Luz describes this view, "the destruction of Jerusalem is understood to be the punishment for the rejection, mistreatment, and murder of the prophets and Jesus' emissaries."[13] At the end of Matthew's Gospel, Jewish chief priests and elders bribe the guards

---

[10] Luz, *Matthew*, vol. 3, 48.

[11] Davies and Allison, *Matthew*, vol. 3, 195–96.

[12] Luz, however, writes of "the most common approach" which thinks of "the first invited guests as the religious establishment—that is… the rejection received from most of the Pharisees, scribes, and chief priests." He points out a major difficulty: "the excuses given by the first invited guests have absolutely no religious character. Nothing leads us to think of Pharisees or scribes" (*Matthew*, vol. 3, 50–51). In a related parable, those who murder the slaves of the vineyard owner and then his son (and heir) likewise do not express themselves in religious terms. But the parable is clearly aimed at the Pharisees (Matt 21:33–46), and has usually been understood in terms of the religious establishment murdering God's emissaries, the OT prophets, and then Jesus himself.

[13] Ibid., 54.

who had been set at the tomb of Jesus to say that his disciples stole the body while they were asleep (Matt 28:11–15).

Here we should recall that the two women who found the tomb open and empty and the disciples sent to Galilee (Matt 28:1, 7, 10) were all Jews. Whatever their terrible failures, the Twelve, identified after the defection of Judas as "the Eleven" (Matt 28:16), were also all Jews. They kept the post-resurrection rendezvous on the mountain and received the commission to evangelize the world, both Gentiles and Jews (Matt 28:16–20). The earliest mission of Jesus's disciples was directed primarily to the Jews; the destruction of Jerusalem "gave impetus to the Gentile mission."[14] If interpreting the parable as Gentiles replacing Jews is not convincing, what of its allegorized form developed by Matthew?

After the surprising failure to secure a single guest from the original list of invitees, the king sent out his slaves to invite to the wedding feast *all* they found along the streets (and not merely some designated guests). (Allegorically, the round-up stands for the universal mission of the church.) This time the mission of the slaves did not fail but immediately proved totally successful. "They gathered all whom they found," even if "all" is at once specified as "*bad and good*," with "bad" coming before "good." This ominous note anticipates what will happen when an improperly dressed guest is identified and excluded (Matt 22:11–13). An attentive reader could remember previous parables found only in Matthew, those of the wheat and weeds and of the fishnet, which represent the just and the unjust co-existing until the full coming of the divine kingdom (Matt 13:24–30, 36–43, 47–50). Good and bad exist together in the crop to be harvested and the catch of fish to be hauled ashore. They will be separated but only at the end.

---

[14] Davies and Allison, *Matthew*, vol. 3, 202.

The parable of the wedding banquet differs, superficially, from those two earlier parables which speak of many weeds and bad fish. Only one guest is evicted for arriving at the feast without the appropriate wedding garment. Here rejection and catastrophe overtake one person, and certainly not all. As regards an incident which involves such a single case, it may seem strange to comment: "many are called, but few are chosen" (Matt 22:8–14). We return below to this question.

Luz finds two further details in the parable less than fully plausible: first, "if one has picked up guests on the street, one cannot then criticize them for coming without a wedding garment." Second, "the table servants (*diakonoi*) perform an unusual function. They become constables who throw a poor condemned man into hell."[15]

Apropos of the first implausible detail, Luz recalls a solution that has made the rounds among some commentators: the substitute guests were provided with wedding garments when they arrived at the marriage feast. The guest evicted had refused to accept the garment which was offered to him. Luz points out, however, that none of the alleged evidence "documents a custom of giving wedding garments to guests to wear. Furthermore, the Matthean text presupposes that the guests themselves are responsible for their wedding garments."[16] After receiving the invitation on the streets, they presumably have time to acquire such a garment or wash a garment in which they could be clothed for the marriage feast. The guest thrown out of the feast had failed to secure and put on special clothing or at least a newly washed garment.[17]

---

[15] Luz, *Matthew*, vol. 3, 46. Davies and Allison agree that the punishment involves banishment to hell: "the outer darkness is hell, not an earthly prison" (*Matthew*, vol. 3, 205).
[16] Ibid., 59, fn. 101.
[17] Ibid., 56, fn. 68.

Davies and Allison continue to find the picture somewhat implausible. How can "guests summoned at a moment's notice be expected to be ready," especially if "it is a question of garments being cleansed for the occasion"?[18] Nevertheless, the stress is on being inappropriately dressed, "an insult to the king and therefore to the [other] guests."[19]

To whom does the warning apply?

Evans appears to limit to Israel the target envisaged by Matthew when the parable moves to the substitute guests: "not all Israel will be saved, some will have to be culled out."[20] He goes on to clarify and modify this view by naming a probable and then a possible group: "the man without the wedding robe *probably* represents Jewish leaders who ignore Jesus' summons to repent and embrace the kingdom of God and, *possibly*, faithless disciples who initially accept Jesus' summons but fail to endure."[21]

Luz declines any talk of probably and possibly. The warning embodies God's judgment on a disobedient people, whether Israelites or members of the Jewish-Gentile church. "Israel's fate" in losing the kingdom is "also a possibility for the church" and "a warning to the church."[22] All should prove their calling through works—that is to say, "working on behalf of their election."[23] As indicated in the parable of the fishnet (Matt 13:47–50), the church is a *corpus permixtum*, a mixture of good and bad members who will be separated only at the final judgment and are "not to be sorted out by anyone

---

[18] Davies and Allison, *Matthew*, vol. 3, 204.
[19] Ibid., 205.
[20] Evans, *Matthew*, 378.
[21] Ibid.
[22] Luz, *Matthew*, vol. 3, 57, 59.
[23] Ibid., 57.

save God at the end."[24]

Here Luz steps aside from a classical explanation stemming from the Reformation: "from Matthew's perspective we are to think of wedding garments as works [see Rev 19:7-9] and not as faith."[25] Those garments represent good works that could be produced at judgment. In particular, the members of the church do not "possess salvation; they are capable of losing it again. They must demonstrate it by their works."[26] They "must walk worthily" of their calling.[27]

Neither Evans nor Luz have any difficulty about one individual representing and symbolizing many others. In the closing section of Matthew's Gospel, groups emerge as in the parable of the vineyard and the tenants (Matt 21:33-46), the parable of the ten bridesmaids (Matt 25:1-13) and the judgment of the nations (Matt 25:31-46). But there are also single individuals who represent others like the rich young man (Matt 19:16-30), the two sons in a parable (Matt 21:28-32), and the unfaithful servant in a parable (Matt 24:45-51). Hence Evans, without pausing to argue, turns one guest lacking a wedding garment into a group who fail that way: "the king identifies those who are not worthy."[28] Davies and Allison pick up an allegorical reference to the last judgment, which extends to those within the church. The one man [without the appropriate garment] obviously stands for the whole class."[29]

Some tension, however, arises in the parable from the plural

---

[24] Davies and Allison, *Matthew*, vol. 3, 203.

[25] Luz, *Matthew*, vol. 3, 59.

[26] Ibid. Davies and Allison identify the wedding garment with the resurrected body or "its garment of glory" (*Matthew*, vol. 3, 204). But we should insist that only God can bring about the glory of a risen body. The parable carries an exhortation to do something which human beings can, with divine help, effect: morally good works.

[27] Davies and Allison, *Matthew*, vol. 3, 207.

[28] Evans, *Matthew*, 378.

[29] Davies and Allison, *Matthew*, vol. 3, 204.

form of the warning, repeated in "many are called but few are chosen." In the case of those first called to the wedding feast, "many are called," but simply none of these—and not simply a few—are finally chosen. In the case of the substitute guests, those invited from off the streets, obviously many are called, yet all but one of these seems chosen. The king finds only one substitute guest wanting; that guest stands alone in being identified as unworthy and excluded from the wedding banquet. As such the plural number in which the apocalyptic warning is expressed does not neatly apply to either group of invitees who enter the parable.

Nevertheless, the lack of such a precise fit does not deter Matthew who draws together the entire parable by adding the traditional warning, "many are called but few are chosen." Luz recognizes how the logion does not fit exactly either the first group of invitees (Matt 22: 3–7) or the second group (Matt 22:9–13).[30] Nevertheless, this apocalyptic warning "brings together the entire parable."[31]

Does the Warning Point to a Well Populated Hell?

Thus far we have situated the warning ("many are called but few are chosen") in its Matthean context. The evangelist has apparently taken from the tradition some authentic words of Jesus to sum up the thrust of the parable.[32] How should we interpret the saying? To put the question in extreme terms: is Jesus predicting that a majority of Christians and/or human beings will finish up in hell?

Davies and Allison rightly understand the warning to be aimed primarily at members of the church. "All are invited but not all will

---

[30] Luz, *Matthew*, vol. 3, 49.

[31] Ibid., 57.

[32] Rudolf Bultmann was inclined to take the saying as authentic: *The History of the Synoptic Tradition*, trans. John Marsh (Oxford: Blackwell, 1963), 105.

attend" the final banquet; "it is not enough just to be called."[33] Matthew uses the saying to check the "self-satisfaction" that election can foster.[34] But some, even many, commentators since the origins of Christianity have gone further, by recognizing here not only a serious moral exhortation but also some kind of factual prediction about a majority of Christians (or perhaps of human beings) failing the test of the last judgment. Does the parable of the marriage feast, when offering a summary preview of what eternal life will bring human beings, support the idea that only a few will be chosen for the joy of the heavenly banquet? Four considerations challenge this conclusion.

First, it is essential, if insufficient, to recall the nature of apocalyptic warnings in the context of semitic speech. The prophecy that Nineveh would be overthrown in forty days (Jonah 3:4) was not literally fulfilled. Through God's mercy the inhabitants of this large city repented of their sins, and they were spared destruction. Such apocalyptic warnings (e.g., about many being called but only few being chosen) or oracles of judgment are always serious ethical and religious warnings but not necessarily predictions about things that literally came about.

Second, we need to locate Matthew 22:14 and, indeed, the entire parable about the royal wedding feast within other passages of the Gospel. We can distinguish three classes of teaching about prospects for a future and final destiny. The parables about the wheat that is mixed with weeds and about the fishnet that brings ashore good and bad fish (see above) obviously imply an abundance of good wheat and fish. Weeds and inedible fish are also present, but it is not the scope of the parables to state their proportion in the complete harvest or the haul of fish. Likewise, the picture of the

---

[33] Davies and Allison, *Matthew*, vol. 3, 207.
[34] Ibid., 208.

last judgment makes no attempt to suggest that those on the left side who face condemnation are more numerous than the "blessed" on the right (Matt 25:31–46). The story works by naming the two groups, without requiring any numerical comparison.

The parable of the bridesmaids might suggest a 50/50 division: five share in the marriage feast and five remain excluded (Matt 25:1–13). Are we supposed to comment: "ten are called and only five are chosen"?

At the end of the sermon on the mount, Jesus warns that "not everyone who says to me, 'Lord, Lord' will enter the kingdom of heaven but only the one who does the will of my Father in heaven." Jesus goes on at once to speak of "many" evildoers whom he will send away at the end (Matt 7:21–23). Numbers and numerical comparisons are left unspecified. In this final chapter of the sermon on the mount, only one passage anticipates the language of "many called" but "few chosen": "the gate is wide and the road is easy that leads to destruction, and there are *many* who take it For the gate is narrow and the road is hard that leads to life, and there are *few* who find it" (Matt 7:13–14).

Such numerical variations in alleged predictions about those who happily pass the test of the last judgment—from some fish in a net and part of the crop at harvest, to half the bridesmaids, to only a few who take the road to life— should prompt caution in pressing one-sidedly the distinction between the "many" and the "few." In short, we should respect the full scope of Matthew's imagery that might bear on the end-time and final judgment.

Third, by placing the story of a marriage feast among the "parables" (Matt 22:1) and then closing it with a saying of Jesus ("many are called but few are chosen"), Matthew himself encourages readers to acknowledge that the whole passage provides "not a report but a picture."³⁵ Parables encourage reflection and aim at transforming present reality by eliciting appropriate responses. Beyond question, Matthew has introduced allegorical elements into the parable. Nevertheless, he does not offer it as a piece of advance information about the eternal fate of human beings. He names it as a parable which highlights the urgent priority of following Christ while it is still possible to make such a decision.

Fourth, we should also respect what Jesus indicated (elsewhere) about the limits in his (human) knowledge of what will come at the end. As incarnate Son he did not know "the day nor the hour" of the *parousia* and final judgment (Mark 13:32). His earthly mission did not require precise knowledge about the timing of the end nor, we should add, about the number of those would pass the test of the judgment to come. Rather he stressed the mysterious uncertainty of the final *kairos*, and encouraged constant and watchful living and doing the will of our loving God.

Years ago Raymond E. Brown exemplified the careful analysis of the Gospel materials required from those who examine Jesus' knowledge: for instance, Jesus' knowledge of the future population of hell.³⁶ Since it was not the mission of Jesus to provide advance coverage by pronouncing on the population of hell, that cannot be the task of biblical experts or other Christians. It should be enough to pray for the final salvation of all people, and commit oneself to facilitating that goal. The good and the bad will be separated only by God at the final judgment.

Coda: this article could be extended by discussing the theme of *reversal* in Matthew. The parable of the marriage banquet (Matt

---

[35] Bovon, *Luke*, vol. 2, 374.
[36] R. E. Brown, "How Much Did Jesus Know?," in *Jesus God and Man: Modern Biblical Reflections* (London: Geoffrey Chapman, 1968), 39–102.

22:1–14) follows two other parables of reversal: the parable of the two sons (21:28–32) and the parable of the wicked tenants of the vineyard (21:33–45). The salvation optimism of Rahner and von Balthasar, to which we alluded at the start, could also be illuminated by exploring the significance of Jesus eating with "tax collectors and sinners" (Matt 9:10–11). Matthew's banquet is presented as a meal of the final, heavenly kingdom to which "everyone," "both good and bad," is invited and at which it is implied that Jesus will preside.

3

THE CHILD AS THE FACE OF GOD (MARK 9:36–37)

Joel Marcus unfolds a series of rich observations when commenting on what he calls "the parable of the child" found in Mark 9:36–37.[1] Let us review the most enlightening of these observations, and then explore in this parable a remarkable feature which Marcus barely touches.

Seven Illuminating Comments and Questions from Marcus

First, in the Markan narrative the parable of the child was delivered by Jesus when he faced the disciples, or at least the Twelve (Mark 9:35), who had started an arrogant dispute over the identity of the greatest among them. Marcus recalls a suggestion from Origen that the question arose naturally from their recent experience: Jesus had taken only three disciples (Peter, James, and John) to join him when he went up a mountain for the transfiguration (Mark 9:2). Did his choice indicate some ranking among the Twelve (Marcus, 673)? Or had the disciples simply drifted away to a frivolous debate about their personal status? At best the debate betrayed inappropriate at-

---

[1] J. Marcus, *Mark 8–16* (New Haven, CT: Yale University Press, 2009), 673–83, at 681–83; hereafter references to this commentary will be provided within the text. Ca-mille Foçant speaks of what Jesus does with the child as "a kind of parable in action" (*The Gospel according to Mark: A Commentary*, trans. Leslie Robert Keylock (Eugene, OR: Pickwick Publications, 2012), 380). Francis J. Moloney writes of "Jesus' symbolic action and his explanation of it" (*The Gospel of Mark: A Commentary* (Peabody, MA: Hendrickson Publishers, 2002), 188).

titudes; at worst it revealed self-assertive rivalry.

Second, occasionally in his commentary, Marcus points out how the language of the evangelist is "susceptible" to a double entendre. Here it is a case of the Greek words *pais* and *paidion* denoting "both slaves and children." The fact that these terms can have both meanings "speaks volumes about the status of children in antiquity" (Marcus, 675; see 681).[2] This must be kept in mind when Jesus proceeds to emphasize the role that a small child can play in mediating God's revelation and salvation. Receiving even a neglected little child and offering it loving hospitality involves receiving God and being open to God's revealing and saving self-communication in Christ.

Third, Marcus draws attention to what could be implied when Jesus embraces a small child, whom Marcus argues to be a boy rather than a girl. Specifying the child's gender, however, is far less important than what the embrace might well imply: "a symbolic act of adoption." "Ancient adoptions sometimes included the gesture of picking up a child, embracing it, or otherwise bringing it into contact with the adoptive parent's body" (Marcus, 675). Jesus may be doing more than welcoming a small child; he may also be adopting it. Jesus provides an object lesson of what he can ask of his followers.[3]

Fourth, Marcus alerts readers to various implications of Jesus' words in Mark 9:37 ("whoever receives one such child in my name receives me"). By proposing that those who receive "a

---

[2] On children in Jewish and ancient society, see Adela Yarbro Collins, *Mark* (Minneapolis: Fortress Press, 2007), 444–46; and Warren Carter, *Households and Discipleship: A Study of Matthew 19–20* (Sheffield: Sheffield Academic Press, 1994), 95–113.

[3] On Jesus and little children, see Simon Légasse, *Jésus et l'enfant: Enfants, 'Petits' et Simples dans la tradition synoptique* (Paris: Gabalda, 1969); and Hans Ruedi Weber, *Jesus and the Children* (Geneva: World Council of Churches, 1980).

humble child" are "actually receiving Jesus," these words reflect, for example, "the common ancient motif of the incognito hero or god, in which gods visit the earth in disguise and receive good or bad treatment, before finally revealing themselves and requiting their erstwhile hosts with rewards or chastisements." A biblical counterpart to this motif showed up in stories of angels being welcomed or treated badly: by Abraham and Sarah (Gen 18:2-15), Lot and the men of Sodom (Gen 19:1-14), Tobit (Tob 12:1-20), and others. The duty of hospitality to strangers could, as Hebrews 13:2 recalls, lead to "some [people] entertaining angels without knowing it" (Marcus, 676).

These undoubted allusions should not lead us to forget what Morna Hooker remarks: "The saying ['whoever receives one such child in my name receives me'] reflects the Jewish belief that a man's agent or representative should be received as the man himself."[4] The parable presents any "such child" as the "agent or representative" of Jesus, who in turn is the "agent or representative" of God. This highlights what is done by the child in acting for and representing Jesus. But what does the child do by way of (a) revealing Jesus and (b) through him, of revealing God? Hooker does not want to neglect (b): "Jesus himself is the envoy and representative of another [namely, God]."[5] Any authentic prophet could, of course, be called "the envoy and representative" of God. Is there more to be said?

That same question comes up when Hooker explains that "in my name probably means simply for my sake." The standard dictionary of New Testament Greek cites Mark 9:37 and agrees that it suggests receiving a child "for my (name's) sake." Yet the diction-

---

[4] M. D. Hooker, *The Gospel According to St Mark* (London: Continuum, 2001; orig. ed. 1981), 228.
[5] Hooker, *Mark*, 228.

ary also allows for receiving a child "when my name is confessed, when I am called upon."[6] "For my sake" focuses on (mere?) motivation, whereas confessing and calling upon the name of Jesus is tantamount to confessing and calling upon Jesus himself—in matters of salvation. This interpretation recognizes his living presence and power, expresses a radical relationship to him, and acknowledges that "Jesus identifies himself with the little ones." "Jesus—and even the Father—will be found," Eduard Schweizer observes, "in these little, helpless ones."[7]

Fifth, Marcus points out that the parable of receiving a small child "is closely related to" the six works of mercy that Matthew lists as the basis for final judgment (Matt 25:31–46). In particular, the duty of offering hospitality to needy strangers of any age (Matt 25:40, 45) yields a partial parallel to receiving children in the name of Jesus (Marcus, 676, 682–83). Nevertheless, what Jesus says about welcoming children enjoys a richer depth of meaning. Matthew's picture of the final judgment makes no suggestion that those who had offered hospitality to a stranger (Matt 25:35) had done this for God who sent Jesus, or that those who had failed to offer hospitality (Matt 25:43) had failed to do so for God who had sent Jesus. Both groups seem surprised that Jesus identified himself (not God) with those in need. But it was Jesus who remained the sole, invisible (but real) co-recipient of such hospitality. Nothing in the account of the final judgment took matters further and claimed that doing something for Jesus was doing something for God, who sent him.

---

[6] See 'onoma', Walter Bauer, Frederick William Danker, William F. Arndt, and F. Wilbur Gingrich, *A Greek-English Lexicon of the New Testament and Other Early Christian Literature* (Chicago: University of Chicago Press, 2000), 711–714, at 714; hereafter BDAG.

[7] Eduard Schweizer, *The Good News according to Mark*, trans. Donald H. Madvig (London: SPCK, 1970), 193.

Sixth, arguing convincingly that "one such child" (Mark 9:37) is to be understood literally and *not totally symbolically* "as if the child were [merely] a representative of Jesus' childlike followers," Marcus asks about the nature of reception that should be offered to little children. He thinks, above all, of welcoming and caring for abandoned and orphaned children. Such children exemplify "a needy person to be served in concrete, nitty-gritty ways," a person who should be the beneficiary of an "act of charity" (Marcus, 681–83). Whatever specific examples of needy children we might offer, the notion of welcoming children seems to be literally intended.[8]

Seventh, Marcus concludes that to receive Jesus by receiving such children "takes on larger dimensions. The one who receives Jesus receives not Jesus alone but God as well." Such a statement is in line with "the strong connection" between the figures of Jesus and God that we find "from the very beginning of the Gospel" of Mark. The way of Jesus the Messiah is "the way of the Lord" (Mark 1:1–3). Marcus also calls attention to the fact that "some of the healing stories have implied that where Jesus is acting, there God is powerfully present" (Mark 2:7, 10; 5:19–20). Finally, the two stories of Jesus' exercising his sovereign power over storms at sea have "portrayed him in ways similar to the depiction of the God of the OT" (Marcus, 683).

Here Marcus expands his reading of the parable of the child to acknowledge that it says something in response to the questions: What is God like? What should we say about God, in the light of the parable of the child? Specifically, God can be identified as being strongly connected with Jesus. This identification allows Jesus to say in effect about those who receive one such a child in his name: they "do not so much receive me as receive the one who

---

[8] BDAG, 221.

sent me" (Marcus, 676).

Receiving Little Children Reduced to a Moral Exhortation?

Marcus goes beyond other exegetes who tend to read the parable of the child as simply a moral exhortation: in the words of Foçant, the followers of Jesus are "called to serve the most insignificant persons in society." Foçant quotes Ulrich C. von Wahle to explain what happens when those followers obey this call: "by receiving the least significant, the disciple receives the most significant." The parable seems to become a matter of good deeds and (the highest) reward: "the reward" is "to receive not only Jesus himself but [also] the Father who sent him."[9]

Rightly claiming that well-connected children who behave in exemplary ways are not envisaged here, Luz draws attention to the general "negative social situation of children in antiquity." They were not considered "full human beings with their own integrity," but "small, insignificant, and without power."[10] Orphaned and homeless children, in particular, embodied the way children lacked social and religious standing. Jesus wanted to turn that situation upside down and called for children to be welcomed as he himself should be welcomed. Since he identified himself with these lowly ones, hospitality should be extended to them as well.

A similar moral exhortation comes from Dennis Nineham. Proposing that "receiving" probably means here "showing kindness to," he comments that "the true disciple achieves greatness not by holding great offices but by doing services to insignificant people such as

---

[9] Foçant, *Gospel according to Mark*, 380.
[10] Luz, *Matthew*, vol. 2, 428–29.

the child."[11] That should be the practice of true disciples, energized by an attitude of service towards lowly and insignificant persons like small children.

John Nolland, commenting on Mark 9:33–37 with the aim of elucidating Matthew's subsequent treatment of this tradition, remarks: "the challenge" is to "disregard one's superior status" and "treat the lowly figure of the child with the respect that would come naturally in relating to Jesus himself".[12] But could it be that *the* ultimate challenge is to recognize in the lowly, vulnerable figure of a child the image and presence not only of Jesus but also and ultimately the image and presence of God, the One who sent Jesus?

God as a Lowly and Vulnerable Child

Here and there the parables of Jesus yield fresh and startling images of God: for example, the image of a woman mixing yeast in three measures of flour until "it was all leavened" (Matt 13:33).[13] While focused on the growth of the divine kingdom in the world, this brief parable presents a woman symbolizing the concerns and activity of God. Three measures of leaven cause a mass of dough to rise and produce 40 litres or 110 pounds of bread. This is much more than the wife of a farmer, if the woman's spouse was that, would normally do. We should imagine some special meal, when a relatively tiny amount of leaven changes a large amount of dough. The parable may seem surprising, given the Old Testament's negative associations of leaven (as being infectious and evil) which continue in the books of the New Testament (e.g., Matt 16:6; Gal 5:9). The language about the woman "hiding" the leaven in the

---

[11] D. E. Nineham, *Saint Mark* (London: Penguin, 1992; orig. ed. 1963), 252.

[12] J. Nolland, *The Gospel of Matthew* (Grand Rapids: Eerdmans, 2005), 733.

[13] Ulrich Luz, endorses the consensus that the parable "goes back to Jesus": *Matthew 8–20*, trans. James E. Crouch (Minneapolis: Fortress Press, 2001), 258.

dough (Matt 13:33) could mitigate the reader's surprise, since the hidden leaven enjoys a certain parallel to the treasure "hidden in a field" (Matt 13:44). In both cases the hidden truth of the kingdom exercises its powerful impact.

This paragraph has drawn on what Luz has to say about the parable of the woman preparing dough for baking.[14] This notable exegete and the sources he cites (from the early Church to contemporary authors) neglect, however, to note how the woman figures forth the divine agent of the kingdom and God's secret work in making the kingdom grow.

We will see below some of the adult human beings whom the Old Testament introduced as images of God. They included women in the labor of childbirth (Is 42:14) and women caring for their babies (Is 49:15–16; 66:13). This was startling enough, given the patriarchal culture that pervaded the ancient world. Jesus' woman preparing the dough belongs with such surprising Old Testament images of God.

In a sense Marcus points us towards only half of the theological teaching conveyed by the parable of the child: there is (1) a "strong connection" between the figures of Jesus and God, and God is "powerfully present" in the activity of Jesus. What might be said about (2), the connection (via the figure of Jesus) between a small child and God? Does a tiny, vulnerable child image forth the very mystery of God?

Apropos of (1), this comment leaves us, of course, with the question: does the witness of Mark lead us to say more about Jesus than we would say about the Elijah and Moses, both present with Jesus at the transfiguration (Mark 9:2–8)? The biblical record attests a

---

[14] Ibid., 257–64.

"strong connection" between these two Old Testament personalities and God.[15] It is also fair to say that God was pictured as "powerfully present" in their activity. What more could Marcus have said about this "connection" with God and the "powerful [divine] presence" in the case of Jesus?

At the close of his comments on the Parable of the Child, Marcus would have been better advised to recall what he had said of the transfiguration. "The divine voice from the cloud" identifies Jesus as God's Son; this is to make it clear that Jesus is more than Elijah and Moses. This title of Son "hints at an identity greater than that of Moses and Elijah" (Marcus, 640). Those who in the name of Jesus welcome a small child are doing more than merely welcoming someone who has a "strong connection" with God and in whose activity God is "powerfully present." They are welcoming the Son who has been sent by God and divinely identified as God's Son,

Old Testament Images of God

The books of the Old Testament picture God in a variety of ways—as warrior king, shepherd, the creator who gives life through his powerful word, the redeemer who rescues his people and individuals, a righteous judge, the loving spouse of his people, a loving father (occasionally), a woman in childbirth or a nursing mother, and so forth.[16] A mysterious transcendence may hide the face of God as in the divine self-presentation in Exodus 3:14 ("I am who I am"), or

---

[15] Rather than "a strong connection," Moloney speaks of "an intimate link" between "receiving the child, receiving Jesus, and receiving the one [God] who sent Jesus" (*The Gospel of Mark*, 188). This observation leaves it open, of course, as to what the intimate link is between Jesus and God, not to mention the direct link between (receiving) the child and (receiving) Jesus and the indirect link between (receiving) the child and (receiving) the One who sent Jesus.

[16] See John J. Scullion, "God in the OT," in David Noel Freedman (ed.), *Anchor Bible Dictionary*, vol. 2 (New York: Doubleday, 1992), 1041–48.

else God is presented with the tender intimacy of a parent who lovingly educates wayward children (Hos 11:1–11) or of a spouse who is eternally faithful to an adulterous people (Hos 2:19).

Ryan P. Bonfiglio goes beyond talking of divine titles and names to distinguish between "*metaphors* of *governance* for God" (king, judge or warrior) and "*metaphors* of *sustenance*" (gardener, parent or shepherd). Bonfiglio also points to the language that conveys the divine activity in the world (as the God who delivers, creates, and blesses) and the divine character (as gracious, merciful, holy, jealous, or hidden and elusive).[17]

In all these metaphors or images God remains an adult figure: as king, shepherd, spouse, parent, mother, and so forth. By way of exception, we have the language of Isaiah concerned, apparently with the birth of Hezekiah (Is 7:14–16). Celebrating seemingly the birth of an heir to the throne, the prophet speaks in exalted terms of "the child born to us" and "the son given to us": "Wonderful Counselor, Mighty God, Everlasting Father and Prince of Peace" (Isa 9:1–7). The prophet uses the newborn child to describe God. But it remains exceptional in the Old Testament to associate children with God. Isaiah does so when an heir to the throne is born.

Jesus proposes something startlingly different when he presents a child as, at least indirectly, representing God. Normally understood to be the last or least of all, children are reckoned in Jesus' parable, albeit indirectly but without qualification, as the greatest of all. Whoever they are. they image forth God. Jesus bears witness to what he has experienced and understood of God: a weak and vulnerable child can be a metaphor for God, and welcoming such a child can be a metaphor for welcoming God. At the end, the parable

---

[17] R. P. Bonfiglio, "God and gods," in Samuel B. Balentine (ed.), *The Oxford Encyclopedia of Bible and Theology*, vol. 1 (New York: Oxford University Press, 2015), 412–26.

of the child proves even more startling than the picture of the last judgment, in which Jesus simply identifies himself with the suffering and the vulnerable (Matt 25:31–46). Holding a small child in his arms, Jesus goes further, and speaks of God as making himself vulnerable and the least. "Those that welcome a little child in my name welcome me; and those who welcome me welcome the One who sent me."

Jesus appeals to the God of his ancestors (Mark 12:26–27), but he radically modifies the divine image, right through to the intimate *Abba* of the Garden of Gethsemane. No longer a divine warrior who could supply effective military defence, God is the loving Father (Mark 14:36) with whom Jesus struggles in prayer.

Jesus preached and practiced other such modifications. They included the metaphor of God as found in the person of a small child. This startling feature of the parable of the child should not be missed. The face of a vulnerable child, who might dismissed as belonging to the lowest class in society, is the face of God. To adapt the language of St Paul (2 Cor 4:6), Jesus invited us to recognize the glory of God on the face of insignificant, weak, little children.

Few have done more than Karl Rahner to spread the language and notion of "the mystery of the child."[18] The parable of the child challenges us by suggesting that the mystery of the child reveals the very mystery of God.

---

[18] Jessie Rogers, "Karl Rahner and Children," *Irish Theological Quarterly* 86 (2021), 111–26.

4

THE FEARFUL SILENCE OF THREE WOMEN (MARK 16:1–8)

The Gospel of Mark, as we have it, ends in a disturbing way.[1] Mary Magdalene, Mary the mother of James, and Salome have discovered the tomb of Jesus to be open and empty. Inside the tomb they meet an angelic figure who announces the resurrection and gives them the instruction: "tell his disciples and Peter that he is going ahead of you to Galilee. There you will see him, as he said" (16:7). But "they went out of the tomb and fled; for trembling (*tromos*) and bewilderment (*ekstasis*) took hold of them. And they said nothing to anyone, for they were afraid (*ephobounto*)" (16:8). How are we to understand this flight and fearful silence of the three women?

Earlier commentators such as Robert Henry Lightfoot, Dennis Nineham, and Rudolf Pesch offered a positive interpretation of this terrified (temporary) silence of the women. It was an appropriate reaction to the revelation of Jesus' resurrection from the dead. Then scholars like Norman Perrin, Morna Hooker, Francis J. Moloney, and Joel Marcus proposed understanding the women's reaction negatively. At the end the women, like the male disciples, failed. But is this view of total failure on the part of all disciples, men *and women*, truly convincing? Should a positive view of the women be reinstated?

---

[1] On variant endings (and theories of lost endings) of Mark, see Joel Marcus, *Mark 8–16* (Newhaven, CT: Yale University Press, 2009), 1088–96.

Lightfoot, Nineham, and Pesch

Lightfoot argued that "the whole tenor" of Mark 16:5–8 suggests "a fear or dread of God," a fear caused by "revelation" which produces the women's amazement, fear, and silent flight. In accounting for the women's emotions and reactions, Lightfoot pointed to the stilling of the storm (Mark 4:35–41): the "physical alarm" of the disciples was "replaced by a much deeper fear." He noted the parallel between the silence of the three women in Mark 16:8 and the "bewildered utterance" of the male disciples in Mark 4:41. These reactions "arise from the same cause, namely, an increasing and involuntary realization of the nature and being of Him with whom they have to do."[2]

Lightfoot went on to recall how various episodes of revelation in Mark's Gospel regularly produce in the disciples or others "fear or astonishment or both together."[3] In a climactic way the reaction of the women at the tomb— their amazement, trembling, fear, and silence— gathers up the emotions caused earlier by the revealing presence of God conveyed through Jesus' actions and teaching.

Dennis Nineham

With considerable attention to Lightfoot's comments, Nineham interprets the fearful silence and flight of the women as expressing "the overwhelming and sheerly supernatural character of that to which" they were responding. Nineham attends not only to protagonists in the narrative but also to the response that could be expected from readers. If they even begin to "understand the full sig-

---

[2] R. H. Lightfoot, *The Gospel Message of St Mark* (Oxford: Oxford University Press, 1950), 88.
[3] Ibid., 90–91.

nificance of what had occurred," they "too will be bound to respond with amazement and godly fear."[4]

Rudolf Pesch

In his own way and without reference to Lightfoot or Nineham, Rudolf Pesch detected in the women's fearful silence "a motif of reaction to the reception of revelation" found in "the [Old Testament] accounts of epiphanies." He referred to such texts as Daniel 7:28.[5] Lightfoot had exemplified the connection between some revealing message from God and human silence by citing passages such as Luke 1:20; and 2 Cor 12:4.[6] Pesch noted that the fear, trembling, and silence of the three women are apocalyptic themes—he cited Daniel 7:15, 28; 8:17, 27, and 10:7—which "underline the meaning of the angel's *revelatory* message."[7]

The "overwhelming secret" communicated by the angel's announcement of Jesus' resurrection produced trembling, ecstatic amazement, and silence. Such a response emphasized "the *mysterium tremendum* of the divine revelation." The women have planned to anoint the corpse of the crucified Jesus. Instead they are "confronted with the message of his resurrection and are torn away from" their normal ways of thinking.[8] Pesch might have used the full account of the Holy coined by Rudolf Otto: *mysterium tremendum et fascinans*.[9] The women go to the tomb drawn unconsciously by the fascinating mystery of God about to be disclosed to them. They flee from the tomb shocked by the awe-inspiring message of

---

[4] D. E. Nineham, *Saint Mark* (London: Penguin, 1963, reprinted 1992), 447–48.
[5] R. Pesch, *Das Markusevangelium*, vol. 2 (Freiburg im Breisgau: Herder, 1977), 536; see also 522; trans. mine.
[6] Lightfoot, *Gospel Message*, 87.
[7] Pesch, *Markusevangelium*, vol. 2, 528; emphasis mine.
[8] Ibid., 535.
[9] R. Otto, *The Idea of the Holy*, trans. John W. Harvey (London: Penguin, 1959).

Jesus' resurrection. The contrasting activity of the women exemplifies Otto's classic thesis about the two-fold human reaction to God and to the revelation of the divine mystery.

Pesch commented that the readers of the Gospel, confronted with the women's response to the "epiphany of God" that has taken place in Jesus' resurrection, are invited to let themselves "be *fascinated* into faith."[10] Here Pesch recalled—for the sake of the Gospel readers— the *fascinans* from Otto's phrase, but ignored the *tremendum*. Surely readers are invited to imitate the women by being both fascinated *and* awe-inspired, and so come to faith (or be strengthened in an Easter faith that already exists). While profitably introducing Otto to illuminate Mark 16:8, Pesch could have deployed more fully the language of *mysterium tremendum et fascinans*.

Norman Perrin, Morna Hooker and Francis Moloney

Norman Perrin was among the first to explain Mark 16:8 as disobedience and failure on the part of three women. Perrin rightly connected the story of the women at Jesus' tomb (Mark 16:1–8) with two other narratives (Mark 15:40–41; 15:42–47). These three narratives (which deal, respectively, with women at the cross, at the burial of Jesus, and at his tomb) are closely related—not least by the fact that two of the three women named in 15:40 turn up again in 15:47 and all three are named again in 16:1. Perrin also noted the progressive failure of Jesus' male disciples that begins at Mark 6:52 and reaches its highpoint with Judas' betrayal, Peter's denial of Jesus, and their total absence at the crucifixion. Meanwhile, women enter Mark's story (from 14:3–9) and "take over the role" one "might have expected to be played" by the male disciples. They remain faithfully present at Jesus' death and burial and are "prepared to play their

---

[10] Pesch, *Markusevangelium*, vol. 2, 541; emphasis mine.

role in anointing him." It is "their great honor to discover the empty tomb and the fact of the resurrection."[11]

Then, like the male disciples before them, "the women also fail their trust" by not delivering "the message entrusted to them." Mark's Gospel ends with total "discipleship failure," as "every disciple fails the master." Perrin admits that this is a "grim picture" and a "dark" and "stark" vision of what Mark intends by the frightened silence of the three women.[12] But is total failure on the part of all the disciples, both male and female, the right vision to be drawn from Mark 16:8?

In her commentary on Mark's Gospel, Morna Hooker agrees with Perrin. She explains the reaction of the women as a final act of disobedience and failure. Mark ends with "the statement that the women disobeyed the divine command because they were afraid"; "their silence is culpable."[13] The male disciples have failed to understand the message and identity of Jesus, who denounces their "hardened" hearts (8:14–21). At the end one of the Twelve betrays Jesus to his enemies, Peter denies him three times, and none of the others have the courage to support him at his death on the cross. The young man who flees naked into the night (14:51–52) symbolizes the way all the male disciples fail Jesus. Having persistently misunderstood and disappointed Jesus, unsurprisingly they all abandon him at the end. Hooker acknowledges that the record of women in Mark's Gospel has been different: "individual women have been

---

[11] N. Perrin, *The Resurrection Narratives: A New Approach* (London: SCM Press, 1977), 31–32.

[12] Ibid., 32–33.

[13] M. D. Hooker, *The Gospel according to St Mark* (London: Continuum, 2001; orig. 1981), 392. It is worth remarking that the evangelist does *not* state that the women "disobeyed" and were "culpable," but only that, after receiving the message from the angel about the resurrection and a rendezvous in Galilee, "they said nothing to anyone" (Mark 16:8). He states what happened without passing a moral judgement on it.

commended for their faith and their actions (5:34; 7:29;12:41–44; 14:5–9); and the women who follow Jesus from Galilee stand alone by him at the end; they alone witness his death (15:40–41) and burial (15:47). But, surprisingly, at this point even they fail." Their fear and failure to deliver the message "demonstrate their inability to believe the good news" of the resurrection of the crucified Jesus.[14] Hooker considers it "ironic that on Easter morning those who had faithfully followed Jesus to his crucifixion should flee from his tomb—just as the [male] disciples fled from arrest (14:50, 52): this stupendous act is too great even for their [the three women's] loyalty."[15]

Hooker's list of references to the faithful activity of women needs to be enlarged by adding details from 1:29–31, the account of Peter's mother-in-law being cured and then "serving" Jesus—the only example from the many people cured in Mark's Gospel who does just that. The full account of the activity of female followers of Jesus in Mark 1–15 remains totally positive. Not a single misstep prepares us for an alleged failure at the end. Such failure would be totally out of character with all that the women associated with Jesus have done since the start of Mark's Gospel.

Nevertheless, Hooker's interpretation has been followed by her former doctoral student, Francis J. Moloney: "The women, who had overcome the scandal of the cross by looking on from afar as Jesus died (15:40–41) and watched where he was buried (15:47), have not

---

[14] Hooker, *St Mark*, 387.

[15] Ibid., 393. But do the male disciples' flight from arrest and the women's flight from the tomb stand in parallel? The men flee from danger at the hands of human beings; the women flee when "confronted with the power of God." Faced with "the mightiest act of all," they flee. This is "precisely how many other characters in the [Mark's] story have reacted when confronted" with the divine power (ibid., 387). Here Hooker herself recognizes that the flight of the men and that of the women are differently motivated; they should not be explained in the same way.

been able to overcome the scandal of the empty tomb and the Easter proclamation. They have joined the [male] disciples in flight and fear."[16] Hence Moloney discusses Mark 16:1–8 under the title "the Failure of the Women."[17] Mark, he insists, proposes that, just as the male disciples failed, "so also the women failed (16:8). In the end, *all human beings fail*...but God succeeds. God has raised Jesus from the dead (16:6)."[18]

Joel Marcus

Marcus recognizes how the women's fear is "a typical biblical reaction to a theophany or angelophany." He points out how Abraham "responds to a covenant-inaugurating theophany with *ekstasis* ('astonishment') and *phobos* ('fear')" (Gen 15:12). Moreover, "when God or an angel appears in the Bible, the recipient of the appearance sometimes becomes mute," for instance, "because of shock" (Dan 10:15). Nevertheless, Marcus claims that it seems that the women in Mark 16:8 remain deliberately silent: "they choose" not to speak.[19] He finds their fear and flight "easy to understand: the women have just encountered an angel, and they have seen a rolled away rock and an empty tomb where they expected a sealed and full one. The sheer unexpectedness of these events and the impression of supernatural power at work help explain their trembling and astonishment."[20]

Marcus suggests, however, that "the muteness of the women in our story seems to arise not from inability to speak but from

---

[16] F. J. Moloney, *The Gospel of Mark: A Commentary* (Peabody, MA: Hendrickson, 2002), 348.
[17] Ibid., 348–52.
[18] Ibid., 352.
[19] J. Marcus, *Mark 8–16* (New Haven, CT: Yale University Press, 2009), 1081–82.
[20] Ibid., 1087.

unwillingness to do so." The "resurrection kerygma" must "now be proclaimed to the whole world," but the women react to the angel's instruction with "fearful silence and flight."[21] "The fleeing [and silent] women provide an image of what not to do, as they run away in fear and squelch the marvelous tidings of the resurrection."[22]

Marcus goes on to qualify his conclusion about the women's allegedly deliberate and disobedient failure to deliver the message. He raises "the question whether the women eventually overcame their fear and told the disciples about the meeting in Galilee, to which they then went and were restored to fellowship with Jesus. The mere existence of the narrative suggests a positive answer."[23] The narrative, I would argue, not only suggests but also requires such a positive answer. If the women never delivered to anyone whatsoever the message about a rendezvous in Galilee and, indeed, about their own experience at the tomb of Jesus, how has Mark come to know about these matters? Apropos of the key instruction of the angel, M. Eugene Boring points out how, "at the narrative level of presenting past events, the reader is aware that the disciples did somehow get the message."[24]

A provisional silence on the part of the women is accounted for by the various astonishing elements in what they experienced at the empty tomb—elements acknowledged by Marcus and just listed above. Their silence was not a deliberate act of disobedience but a stunned, temporary silence produced by the unexpected discovery and bewildering encounter at the tomb of Jesus. Timothy Dwyer il-

---

[21] Ibid.
[22] Ibid., 1093.
[23] Ibid., 1095.
[24] M. E. Boring, *Mark: A Commentary* (Louisville, KY: Westminster John Knox), 449, fn. 16.

lustrates how in biblical stories silence, at least for a time, can "result from a divine encounter."[25] The silence of the women, he proposes, is best understood as provisional: in due course they spoke to the male disciples.[26] The women remained silent with inappropriate persons, until their message could be passed on "to the appropriate audience, the disciples."[27]

Early in Mark's Gospel, Jesus cured a leper and instructed him to "say nothing to any one" as he went off to show himself to a representative of the priestly establishment (Mark 1:44). He was to remain silent until he reached the appropriate person, a priest in Jerusalem. Now the three women, although not explicitly so instructed, "said nothing to any one" as they ran to bring the angel's message to the appropriate persons, Peter and the other male disciples.

The temporary silence of the women belongs to three dramatic contrasts which heighten the numinous nature of the revelation expressed by Mark16:1–8. A first contrast pits not only the *darkness* of the night (between the Saturday and the Sunday of the resurrection) but also the darkness that enveloped the earth at the crucifixion (Mark 15:33) against the *light* of the sun that has just risen when the women go to visit the tomb (Mark 16:2). The second contrast emerges once the women enter the tomb itself. The *absence* of Jesus' body is set over against the *presence* of Jesus mediated through an interpreting angel in the form of a well-dressed "young man." A third contrast sets the confident *words* of the heavenly figure ("he has been raised; he is not here; see the place where they laid him"; and the instruction about the rendezvous in Galilee) against the

---

[25] T. Dwyer, *The Motif of Wonder in the Gospel of Mark* (Sheffield: Sheffield Academic Press, 1996), 189.
[26] Ibid., 191–92.
[27] J. Lee Magness, *Sense and Absence: Structure and Suspension in the Ending of Mark's Gospel* (Atlanta: Scholars Press, 1986), 100.

silence of the women when they flee from the tomb.[28] Their provisional silence belongs to an appropriately dramatic way of using contrasts to narrate the climactic revelation of Jesus' resurrection from the dead, and should not be taken to be a disobedient refusal to pass on the angelic message.

Some readers may wonder why I have not discussed the hypothesis which explains the women's silence as "a later-first-century attempt to explain why no one had previously heard the story about the empty tomb, which according to this theory had recently been concocted, either by Mark or by a predecessor."[29] Marcus did not find those who argue for the later invention of an empty tomb story to be convincing. Neither have I. Both before and after his 2009 commentary appeared, I have argued against those who hold such a later invention view.[30]

Camille Foçant

Besides respecting the narrative of Mark 16:1–8, we should also note what it can ask of its readers and hearers—something that J. Lee Magness called "the completion of the story by the readers and their dramatic participation in its conclusion."[31] We also saw above how Nineham and Pesch introduced the role of readers into their interpretation of Mark 16:1–8.

Like other commentators, Camille Foçant recognizes how "the mention of Galilee" in Mark 16:7 recalls "the start of the gospel nar-

---

[28] G. O'Collins, *Easter Faith: Believing in the Risen Jesus* (London: Darton, Longman & Todd, 2003), 72–73.

[29] Marcus, *Mark 8–16*, 1082.

[30] G. O'Collins, *Interpreting the Resurrection* (Mahwah, NJ: Paulist Press, 1988), 53–58; O'Collins, *Easter Faith*, 66–71; O'Collins, *Believing in the Resurrection* (Mahwah, NJ: Paulist Press, 2012), 80–91.

[31] Magness, *Sense and Absence*, 102.

rative that begins with the preaching in Galilee." This carries momentous implications for readers of the gospel. In a striking reversal and extension, "the epilogue of the gospel [Mark 16:1–8] thus constitutes a prologue to the work of the reader" (reversal). Moreover, "where the work of the narrator ends, that of the reader begins" (extension). Readers are invited to complete the story. They are led to register themselves "personally in the evangelical drama and assume it."[32]

Thus the (provisional) silence of the three women becomes an invitation to speak. Readers can become "voices crying out in the wilderness" (Mark 1:3) and play their role "in the history of the gospel kerygma."[33]

A positive interpretation of the women's fearful silence in Mark 16:8 should be reinstated. It embodies an appropriate reaction to the unique divine revelation conveyed in the resurrection of the crucified Jesus. The comments of Nineham, Pesch, Magness, and Foçant add to this, by calling on us to acknowledge in the enigmatic final verse of Mark an invitation to complete what we read by living and proclaiming the resurrection.

[This chapter already appeared substantially in my *Illuminating the New Testament: The Gospels, Acts, and Paul* (Mahwah, NJ: Paulist Press, 2022), 35–43. The repetition is motivated by the desire to win over more readers to its views of divine revelation and the ministry of women for the church and the world.]

---

[32] C. Foçant, *The Gospel According to Mark: A Commentary*, trans. Leslie Robert Keylock (Eugene, OR: Pickwick Publications, 2012), 661.
[33] Ibid., 662.

5

THE VIRGINAL CONCEPTION AND ITS MEANINGS

In *The Gospel according to Judas*, Jeffrey Archer, assisted by Francis J. Moloney, launched another attempt, albeit a novelistic attempt, to rehabilitate Judas Iscariot.[1] As recounted by a fictitious son of Judas, Benjamin Iscariot, Judas wanted to rescue Jesus from a dangerous situation in Jerusalem and send him home safe to Galilee. But he was double-crossed by a sinister figure called "the Scribe," who arrested Jesus and hurried him off to be tried by Caiaphas, handed over to the Romans, and sentenced to death on a cross. This imaginative exercise turns Judas into a tragic hero who could not undo the terrible deed he had been tricked into doing.

An introductory note describes the joint project of a novelist and a biblical scholar: "Archer would write a story for twenty-first century readers, while Moloney would ensure that the result would be credible to a first-century Christian or Jew. But they take too many liberties with the given data to be convincing.[2] One such liberty concerns the virginal conception of Jesus.

Judas against the Virginal Conception

Judas is recalled by Archer/Moloney as flatly denying the virginal conception. According to Judas, Jesus was "the first born of the lawful wedlock between his father, Joseph, and his mother, Mary." Ju-

---
[1] London: Macmillan, 2007.
[2] See my review of their book in *The Pastoral Review* 3 (2007), 83–85.

das added: "some of the stories about Jesus' birth...were nothing more than Greek myths that tell of gods in heaven who produce offspring following a union with women of this earth."[3] In the glossary, a note justifies this denial of the virginal conception by referring readers to Genesis 6:1–4, a piece of Near-Eastern (not Greek) mythology that tells of sexual unions between angels ("the sons of God") and women ("the daughters of men"). This old myth about a lustful breaking of boundaries that separate heaven and earth seems to have originally intended to account for the existence of the Nephilim, tall men who were famous warriors and credited with superhuman power (Num 13:33; Deut 2:10–11). In the context of Genesis 6, this Near-Eastern myth is cited to illustrate the increase of sin and violence that led up to the great flood (Gen 6:11).

Would a first-century Jew like Judas have dismissed the virginal conception as "nothing more" than a "Greek myth?" It seems doubtful that, in the time before AD 70 and the fall of Jerusalem, Jews in Palestine, would have known much of these myths, and so be in a position to dismiss the virginal conception as just another version of such legends.'[4] What is, however, clearly documented is that some Jews alleged that Mary committed adultery and had a child (Jesus) as the result of an affair with a soldier called Panthera. When writing around 177–80 his *True Discourse* (1.28, 32), the pagan author Celsus drew on Jewish sources to make this charge.[5] What is not clear, however, is whether this charge of illegitimacy circulated before Matthew and Luke wrote their Gospels in the late first century

---

[3] *Gospel according to Judas*, 4–5.
[4] See R. E. Brown, *The Birth of the Messiah*; new edn (Doubleday: New York, 1993), 522–23.
[5] See H. Chadwick, *Origen Contra Celsum*; paperback edn (Cambridge: Cambridge University Press, 1980), 28, 31–32.

or whether it arose, polemically, in response to their Gospels. All in all, it would have been more plausible (and less blatantly anachronistic) for Archer and Moloney to have represented Judas dismissing the virginal conception as a case of illegitimacy rather than doing so on the grounds of its being a mere "Greek myth" that crept into the Gospel stories of the origin of Jesus.

When we examine Greek (and Roman) myths about Zeus and other deities coupling with women and producing remarkable offspring, we find stories about legendary heroes and, occasionally, about remarkable human beings who actually existed. Thus Zeus was supposed to have arrived in a shower of gold to impregnate Danaë and beget Perseus, a mythical Greek hero who slew Medusa, saved Andromeda from a sea-monster, and became king of Tiryns. When Zeus came in his true shape to another woman, Semele, she died but their offspring lived and was known as Dionysus (or Bacchus), the god of wine. The god of wisdom, Phoebus Apollo, was sometimes credited with supplying Amphictione, the mother of Plato, with superior, divine sperm for the conception of her brilliant offspring. All these Graeco-Roman myths name some particular individual, generally a legendary hero, as the offspring of intercourse between a god and a woman. As far as I know, such myths never purported to explain the origin of a group of people like the Nephilim, famous warriors of gigantic stature. It seems quite gratuitous to associate these myths with Genesis 6 and its reference to the origin of the Nephilim. Let us put aside this strange reference that Archer and Moloney provide to back up their picture of Judas dismissing the virginal conception of Jesus as nothing more a Greek myth. What of the Graeco-Roman myths themselves? Can they throw any light on the narratives of the virginal conception that we read in the Gospels of Matthew and Luke?

Graeco-Roman Myths

Some writers continue to claim that early Christians fashioned the virginal conception stories (picked up later by Matthew and Luke) by borrowing from Graeco-Roman legends about the extraordinary birth of mythical or actual heroes. Since they acknowledged the divine origin and status of Jesus, Christians supposedly took over and applied to him current legends about the conception and birth of such heroic figures as Heracles, Romulus, Remus, Plato, and Alexander the Great.

Three groups of notable difficulties have rightly been raised against this hypothesis. First, is there any hard evidence that such legends were known to the earliest, Palestinian Christians during the years leading up to the composition of Matthew and Luke? Certainly in the second century, the writings of Christians like Justin Martyr (d. around 165) and Irenaeus (d. around 200) show that they were acquainted with Graeco-Roman legendary accounts about the extraordinary conception and birth of mythical or actual heroes. But no such clear evidence exists that the eyewitnesses of the life of Jesus, associates of such eyewitnesses, and the communities (and individuals) that Matthew and Luke drew from when writing their Gospels knew such Graeco-Roman myths.[6] Some writers have bravely affirmed that Graeco-Roman thought forms and myths affected the composition of Mark, the first Gospel to be written and on which Matthew and Luke drew. If Mark was influenced by Graeco-Roman legends, one might suppose that the two Gospels which followed him might well display similar influences. But the alleged

---

[6] On the composition of the four Gospels, see Richard Bauckham, *Jesus and the Eyewitnesses: The Gospels as Eyewitness Testimony* (Grand Rapids: Eerdmans, 2006; 2nd edn, 2017).

evidence for such Graeco-Roman influence on Mark is concocted rather than detected.[7]

Second, would the Graeco-Roman myths about Zeus and other gods impregnating women and producing remarkable offspring have proved acceptable models to be adopted by early Christians, whether of Jewish or Gentile origin, when they recounted the conception and birth of Jesus? Is this plausible? The New Testament evidence is overwhelmingly clear: the first Christians, whether Jew or Gentile, were immersed in the Old Testament scriptures and maintained the essence of Jewish faith in one God (even if now they acknowledged some measure of "personal" distinctions between Father, Son, and Holy Spirit within the unity of the divine life (e.g., 2 Cor 13:13; Matt 28:19). This Jewish faith in YHWH which the first Christians inherited simply excluded any notion of God having a female consort, let alone indulging in promiscuous sexual conduct. Nowhere do the Jewish scriptures attribute to YHWH the sexual activity and trickery ascribed to Zeus and other deities who were said to have fathered mythical heroes and exceptional human beings. There is not the slightest hint that the first Christians ever wavered in maintaining the Jewish image of God as being utterly beyond sexual activity. It seems unimaginable that early Christians, coming from a Jewish background or at least nourished by Jewish scriptures, would have considered Graeco-Roman legends about the sexual performances of the gods appropriate sources for illuminating the human origin of Jesus. When we come to the second century, we find Justin Martyr dismissing the promiscuous capers of Zeus in Greek mythology as loathsome and worthy only of a de-

---

[7] For details, see G. O'Collins, *Easter Faith* (London: Darton, Longman & Todd, 2003), 48–49, 67–69, 112.

ity "overcome by the love of evil and shameful pleasure" (*First Apology*, 21).

Third, the thesis of borrowed legends crumbles dramatically, once we examine the alleged parallels. Over and over again the Graeco-Roman myths show themselves startlingly different from the accounts of Jesus' virginal conception found in Matthew and Luke. The Graeco-Roman stories repeatedly tell of sexual intercourse between a god and a woman, who is sometimes tricked into having relations with the god in question or even raped by him. Those myths remain unlike the Annunciation story, in which Mary's conscious agreement features prominently and there is no sexual intercourse (Luke 1:26–38). The Graeco-Roman legends generally turn mothers of mythical heroes, such as Danaë (who begets Perseus) into mere tools of divine passion and projects. The smutty tone of these legends, which often feature mythical figures who (unlike Mary and Jesus) do not belong to human history, can verge on soft pornography. Let me cite three examples.

Diodorus Siculus, a first-century BC writer, recounted the legend of the conception, birth, and subsequent "labors" of Heracles. Supposedly the great-granddaughter of Zeus, Alkmene "was taken by Zeus through a deceit" and she gave birth to Heracles. Thus this hero, according to his mythical family tree, was both the son and the great-great-grandson of Zeus, "the greatest of the gods." Diodorus described the episode as follows: "When Zeus lay with Alkmene, he tripled the length of the night and, in the increased length of time spent in begetting the child, he foreshadowed the exceptional power of the child who was to be begotten." Since Zeus "could never hope to seduce her because of her self-control," he "chose deceit. By this means he tricked Alkmene [and her husband] in every way." Hera, Zeus' wife, was naturally jealous and furious at what had happened.

She succeeded in stopping for a time the labor pains of Alkmene. After Heracles was eventually born, Hera even sent "two snakes to destroy the baby, but the child did not panic. He grabbed the neck of each snake in his two hands and strangled them" (*Universal History*, 4.9.1–10). It is bizarre to imagine that this legend of Heracles's conception and birth served as a workable model for the accounts provided by Matthew and Luke about the virginal conception and birth of Jesus.

Livy (d. AD 12 or 17) tells briefly a story of the conception and birth of the legendary founders of Rome, Romulus and Remus. Their mother, Rhea Silvia, had been forced by her wicked uncle who had usurped the throne of Alba Longa, to become a vestal virgin. Then she "was violated and gave birth to twins. She named Mars as their father, either because she believed that, or because the fault might appear less heinous if a deity were cause of it." The cruel king threw her into prison and had the babies left in a cradle on the banks of the Tiber. They were suckled by a kindly she-wolf, and grew up to found the city of Rome (*The History of Rome*, 1.4). A Greek writer, Dionysius of Halicarnassus (d. early first century AD), gives three versions of how Rhea Silvia was violated in the course of her duties as a vestal virgin. The three versions ascribe the rape, respectively, to one of her suitors, to her evil uncle (Amulius), or to the god Mars (*Roman Antiquities*, 1.76–77). Once again we would require a reckless leap of the historical imagination to think that these stories about Romulus and Remus furnished a source for early Christians bent on creating a "fitting" account of Jesus' conception and birth.

What of Graeco-Roman legends about the origin of such genuinely historical figures as Plato and Alexander the Great? The god of wisdom, Phoebus Apollo, was sometimes credited with providing Amphictione, the mother of Plato, with superior, divine sperm for the conception of her brilliant offspring. To bring about the desired effect from this sperm, her human husband was prevented from having sexual intercourse with her.[8]

Even during her lifetime some credulous people were led to believe that the mother of Alexander the Great, Olympias, had conceived him through intercourse with Zeus. The god appeared in the form of "a great snake" (a classic penis symbol) and wound himself around her body while Olympias was asleep (Plutarch, "Alexander," *Parallel Lives*, 2.1–3.2). Suetonius (b. about AD 69), drawing on an earlier Greek source, tells a similar story about the origin of Augustus Caesar. The god Apollo assumed the form of a snake and came in the middle of the night, when she was asleep, to impregnate Atia, the mother of the future Emperor Augustus (*Lives of the Caesars*, 2.94.4). These stories about what happened during the night to the sleeping Olympias and Atia stand in striking contrast with the Annunciation story in Luke's Gospel. Mary is fully awake, accepts the divine invitation to collaborate in the incarnation, and does so without any sexual intercourse taking place. Whatever the historical status of some particular details in Luke's text, it stands worlds apart from the myths told by Plutarch and Suetonius about Olympias and Atia, respectively.

The denial of the virginal conception of Jesus attributed to Judas in *The Gospel according to Judas* belongs in a long sequence that goes back to the second century. The latest denial seems no more persuasive than the earlier ones. Yet it leaves us with a challenge. All who agree with Raymond Brown in arguing that "both Matthew and Luke regarded the virginal conception as historical,[9] and in maintaining the traditional faith about the virginal conception

---

[8] See Chadwick, *Origen Contra Celsum*, 321, n. 12.
[9] R. Brown, *Birth of the Messiah*, 517.

hold, in effect, that the conception of Jesus took place not through normal sexual intercourse but through a special intervention of the Holy Spirit. In holding this belief, Christians claim a unique divine action that has happened only once in human history and that differs, for instance, from the miraculous activity of Jesus' ministry, which finds some parallels in the Old Testament, in the Acts of the Apostles, and in the ongoing story of Christianity. In the case of the virginal conception, however, we deal with a special divine action that is the only one of its kind. The challenge is to show how the religious significance of this unique conception. It is not enough merely to uphold the fact of the virginal conception. One must also show how it is religiously illuminating, a truth that has deep bearing on the history of our salvation. Luke can point us in the right direction here and lead us towards four conclusions.

The Virginal Conception in its Religious Significance

First of all, Luke places his account of the virginal conception within an Old Testament background. He looks back to various extraordinary conceptions in Jewish history and to great persons born from the so far barren wombs of older women. His genealogy of Jesus (Luke 3:23–37) evokes the story of Isaac and Jacob, who were born to previously childless mothers. Even more clearly by calling to mind in the *Magnificat* (Luke 1:46–55) the prayer of Hannah (1 Sam 2:1–10) the story of a woman who late in life conceived and gave birth to Samuel, a remarkable prophetic and priestly figure, Luke suggests how such births prefigure the virginal conception of Jesus.

The evangelist does not take up Isaiah 7:14. Unlike the Old Testament texts about older, childless women like Sarah (the mother of Isaac), Rebecca (the mother of Jacob), and Hannah, that verse speaks of a young woman of marriageable age who is presumably fertile. Nor does Luke find any texts in the Old Testament that refer to someone being conceived and born through the power of the Holy Spirit. The messianic king to come from the house of David will enjoy six gifts from the divine Spirit (Isa 11:1–2), but it is never said that he would be conceived through the Spirit. What Luke recalls are passages about some older women who gave birth to a son who played a remarkable role in salvation history.

The climactic example of a barren woman conceiving and giving birth to an extraordinary son comes with the promise of John the Baptist's conception (Luke 1:5–17). Clearly Luke sees nothing impure about married love and the normal way of conception; great joy follows the sexual union of the aged Zechariah and Elizabeth and the birth of their son (Luke 1:58). But Luke acknowledges a kind of quantum jump when the divinely caused conception of Jesus brings a new, unexpected life from a young virgin. The story of salvation history shows here discontinuity as well as continuity—something startlingly new standing within but also bringing a dramatic change to a long-standing divine pattern.

In two books, his Gospel and the Acts of the Apostles, Luke reports various miracles worked not only by Jesus but also by his followers—in particular, by Peter and Paul. Like Jesus the apostles heal cripples, drive out demons, and even bring the dead back to life (e.g., Acts 3:1–10; 5:14–16; 8:4–8; 9:32–43; 14:8–10). But Luke never claims that any of Jesus' followers ever brought about, through the power of the Holy Spirit, a virginal conception. Jesus' virginal conception stands apart, a unique action of God that may not be repeated, as are the characteristic miracles worked by Jesus in his ministry (see Luke 7:22–23). Like his glorious resurrection from the dead, his virginal conception towers above the "normal" miracles attributed to Jesus and his followers. The virginal conception of Jesus and his resurrection from the dead (along with the outpouring of the Holy Spirit) mark the beginning and the end of the central climax of salvation history: the coming of the Son of the God.

We can express this imaginatively by linking the womb of Mary in which the Son of God was conceived with the tomb in which he was buried. That hollowed out vessel received his body after the crucifixion and like a womb held it for three days until he rose, newly and gloriously alive. Thus a womb at the start and a tomb at the end mark the beginning and the end, respectively, of the first coming of the Son of God.

A second theme that emerges naturally from Luke's account of the Annunciation was the *double generation* of the Son. As the Council of Chalcedon put matters through its definition of 451, in his divinity the Son was born of the Father "before all ages" and in his humanity was born of the Virgin Mary "in the last days."[10] The theme of the double, eternal/temporal generation flowered early with Irenaeus and was developed by such fathers of the church as St Cyril of Jerusalem, St Cyril of Alexandria, and St Leo the Great before the language passed into the definition of Chalcedon.[11]

As one might expect, St Augustine of Hippo articulated the double generation with brilliant concision and did so in a way that brought out the redemptive truth of the virginal conception. In a Christmas homily preached some time after 511/12, he declared: "Christ was born both from a father and a mother, both without a father and without a mother. From the Father he was born God, from the mother he was born a man; without a mother he was born

---

[10] Heinrich. Denzinger and Peter Hünermann (eds), *Enchiridion Symbolorum, Definitionum et Declarationum,* 43rd edn (San Francisco: Ignatius Press, 2012), nr 301.

[11] See G. O'Collins, *Christology: A Biblical, Historical and Systematic Study of Jesus*; 2nd edn (Oxford: Oxford University Press, 2009), 171.

God; without a father he was born a man" (*Sermo* 184.2; see 190.2; 195.1).

Through the words of Gabriel to Mary, Luke states the double generation: "you will conceive in your womb and bear a son" and "he will be called the Son of the Most High" (Luke 1:31–32). Thus the virginal conception expresses the human and divine origin of Jesus. The fact that he was born of a woman points to his humanity. The fact that he was conceived and born of a virgin points to his divinity and his eternal, personal origin as the Son of God. Jesus has a human mother but no (biological) human father—a startling sign of his divine generation by the Father within the eternal life of God.

Third, Luke's presentation of the virginal conception also yields meaning about Jesus' *relationship with the Spirit*. Gabriel says to Mary: "the Holy Spirit will come upon you." Christians experienced the outpouring of the Spirit in the aftermath of Jesus' resurrection from the dead. They came to appreciate how the Spirit, sent to them by the risen Christ or in his name, had been actively present in the whole of Christ's life—not only at his baptism and subsequent ministry but also at his conception. In other words, the risen Christ blessed his followers with the Holy Spirit. In his entire earthly existence he had been uniquely blessed by the Spirit—right from his very conception when he came into the created world through the Spirit's power.

Thus the virginal conception plays its part in revealing and clarifying that central truth: from the beginning to the end of Jesus' history, the Trinity is manifested. His total history discloses the God who is Father, Son, and Holy Spirit. We would miss something essential about the virginal conception, if we were to ignore its "trinitarian face." Christian artists have led the way here. Master Bertram of Minden (d. about 1415), Hubert and Jan van Eych (in their 1432 altarpiece in the St Bavo Cathedral, Ghent) and Fra Lippo Lippi introduce the Holy Spirit and God the Father into their representations of the Annunciation.

A fourth theological reflection on the virginal conception takes up the prior initiative of God embodied in the presence and promise conveyed by Gabriel. By opening the climactic phase of redemption or new creation, the conception of Christ exemplifies the truth that salvation comes as divine gift. Human beings cannot inaugurate and carry through their own redemption. Like the original creation of the universe, the new creation is divine work and pure grace—to be received on the human side, just as Mary received the new life in her womb.

This new creation more than reverses the harm caused by human sin. Once again great artists proved alert to the redemptive role of the virginal conception, In a famous altarpiece, Bertram of Minden set in parallel the creation and fall of our first parents with scenes of the Annunciation and Nativity. Beato Angelico, in one version he painted of the Annunciation (now in Cortona), introduced on the upper left the tiny figures of Adam and Eve. Their fall into sin produced and symbolized the human need for redemption, which God began to meet decisively by sending Gabriel to the Virgin Mary. In another painting of the Annunciation (now in the Prado), Beato Angelico included a representation of Adam and Eve being driven out of the garden of paradise.

One can cite many other works of art that reveal sensitivity to the place of the virginal conception in the whole divine plan to overcome sin and evil and bring the new life of grace. Examples of such insight are not lacking today. The Church of Saint Lawrence in Huntington, Connecticut, displays a vividly beautiful, stained glass window of the Annunciation. On the lower left, below the figures of Mary and Gabriel, there is small, red-colored representation of a snake. It recalls the serpent that tempted Eve in the Garden of Eden, the serpent whose head would be crushed by the New Eve (Gen 3:15). At the Annunciation, Mary was called by God to play her part towards undoing the harm caused by the first Eve.

To conclude. The Archer/Moloney *The Gospel according to Judas* is certainly not the first attempt to rehabilitate Judas Iscariot religiously. It seems, however, the first time that Judas has been represented as dismissing the virginal conception of Jesus. But this rejection of the virginal conception is no more convincing than earlier ones. I do not want to credit this novel with more importance than it deserves. Yet it can have its value by encouraging us to reflect on the rich theological significance of the way in which Jesus was conceived and entered our human scene. The more we appreciate the meaningfulness of the virginal conception in the overall pattern of God's plan of salvation, the more credible this unique conception will be seen to be.

6

BELIEVING AS VERBAL IN JOHN'S GOSPEL

In *Jesus in John's Gospel* William Loader encourages readers to hear "the questions which the text of the Gospel raises."[1] Apropos of the relation of believers to Jesus, the Fourth Gospel raises a serious question by never using the noun "faith (*pistis*)" but always the verb "believe (*pisteuein*)" and does so at least 96 times (from 1:7–20:31).[2] John shows a similar verbal choice for the closely associated verb "knowing (*ginōskein*)" (e.g., John 6:69), employing it 56 times, while avoiding completely the noun "knowledge (*gnōsis*)."

The use of the verb *pisteuein* made by the author of John differs from the way in which some other terms are handled: for instance, he employs not only the verbs "live (*zēn*)," "glorify (*doxazein*)," and "illuminate (*phōtizein*)," but also the nouns "life (*zōē*)," "glory

---

[1] W. Loader, *Jesus in John's Gospel: Structure and Issues in Johannine Christology* (Grand Rapids: Eerdmans, 2017), 8.

[2] His decisions about variant readings led Rudolf Schnackenburg, *The Gospel According To St John*, vol. 1, trans. Kevin Smyth (London: Burns & Oates, 1968) to list 98 occurrences of *pisteuein* in the Fourth Gospel (558). The count of 96 is endorsed by Walter Bauer, Frederick W. Danker, William E. Arndt, and E. Wilbur Gingrich, *Greek-English Lexicon of the New Testament and Other Early Christian Literature* (3rd edn; Chicago: Chicago University Press, 2000), 918. Apropos of *pisteuein*, Andreas J. Koestenberger remarks: "apart from 'Jesus' (237 times) and 'Father' (136 times), there is no theologically significant word that occurs more frequently in John's Gospel than the word 'believe'" (*Encountering John: The Gospel in Historical, Literary, and Literary Perspective* (Grand Rapids: Baker Academic, 2013), 46),

(*doxa*)," and "light (*phōs*)."³ Why does he also adopt nouns in these particular cases, if, in what looks like an analogous case, he completely avoids the noun *pistis*?

John's preference for the verb *pisteuein* over the noun *pistis* sets him apart from the apostle Paul. His seven certainly authentic letters (Romans, 1 and 2 Corinthians, Galatians, Philippians, 1 Thessalonians, and Philemon) introduce 101 times the noun *pistis* (with 72 occurrences in Romans and Galatians) but only 33 times the verb *pisteuein*.

These findings from the text of John's Gospel raise the question: Why this total preference for the verb "believe" over the noun "faith" (but a willingness to adopt a noun in three other, apparently parallel, cases)? I have not been able to find a commentator who fully and satisfactorily examines John's 'verbal' preference for "to believe." Loader himself speaks of "a progression to full faith," the "journey" of faith, the "ongoing faith relationship," which "continues," "grows," and advances beyond a faith that is merely based on miracles.⁴ This language summarizes the dynamic Johannine vision of faith, even if Loader neither appeals to statistics demonstrating how complete was John's verbal preference nor reflects at depth on the significance of persistently choosing a verb (*pisteuein*) over an equally available noun (*pistis*).

What of Loader's predecessors, who might have examined John's verbal emphasis for *pisteuein*? We begin with Rudolf Bultmann, not least because of the considerable attention Loader paid to his classic

---

³ John employs the verbs "live (*zēn*)" 16 times, "glorify (*doxazein*)" 23 times, and "illuminate (*phōtizein*)" once, and uses the corresponding nouns "life (*zōē*) 36 times, "glory (*doxa*)" 19 times, and "light (*phōs*)" 23 times. In the case of these three verbs, but not *pisteuein*, we *also* find the corresponding nouns. Can there be an explanation for this?

⁴ Loader, *Jesus in John's Gospel*, 293.

work on the Fourth Gospel.⁵ We can then take up other scholars who led Johannine scholarship in the twentieth century.

Bultmann, Dodd, Barrett, Schnackenburg, Brown

Bultmann

In various places, Bultmann presents the vision of faith found in John's Gospel.⁶ In the *Theology of the New Testament*, for instance, he spends five pages on "faith as the hearing of the word," and dedicates the rest of the chapter to "faith as eschatological existence."⁷ As usual, Bultmann offers much for reflection: for instance, on other verbs which more or less mean the same thing as to believe—to "abide in" (e.g., John 15:4–7),⁸ "come" (e.g., 5:40; 6:35; 7:37), "follow" (e.g., 1:43), "accept" (e.g., 1:1–12), "hear" (e.g., 4:42; 5:24), "see," as expressed by several Greek verbs (e.g., *theasthai* 1:14), and "know" (e.g., 6:69). But Bultmann shows little concern to compare statistics and explain the remarkable dominance of the verb *pisteuein* in the face of the total absence in John's Gospel of the noun *pistis*.

Bultmann hints at the verbal quality of faith in the language of the Fourth Gospel. Apropos of the Revealer's gift of "*chara* (joy)," he

---

⁵ In *Jesus in John's Gospel*, Loader dedicates the first ten pages to Bultmann. The closing index of names shows that this book makes Bultmann one of its most cited commentators on John.

⁶ *The Gospel of John: A Commentary*, trans. G. R. Beasley-Murray, R. W. N. Hoare, and J. K. Riches (Oxford: Basil Blackwell, 1971; German orig., 1941); Bultmann, *Theology of the New Testament*, vol. 2, trans. Kendrick Grobel (London: SCM Press, 1955; German orig., 1948), 70–92; Bultmann, "*pisteuō*" etc., in Gerhard Kittel et al. (eds), *Theological Dictionary of the New Testament*, vol. 6, trans. Geoffrey Bromiley (Grand Rapids: Eerdmans, 1964), 174–228.

⁷ *Theology of the New Testament*, vol. 2, 70–74, 75–92.

⁸ "Remaining in" Jesus' is "virtually interchangeable" with *pisteuein*; it "signals a steadfast persevering that yields the reciprocal results of relationship" (Dennis R. Lindsay, "Believing in Jesus: John's Provocative Theology of Faith," *Restoration Quarterly* 58 (2016), 193–209, at 200).

remarks that it "is never a definitively realized state, but always lies ahead of the believer as something to be realized." Joy "can never become a static condition."[9]

Primarily Bultmann is concerned to present faith as hearing the word that leads to an eschatological existence.[10] Those who are incapable of hearing Jesus' word cannot believe him or believe in him (John 8:43, 45–47). The sheep who "hear" their shepherd, however. can follow him (John 10:5, 16, 27).

It is more in the area of *revelation* (rather than that of any responding human faith) that Bultmann has permanently enriched Johannine scholarship. His commentary on John's Gospel successfully uses the theme of divine self-revelation when presenting the structure of that gospel. Debates over such matters as Bultmann's view of faith, still less of sources, should not be allowed to obscure his contribution to a biblical understanding of revelation.[11]

Dodd and Barrett

In *The Interpretation of the Fourth Gospel*, C. H. Dodd had noted the close association between the verbs *pisteuein* and *ginōskein*: for instance, in Peter's words to Jesus, "we have come to believe and to know that you are the Holy One of God" (John 6:69). Dodd comments: "along with *ginōskein* the evangelist used the term *pisteuein*, which is in fact considerably more frequent in the gospel."[12] Yes, indeed: *pisteuein* is found in John at least 96 times, whereas *ginōskein* turns up only 56 times.

---

[9] Bultmann, *Theology of the New Testament*, vol. 2, 83.
[10] Ibid., 70–92.
[11] Ibid., 49–69.
[12] C. H. Dodd, *The Interpretation of the Fourth Gospel* (Cambridge: Cambridge University Press, 1953), 179.

Without being truly synonymous for John, the two verbs overlap in meaning. The deep personal *relationship* experienced through knowing Jesus converges with the new *recognition* and radical allegiance brought through believing in him. It is Jesus himself who provides the one major exception to the synonymous parallelism between the two verbs. While he is said to "know" God (e.g., John 7:29; 8:55; 10:15), he is never said to believe in God.

Here one should add that, just as the Fourth Gospel never introduces the noun *pistis* along with the verb *pisteuein*, so it never introduces the noun *gnōsis* along with *ginōskein*. John not only understands the knowledge of God as similar to (or even identical with) the process of seeing or believing in God revealed in Jesus but also prefers to express it through a verb and never through a noun. How might we interpret this particular verbal preference?

Commenting on the Fourth Gospel, C. K. Barrett remarks that "in John as in Paul the real medium of salvation is faith".[13] Yet he recognizes that their formulations are "quite different." John's Gospel, for instance, "never uses the noun *pistis*." He also notes that the noun "*gnōsis* does not appear in the gospel."[14] Barrett hints at the significance of the verbal usage "*pisteuein*," but it is only a passing hint. The "present (continuous) tense" of *pisteuein* in John 6:29 does not point to "an *act* of faith but [to] a *life* of faith."[15]

Barrett expresses as nouns what believing conveys: as "allegiance and assent," faith involves "the means of life and regeneration."[16] Here four nouns are deployed to describe what John always expresses verbally.

---

[13] C. K. Barrett, *The Gospel According to St John*, 2nd edn (London: SPCK, 1978; first publ. 1955), 81.
[14] Ibid.
[15] Ibid., 287.
[16] Ibid., 163–64.

Schnackenburg

Among the classical Johannine scholars of the mid-twentieth century, Schnackenburg comes perhaps closest to addressing fully the question that has prompted this essay: Why does the Fourth Gospel constantly prefer the verb *pisteuein* over the noun *pistis*? While helpfully remarking that the verb turns up 98 times in John, Schnackenburg speaks of the noun when he comments: "Throughout the whole of the Gospel one can recognize the supreme importance which the evangelist accords to *faith*."[17] Yet what could be the importance suggested by the evangelist through constantly preferring the verb "to believe" (or one of its equivalents) over the noun "faith"?

This question becomes more urgent when Schnackenburg supplies statistics that reveal a significant contrast between John and Paul. The full Pauline corpus chooses the noun *pistis* 142 times and the verb *pisteuein* only 54 times. Schnackenburg looks elsewhere for the contrast between John and Paul: "faith is equally emphasized by Paul and John, although the accents are different."[18] What are these different accents?

Schnackenburg writes: "[in John, faith] appears as a fundamental and comprehensive decision and attitude towards the eschatological envoy of God and his saving revelation. Hence "faith in John has attained a markedly theological eminence, in which it resembles that of Paul." In "contrast to Paul, for whom faith in the crucified and risen Lord is all-important, John brings faith into his account of the earthly work of Jesus and makes it unfold in the encounter with the redeemer during his life in this

---

[17] Schnackenburg, 'The Notion of Faith in the Fourth Gospel', *Gospel According to John*, vol. 1, 558–75, at 558.
[18] Ibid, 558.

world." Having provided some relevant statistics, Schnackenburg might have found a difference between Paul and John *also* in the verbal quality of Johannine faith and what that might signify. At best he merely implies this when he writes of the Fourth Evangelist describing the "coming and growth of faith."[19] This is a growth in attaching oneself to Jesus. In the words of Schnackenburg, "to believe means to accept the self-revelation of Jesus and to attach oneself to this unique mediator of salvation to attain eternal life."[20]

In his excursus on faith, Schnackenburg sets himself to illuminate the Fourth Evangelist's "interest in the call to faith, the awakening of faith, the pedagogy of faith," and deep "theological conception of faith."[21] Is there no need to investigate also the *verbal* characteristics of John's presentation of faith?

In fact, Schnackenburg offers some eloquent pages summarizing the Fourth Gospel's message of the "genesis and growth of faith," along with "the testing and triumph of faith." He does this by citing individuals like Nicodemus and the man born blind who come to believe in Jesus, as well as groups who do so like the people of Sychar.[22] Attention to Greek syntax could have led him to appreciate the way in which John's view of the dynamic nature of faith was reinforced by a massive use of verb *pisteuein* and related verbs.

Brown

Raymond E. Brown belongs among the leading figures who shaped Johannine studies for those who came after them in the twentieth century. The first volume of his two-volume Anchor Bible com-

---

[19] Ibid.
[20] Ibid., 560.
[21] Ibid., 559.
[22] Ibid., 569–73.

mentary on the Fourth Gospel contains an appendix on "to believe (*pisteuein*)" and closely associated verbs for knowing, not only "*ginōskein*" (see Dodd above) but also "*eidenai*" (which is used 85 times in John).[23]

Brown found "knowing" and "believing to be frequently interchangeable. The important exception comes with Jesus himself.[24] He "knows" God but is never said to believe in God (see Barrett above).

Unlike Bultmann, Dodd, and Barrett, Brown provided statistics for the frequency of "*pisteuein*" in the Fourth Gospel—he counted 98 times—and mentioned the non-appearance of the noun *pistis* in that gospel. He judged this "another example of the Johannine preference for verbs and action," and briefly comments on its significance: "that John prefers the verb *pisteuein* to the noun shows that the evangelist is not thinking of faith as an internal disposition, but as an active commitment."[25] Likewise, Brown wrote of a "preference for verbs" being shown in "the Johannine writings" by the fact that neither the Gospel nor the letters and the Book of Revelation ever "use the noun *gnosis*."[26]

Yes, verbs are preferred in the Fourth Gospel and the Johannine writings generally. But it is just that—a preference and not a monopoly. We have seen how, while John uses the verb *doxazein* with slightly more frequency (23 times) than the corresponding noun *doxa* (19 times), he introduces the noun *zōē* much more often (36 times) than the corresponding verb *zēn* (16 times). The noun *phōs* at 23 times completely outnumbers its corresponding verb, *phōtizein*

---

[23] R. E. Brown, *The Gospel According to John*, vol. 1 (New York: Doubleday, 1966), 512–14.
[24] Ibid., 514.
[25] Ibid., 512.
[26] Ibid., 514.

(used only once). When presenting in appendixes *doxa*, *zōē*, and *phōs*, Brown does not mention the ratio of nouns to corresponding verbs.[27] Moreover, to explain the general preference, Brown says only a little by contrasting an "active commitment" with an "internal disposition."

Culpepper, Keener, Köstenberger, and Lincoln

Before investigating further whether more recent Johannine scholars have noticed how the Fourth Gospel used *pisteuein* at least 96 times and how they might have interpreted this "verbal" version of faith, let me pause to sum up my own view of believing as found in John's Gospel. It shares much with the classical commentators, from Bultmann to Brown.

Drawn by divine grace to the person of Jesus (John 6:44) and accepting the "signs" of God's presence in his ministry, believers give him their allegiance by responding to the divine self-revelation he embodies. Through accepting the truth he brings, they become his disciples. "Knowing" highlights more what they receive; "believing" draws attention to their freely adopted relationship of discipleship. The interchangeable status of these two terms does not obliterate all distinctions. To know and believe in Jesus is to begin a journey towards the fullness of eternal life.

Culpepper

In the 1980s Alan Culpepper's *Anatomy of the Fourth Gospel: A Study in Literary Design* observed the "progress" in divine revelation and corresponding human faith: "in John's story" the "disciples and [other] believers do not have to understand perfectly or even adequately. As long as they follow the revealer, revelation

---

[27] Ibid., 503–04, 505–08, and 515–16, respectively.

is in progress. We may be dealing with a positive "commitment" to Jesus despite misunderstanding,[28] or with failures, even a total regression when many disciples cease to follow Jesus (John 6:66).

In the Fourth Gospel's vision of faith, "the Beloved Disciple represents the paradigm of authentic faith." His witness was true and "his place was the bosom of the Lord."[29] At the other extreme, the man disabled for 38 years (John 5:1–18) "represents those whom even the signs cannot lead to authentic faith."[30] The man born blind (John 9:1–41) is a model of someone coming from signs and through Jesus' words "to an authentic faith."[31]

Culpepper's discussion of faith is enhanced by his noting how disciples, right from the case of Andrew, have the task of bringing faith to others. He becomes a disciple and at once shares faith in Jesus with his brother Peter (John 1:40–42). Culpepper sketches this function of the disciples and includes a relevant statistic: the Fourth Gospel refers 78 times to "disciples (*mathētai*)."[32] Culpepper does not press on to mention that this function of the disciples leads others to believe (*pisteuein*), a verb that occurs at least 96 times in John. Bringing others to believe and believing itself belong with each other (see John 2:11).

Keener and *Köstenberger*

In a two-volume commentary on John, Craig S. Keener does not go far in examining the evangelist's predilection for the verb *pisteuein*. He writes of the personal relationship between believers and Jesus,

---

[28] (Philadelphia: Fortress Press, 1983), 115, 147.
[29] Ibid., 226–27.
[30] Ibid., 138.
[31] Ibid., 147.
[32] Ibid., 115.

remarks how the Gospel employs the verb 98 times,[33] and more or less leaves it at that.

A year later Andreas J. Köstenberger, perhaps aware of the lack of uniformity in counting occurrences in John of *pisteuein* (98 or 96), speaks of nearly one hundred occurrences, notes the total absence of the noun *pistis*, and offers a brief reason for the evangelist's preference: "he is much more concerned about active, relational trust in Jesus Christ."[34]

Lincoln

Andrew Lincoln dwells on the response that readers make to the Fourth Gospel's stories of faith: they can identify with "the role of Jesus' followers in the narrative" and "be confirmed in the appropriate beliefs about his identity."[35] Lincoln provides statistics for the occurrences of the noun "glory (*doxa*)" and the verb "glorify (*doxazein*)": "the noun 'glory' occurs 19 times while the verb 'to glorify' is to be found 23 times."[36] While John 1:14 ("we saw his glory") illustrates how "seeing is the perception of faith," an inadequate belief "fails to see through the signs to what they signify—the glory of Jesus in his oneness with God."[37]

In other words, Lincoln understands John to expect an "appropriate response to Jesus' performance of signs." That response is nothing less than "belief in the one who performs them,"[38], or, as we should say in the light of the evangelist's total preference for the

---

[33] *The Gospel of John: A Commentary*, vol. 1 (Peabody, MA: Hendrickson, 2003), 326.
[34] *John: Baker Exegetical Commentary on the New Testament* (Grand Rapids: Baker Academic, 2004), 34.
[35] A. T. Lincoln, *The Gospel According to Saint John* (London: Continuum, 2005), 87.
[36] Ibid., 105.
[37] Ibid., 104, 145.
[38] Ibid., 188.

verb *pisteuein* over the noun *pistis*, believing in the one who performs the signs.

Byrne, Morgan, van Deventer

Byrne

Recent works dedicated to John remark on that Gospel's notable use of the verb "to believe (*pisteuein*)." In *Life Abounding: A Reading of John's Gospel*, Brendan Byrne accurately observes that, while there are many references to faith in the verbal form (*pisteuein*), John never employs the noun *pistis*. "This," he adds, "lends the sense that, rather than simply an internal disposition, faith is dynamic personal commitment, above all to the person of Jesus."[39]

The title of Byrne's work, *Life Abounding*, which can be nothing less than Life shared, joined a remark by Teresa Morgan in prompting me to suspect why the noun *pistis* is totally absent from John's Gospel, whereas the verb *pisteuein* occurs nearly one hundred times. I will explain this below.

Morgan

In her magisterial study, *Roman Faith and Christian Faith: Pistis and Fides in the Early Roman Empire and Early Churches*,[40] Teresa Morgan dedicates nearly fifty pages to the usage of *pisteuein* in the Johannine corpus. She has already shown how the noun "*pistis* has a very wide range of meanings," unlike the verb *pisteuein* which "has a much narrower range of meaning." She does not press the point, and even suggests that the "absence of *pistis* in

---

[39] (Collegeville, MN: Liturgical Press, 2014), 355.
[40] (Oxford: Oxford University Press, 2015), 392–443.

John's Gospel remains ultimately a puzzle."[41] Yet, I would argue, her comment on usage, and, specifically, on the usage of the verb, offers a contributory reason why John employs the verb nearly one hundred times and never introduces the noun. The evangelist has a thoroughly Christocentric view of trusting/believing as focused "narrowly" on (often *eis*) the person of Jesus (e.g. 1:12; 2:11). The "very wide range of meanings" attached to noun *pistis* might obscure the particular, personal meaning that the evangelist intends.

Morgan points out that John shows "a strong preference for couching key concepts in verbs rather than nouns."[42] In general this is true, but we need to explain why the evangelist sometimes couches key concepts as nouns as well as verbs. We saw at the beginning of this chapter how key concepts expressed in verbs (above all, *zēn* and *doxazein*) go hand in hand with the nouns for life and glory (*zōē* and *doxa*). Without attending to these examples, Morgan herself adds two other examples: the verb *agapein* and the noun for love (*agapē*); and the verb/noun for truth. While the verb *alētheuein* (be truthful), itself a rarity in Greek, occurs only twice in the New Testament (Gal 4:16; Eph 4:15), John's Gospel contains 25 times the noun for truth (*alētheia*).[43] Doing the truth and being in the truth are, Morgan reflects, alternate ways of "experiencing the idea of divine *participation*."[44]

Here "participation" leapt off the page for me. Below I want to take up this notion and go beyond Morgan in suggesting why the Fourth Gospel makes room for the nouns *zōē*, *doxa*, *agapē*, and

---

[41] Ibid., 395, 397.
[42] Ibid., 395.
[43] Ibid., 396, n. 14.
[44] Ibid., 432; italics mine.

alētheia but not for the noun *pistis*. Believers can participate in the "abounding" Life, Glory, Love and Truth that is to be attributed to the person of Jesus. But there is no abounding faith in which they can share. They are called (or "drawn," John 6:44; see 12:32) to initiate the process of *pisteuein*, a relationship of believing in the person of Jesus, now revealed to them.

Morgan finds positive and negative "traces" of changes and "developments" in the trusting/believing that constitutes *pisteuein*. "To the end of the Gospel," the disciples "continue to misunderstand and fail Jesus." In short, she concludes, "*pisteuein* is perhaps work in progress for all Jesus' followers."[45] I would remove the "perhaps"; the evidence which Morgan cites establishes that believing is truly work in progress for the disciples as a whole (e.g., John 14:8–14; 20:8–9).

Van Deventer

A recent article by Cornelia van Deventer, "The Mosaic of Belief in the Fourth Gospel," offers an up-to-date, two-page bibliography on believing in John.[46] She sketches helpfully both portraits of belief and distorted portraits of belief to be found in John, writing of a mosaic "of performative responses to Jesus (and God)."[47] In the sense promoted by modern analytic philosophy, performatives are speech acts that describe reality and change the reality they describe. "I take you to be my lawful wedded husband" would be an example easy to hand. Those words, by helping to

---

[45] Ibid., 406–07.
[46] *Neotestamentica* 55 (2021), 155–70. Catrin H. Williams provides another bibliography that serves the scope of my article: "Faith, Eternal Life and Spirit in the Gospel of John," in Judith M. Lieu and Martinus C. de Boer (eds), *The Oxford Handbook of Johannine Studies* (Oxford: Oxford University Press, 2018), 347–62, at 359–62.
[47] Van Deventer, "The Mosaic of Belief," 165.

create a marriage bond, change an existing reality and describe a new reality. I think van Deventer seems to have in mind the less technical sense of any performances that express what believing in Christ entails.

Among the scholars mentioned in this article, she stands out for using experts in New Testament syntax. They note, for instance, that all the occurrences of the participle *ho pisteuōn* in John's Gospel are "in the present." This illustrates the progressive, continuous actions of believers, which move them beyond a merely "once-off" action.[48]

Daniel Wallace

Experts in New Testament syntax illuminate for us what is at stake when the Fourth Gospel studiously avoids the noun *pistis* and employs the verb *pisteuein* at least 96 times, making it (after "Jesus" and "Father") the third commonest theological term in this Gospel. Let us take up one of the experts van Deventer mentions, Daniel B. Wallace.[49] His monumental study of the exegetical syntax of the New Testament, taken with the *Oxford Dictionary of English* (3rd ed. 2010; hereafter OED), sheds further light on John's total preference for the verb.

The OED describes a *noun* as follows: "a word (other than a pronoun) used to identify one of a class of people, places or things or to name a particular one of these."[50] This description of "noun" fits not only contemporary English but also the Greek used in the New Testament. By speaking of classes of "peoples, places or things," this

---

[48] Ibid.; this recalls how appropriate the present tense is for pointing to the ongoing life of faith.
[49] *Greek Grammar: Beyond the Basics* (Grand Rapids: Zondervan, 1996).
[50] OED, 1214.

description illustrates, rather than any particular identification, the "very wide range of meanings" that Morgan assigns to such nouns as *pistis* in Greek and *fides* in Latin.[51]

A *verb*, according to the OED, is "a word used to describe an action, state or occurrence and forming the main part of the predicate of a sentence."[52] This language is paralleled by Wallace's account of New Testament verbs in the active voice: "the subject *performs, produces*, or *experiences the action* or exists in the *state* expressed by the verb."[53] Wallace highlights how verbs point to experiences and actions (physical, mental, or both) even more than to states in which the subject exists.

Add the fact that many of the occurrences of the verb *pisteuein* (e.g., 1:7, 12; 11:26; 20:31) in the Fourth Gospel are found in the *present* tense (e.g., 14:1) and so, in Wallace's words, "represent an activity as in process" (or in progress).[54] Once again his observation converges with what the OED says, this time with what it says of the present tense as "expressing an action as now going on or habitually performed, or as a condition now existing."[55]

There is a convergence between the use of verbs with active meaning and often in the present tense in both New Testament Greek and contemporary English. This opens up possibilities for those who

---

[51] In *Through the Looking-Glass* (Ch. 6), Humpty Dumpty tells Alice that verbs are "the proudest, *unlike* adjectives and nouns, which we can do anything with and make mean what we choose them to mean." This passage is often quoted as it were simply about choosing to make "words" mean what we like. But its remarks about the difference between "verbs," on the one hand, and "adjectives and nouns," on the other, should not be ignored; they suggest something about the conditions John's total preference for the verb *pisteuein* and total avoidance of the noun *pistis*.

[52] "Verb," OED, 1972.

[53] Wallace, *Greek Grammar*, 410.

[54] Ibid., 514.

[55] "Present," OED, 1404.

wish to explain John's remarkable use of the verb *pisteuein*. Repeating this verb nearly one hundred times, the evangelist emphasizes the activity of believing. Employing the verb in the present tense supports the idea of believing as an action or process now going on. Believing is an active performance more than a possession or internal possession (Brown and Byrne above), which would be better expressed by employing a noun.[56]

Typically, *pisteuein* in John's Gospel indicates acknowledging or confessing Jesus as the saving Revealer come from the Father (4: 42), believing him to be the Christ and Son of God (11:26; 20:31), entrusting oneself to him as a disciple (1:37), and entering a personal relationship with him (1:7,12; 2:23). That relationship is a gift from God (6:44), a process that can emerge and grow very quickly (as in the case of the Samaritan woman) or quite slowly (as is the case with Nicodemus). It can also be broken off (6:66). Believing is not an unconditionally stable and assured gift.

Subject of Faith

We noted above how John, while expressing key theological ideas through several verbs ("live," "glorify," and "illuminate"), was also ready to employ the corresponding nouns: "*zōē* (life)," "*doxa* (glory)," and "*phōs* (light)." The evangelist believed and knew that the incarnate Word or Son of God was to be identified unconditionally as Life, Glory, and Light (John 1:4–5; 2:11). He is the subject who enjoys abounding Life, Glory, and Light. Nouns could express satisfactorily that unconditional, eternal existence of Life, Glory,

---

[56] Williams speaks felicitously of "the journey" to/of faith: "a journey of faith [better believing] implies progressive stages"; "Faith, Eternal Life and the Spirit," 351.

and Light. Right from the start, the Gospel of John made it clear that human beings are called to share in the divine Life that reveals itself as Light: "in him [the Word] was Life and the Life was the Light of human beings" (1:4).

But there was and is no such thing as an unconditional faith, embodied absolutely in the incarnate Son of God and shared by human subjects—analogously to the way they could share in his Life (6:35), recognize his Glory (2:11), and walk no longer in the darkness (1:5) but in his Light (11:9). The Fourth Gospel could proclaim "I am the Light of the world," but not "I am Faith of the world." The evangelist knew that believing was a relational process into which the disciples of Jesus entered, a performance in active progress that could not be deemed unconditional and absolute. There was nothing conditional or relative about Jesus' own total commitment to the Father and the divine will (8:29).

Significantly it was only once in John's Gospel that Jesus presented himself as the subject of "*pisteuein*," and he did so in a negative sense. While "many believed in him when they saw the signs that he did, he did not entrust himself (*ouk episteuen auton*) to them because he knew (*ginōskein*) them all" (2:23–24). Although his signs had triggered in them a relationship of faith with Jesus, it fell short of genuine belief, being an imperfect, inadequate faith or even only "the appearance of faith."[57] Jesus knew that, and his knowledge ruled out crediting them with the advanced faith that he looked for. Here, unlike some other contexts where knowing ran parallel to believing, his knowing them ruled out believing (or having faith) in them and entrusting himself to them.

---

[57] See the comment of Barrett: "Jesus has divine knowledge and is not misled by appearances, even by the appearance of faith" (*Gospel According to St John*, 202); see also Tony Costa, "The Use of *Pisteuō* in the Gospel of John," *Conspectus* 32 (2021), 93–109, at 96–97.

Conclusion

This article has aimed at suggesting answers to two interrelated questions: Why does the Fourth Gospel employ the verb *"pisteuein"* nearly one hundred times and thus making it a key theological term, surpassed only by "Jesus" and "Father"? Why does John totally avoid employing the noun *"pistis"*?

The answers given to the two questions have been facilitated by attending to the syntax of New Testament, the kind of help provided by Daniel Wallace's account of differences in the usage of verbs and nouns. John does *not* systematically avoid such nouns as "Life." "Glory," "Light," "Truth," and "Love"; he knows how the personal fullness of these realities can be identified: Jesus is Life, Glory, Light, Truth, and Love in infinite abundance. But, given the process- or journey-nature of faith, the evangelist refrains from writing of Jesus as faith in abundance or faith itself. At the same time, the thoroughly Christocentric character of the Fourth Gospel requires repeating the theme of entering into and growing in a believing/trusting relationship with Jesus that will endure and move beyond an imperfect relationship merely based on the signs Jesus did.

Those who understand believing in John's Gospel as initiating an ongoing relationship with Jesus will adjust accordingly their vision of *ministry and leadership* in the church. For the moment I leave it to someone else to make this application, which already characterizes much of what we can glean from Dorothy Lee's recent book, *The Ministry of Women in the New Testament: reclaiming the biblical vision for church leadership.*[58]

---

[58] Grand Rapids: Baker Academic, 2021.

7

TRANSLATING JOHN 21:14 AND ITS SIGNIFICANCE

The two verbs in the passive voice used by John 21:14 (the main verb *ephanerōthē* and the participle *egertheis*) have been rendered differently by modern scholars. Their translations fall into three groups.

First, some versions understand both verbs to be in the active (or middle/intransitive) voice. For instance, the Jerusalem Bible of 1966 (JB) translates the verse, "this was the third time that Jesus showed himself to the disciples after rising from the dead." Second, other versions render the main verb in the active (or middle/intransitive) voice but render the participle in the passive: for instance, the New International Version of 1973 (NIV; rev. 1978 and 1983) translates, "this was now the third time Jesus appeared to his disciples after he was raised [by God] from the dead." Third, yet other versions render both verbs in the passive: for instance, the English Standard Version of 2001 (ESV; rev. 2007, 2011, and 2016) translates, "this was now the third time that Jesus was revealed [by God] to the disciples after he was raised [by God] from the dead."

These differences raise three questions. First, what translations are made possible or even favored by the syntax of New Testament

Greek, as found in John's Gospel? Second, are recent commentaries on the Fourth Gospel interested in the appropriate translation of John 21:14? Do they shed any light on the preferable rendering of the main verb and participle found in the verse? Third, is the verse's translation of relatively minor importance or does it carry any serious theological significance?

Relevant Syntax of New Testament Greek

Daniel B. Wallace defines what "voice" means when we distinguish between the active, passive, or middle voice: "Voice is that property of the verb which indicates how the subject is related to the action (or state) expressed by the verb. In general, the voice of the verb may indicate that the subject is *doing* the action (active), *receiving* the action (passive), or both doing and receiving (at least the results of) the action (middle)."[1] It is the middle voice that calls for attention.

What Wallace calls the "direct middle" (also known as the "reflexive or direct reflexive") is defined by him as follows: "with the direct middle, the subject acts on himself or herself. The genius of the middle can be most clearly seen by this use."[2] We should consider this possibility when translating the two verbs found in John 21:14.

The pericope which the main verb *ephanerōthē* ends (John 21:1–14) begins with the same verb occurring twice but in the active voice *ephanerōsen* (John 21:1): "after these things Jesus revealed himself again to the disciples by the sea of Tiberias; he revealed [himself] in this way" (my trans.). Edward W. Klink III rightly comments: 21:14

---

[1] D. B. Wallace, *Greek Grammar: Beyond the Basics: An Exegetical Syntax of the New Testament* (Grand Rapids: Zondervan, 1996), 408; ital. orig.
[2] Ibid., 416.

forms "an *inclusio* with what is now the third use of the verb," employed in recalling the "third" appearance of Jesus to the disciples.³ Klink does not press on and note a conclusion suggested by the presence of an inclusion.

Recognizing the occurrence of the same verb (vs. 14) after its repeated, emphatic usage in vs. 1 ("he revealed himself") encourages translating it reflexively or as a direct middle in vs. 14. While passive in form in vs. 14, the verb is not passive in meaning: Jesus the subject acts on himself. He both performs the action (revealing himself) and receives the action or rather its results (his being revealed to the seven disciples).

Understanding in this way the main verb in John 21:14 (*ephanerōthē*) affects the translation of the passive participle associated with it (*egertheis*). The association suggests also rendering the participle reflexively or as a direct middle: "after rising/having risen from the dead." Like *ephanerōthē*, the participle *egertheis*, while passive in form or voice, is active or middle in meaning.

But it does not occur to Klink to make this move. Without discussion he finds the participle passive in voice and so passive in meaning: "this is now the third time Jesus appeared to his disciples after he was raised [by God, the unexpressed but implied agent] from the dead."⁴ Does such a passive account sound strange in

---

³ E. W. Klink, *John* (Grand Rapids: Zondervan, 2016), 904. Charles H. Talbert also noted that John 21:1–14 was a unit held together by an "inclusion" (*Reading John* (London: SPCK, 1992), 258). Mark W. G. Stibbe went beyond Klink and Talbert to remark that the same verb and the same noun, occurring both at the beginning (21:1) and the end (21:14) of this passage, *phaneroō* (reveal) and *mathētai* (disciples), worked together to construct the inclusion: *John* (Sheffield: JSOT Press, 1993), 212. D. A. Carson, *The Gospel According to John* (Grand Rapids: Eerdmans, 1991), 674–75 and Raymond E. Brown, *The Gospel According to John*, vol. 2 (1970), 1083 also note how an inclusion unites 21:1 and 21:14.

⁴ Klink, *John*, 904.

John, the Gospel that highlights the activity of Christ in his own resurrection (John 10:18), and even identifies him as "I am the resurrection" (John 11:25)? Both verbs in John 21:14 are passive in form. Yet could they have laid aside its original force and replaced it with an active or middle meaning: "Jesus rose and revealed himself," rather than "was raised by God" and "was revealed by God"?

Commentaries on John 21:14

When translating John 21:14, commentaries also fall into the same three classes as the translations. First, only a few render both the main verb and the participle in the active or middle voice. Thus far I have discovered this rendering coming only from a recent German commentator, Hartwig Thyen: "Dies war das dritte Mal, dass Jesus sich seinen Jüngern offenbarte, nachdem er von den Toten auferstanden war (this was the third time that Jesus revealed himself to his disciples after he was risen from the dead)."[5] Those translators who render the participle *egertheis* by the noun "resurrection" also refrain from accepting a passive rendering.[6]

Second, a good number of scholars join Klink in representing the main verb in the active or middle voice but without also expressing the participle in the active or middle voice. Thus Ben Witherington translates: "this was now the third time that Jesus appeared to the disciples when he was raised [by God] from the dead."[7] Klaus Wengst opts for a similar combination of active and

---

[5] H. Thyen, *Das Johannesevangelium* (Tübingen: Mohr Siebeck, 2005), 771.

[6] This is the solution taken by Brown: "now this was the third time that Jesus revealed himself to the disciples after his resurrection from the dead" (*The Gospel According to John*, vol. 2, 1066).

[7] B. Witherington, *John's Wisdom: A Commentary on the Fourth Gospel* (Cambridge: Lutterworth Press, 1995), 353. Willard M. Swartley translates similarly: this was "now the third time that Jesus appeared to his disciples after he was raised from the dead"

passive: "das war schon das dritte Mal, dass Jesus sich seinen Schülern zeigte, nachdem er von den Toten auferweckt worden war (this was already the third time that Jesus showed himself to his disciples after he had been woken/raised [by God] from the dead)."[8] Rodney A. Whitacre likewise renders the main verb in the middle (intransitive), but the participle in the passive: "this was now the third time Jesus appeared to his disciples after he was raised [by God] from the dead."[9]

Third, not a few commentators find a passive meaning in both the verb and the participle. Andrew Lincoln does his exegesis on the basis of such a translation: "this was now the third time Jesus was revealed [by God] to the disciples after being raised [by God] from the dead."[10] In modern times the Revised Standard Version (RSV of 1946, rev. 1952 and 1971), by also rendering the main verb as passive in meaning, had its particular influence on English-speaking commentaries: "this was now the third time that Jesus was revealed [by God] to the disciples after he was raised [by God] from the dead." This is also, word for word, the translation of John 21:14 found in the commentary on the Fourth Gospel by Francis J. Moloney.[11] In an earlier generation of German scholars, the double passive meaning shaped the rendering offered by Rudolf Schnackenburg and followed in the English translation of his *magnum opus*: "this was now the third time that Jesus was revealed [by God] to the disciples after he was raised [by God] from the dead."[12]

(*John* (Harrisonburg, VA: Herald Press, 2013), 482).

[8] K. Wengst, *Das Johannesevangelium*, vol. 2 (Stuttgart: Kohlhammer, 2001), 309.

[9] R. A. Whitacre, *John* (Downers Grove, ILL: InterVarsity Press. 1999), 493.

[10] A. T. Lincoln, *The Gospel According to St John* (London: Continuum, 2005), 510.

[11] F. J. Moloney, *The Gospel of John* (Collegeville, MN: Liturgical Press, 1998), 547.

[12] R. Schnackenburg, *The Gospel According to St John*, vol. 3, trans. David Smith and G. A. Kon (New York: Crossroad, 1987), 351.

Among the commentators on John's Gospel, I have come across only one, Raymond Brown, who recognizes the way in which Greek syntactical usage, not to mention the inclusive structure of 21:1–14, opens up differing translations of both verbs in 21:14. Passive in form, these verbs could both be active or middle/reflexive in meaning. But commentators, apart from Brown (to whom we return below), never raise this possibility.

The way in which the evangelist names the risen Christ's appearance as "the third time" he appeared to his disciples "ties the present account in with" previous appearances.[13] This link regularly captures and even monopolizes the attention of commentators.[14] They recall the previous appearances in Chapter 20.[15] Remembering, in particular, the appearance to Mary Magdalene in 20:11–18, they point out that, strictly speaking, the appearance to the seven disciples on the shore of Lake Tiberias is the fourth time that the risen Jesus revealed himself. This prompts Moloney into claiming that "the number given for Jesus' post-resurrection appearances (vs. 14) is incorrect."[16] Lincoln justifies the reference to the "third" appearance, however, by arguing that John's Gospel is counting the group appearances (20:19–23; 20:26–29; and now 21:4–14): "the reference is to the appearance to a group and does not include the appearance to the individual woman, Mary Magdalene."[17] A classic commentary by Brooke Foss Westcott had

---

[13] Andreas J. Köstenberger, *John* (Grand Rapids: Baker Academic, 2004), 594.

[14] Craig S. Keener is the only major commentator on John that I have discovered to have nothing specific to say about vs. 14 when he exegetes John 21:1–14: *The Gospel of John*, vol. 2 (Peabody, MA: Hendrickson, 2003), 1225–33.

[15] See Urban C. von Wahlde, *The Gospel and Letters of John*, vol. 2 (Grand Rapids: Eerdmans, 2010), 889.

[16] Moloney, *The Gospel of John*, 551.

[17] Lincoln, *The Gospel According to St John*, 514.

offered the same explanation: "the third time most probably refers to the manifestations to the disciples in a body."[18]

C. K. Barrett makes the unfortunate suggestion that the failure to count the first appearance to Mary Magdalene was "perhaps" due to her not being a disciple,[19] rather than to her not being present when the risen Jesus appeared to groups of disciples. Köstenberger's comment, that the episode with Mary Magdalene was not counted because she was "not one of the Twelve," is likewise a bit strange (*John*, 594, fn. 38). John's Gospel hardly recognizes the existence of "the Twelve"; it acknowledges them in a bad light by using the term only in connection with the traitor Judas (6:67, 70, 71) and the doubting Thomas (20:24). John's Gospel never uses the term *apostolos*, except for the parabolic comparison, "no messenger (*apostolos*) is greater than the one who sent him" (13:16). There might be an implicit, secondary reference in 21:14 to the disciples as "apostles" sent to preach the resurrection. All in all, the Fourth Gospel speaks rather of "the disciples"; in the Easter chapters it does so, for instance, eleven times in Chapter 20 and ten times in Chapter 21.

Wengst considers that 21:14 aims at bringing the narrative into relation with Chapter 20. Talk of the "third" appearance obviously leaves aside the appearance to Mary Magdalene (20:11–18), but does not intend to downplay her. Rather, the evangelist is con-

---

[18] B. F. Westcott, *The Gospel According to St John* (London: John Murray, 1882), 302. Westcott followed the translation of the King James Bible of 1611, which rendered actively both the main verb and the participle in John 21:14: "This is now the third time that Jesus showed himself to his disciples, after that he was risen from the dead."

[19] Barrett, *The Gospel According to John*, 582. The possibility of Mary Magdalene not being reckoned a "disciple" was repeated by Carson, *The Gospel According to John*, 675. On the identity of the disciples (*mathētai*), see Walter Bauer, Frederick William Danker, William E. Arndt, and F. Wilbur Gingrich, *A Greek-English Lexicon of the New Testament and Other Early Christian Literature*, 3rd edn (Chicago: University of Chicago Press, 2000), 609–10; hereafter BDAG. John can write of "a large number of disciples" (6:66); they are not limited to the core group of "the Twelve."

cerned with counting appearances to groups of disciples.[20] Whitacre agrees: "John is counting appearances to the disciples as a group, which would not include Jesus' appearance to Mary Magdalene."[21]

The "third" appearance prompts some commentators to think of Simon Peter—his threefold denial of Jesus (John 18:15–18, 25–27), his being present at two earlier appearances of the risen Christ (20:19–23, 24–29) and now, very prominently, at a third appearance of Jesus. Swartley finds "the count of three times" to be "important," even more because Jesus is about to "restore and commission" Peter through three, striking questions.[22]

Whitacre rightly adds another name alongside that of Peter: vs 14 "signals a transition. This story has focused on Jesus' love and lordship, but Peter and the Beloved Disciple have also been featured. Now we will see Jesus' love and lordship in action in their lives specifically."[23]

The reference to the "third time" prompts a rich reflection from Thyen. He interprets this "third time" as opening the history of the risen Jesus' coming to his followers: "die lange, bis am Ende der Weltzeit währende Geschichte seines Kommens zu den Seinen eröffnet. Jetzt ist die Zeit, da die Jünger im Licht seiner Auferstehung erst die ganze Wahrheit seines irdischen Weges begreifen (2:22) (the long history of his coming to his own, which lasts right to the end of the world's time, opens. Now is the time for the disciples, in the light of his resurrection, to grasp for the first time the whole truth of his earthly journey (John 2:22))."[24] This beautiful, community-related reflection picks up and devel-

---

[20] Wengst, *Das Johannesevangelium*, vol. 2, 317.
[21] Whitacre, *John*, 493.
[22] Swartley, *John*, 482.
[23] Whitacre, *John*, 494.
[24] Thyen, *Das Johannesevangelium*, 786.

ops the language of Schnackenburg: "the appearance to the disciples on that day becomes, still more than the two previously related [appearances], the revelation to the whole later fellowship of disciples."[25]

To complete this account of what commentators have made of John 21:14 and their failure to consider the importance of appropriately translating its main verb (*ephanerōthē*) and the phrase *egertheis ek nekrōn*, we should mention that Schnackenburg refers to passages where "raised from the dead" has already been used: 2:22; 12:9; 12:17; and 20:9. These references need to be qualified. In 2:22 ("when therefore he [Jesus] rose from the dead," trans. mine), the verb *ēgerthē* is passive in voice but, arguably, active or middle (intransitive) in meaning. Pointedly the REB does not translate "when therefore he was raised from the dead," but uses a noun that leaves matters open, "after his resurrection." John 12:9 and 12:17 refer to Jesus' action in raising Lazarus from the dead, whereas 20:9 uses the infinitive of *anistēmi*: "they [Peter and the Beloved Disciple] did not yet know the Scripture that he [Jesus] must rise (*anistēnai*) from the dead" (trans. mine), not "be raised (*egerthēnai*) from the dead." Unlike other commentators, with the exception of Brown,[26] Schnackenburg alerts readers to these earlier verses which could throw light on the meaning of 21:14 and could suggest Jesus' active role in his own resurrection ("after he rose from the dead"). But, as we saw above, Schnackenburg translates as passive in meaning both the main verb and the aorist participle: "this was now the third time that Jesus was revealed [by God] to the disciples after he was raised [by God] from the dead."

At the end, Raymond Brown seems to have been the only com-

---

[25] Schnackenburg, *The Gospel According to St John*, vol, 3, 360.
[26] Brown, *The Gospel According to John*, vol. 2, 1077.

mentator alert to the possible translations of 21:14 which Greek syntax offered. These possibilities were already on display in what he understands 2:22 to say about the resurrection of Jesus: "*ēgerthē*" is "passive in form" but is to be translated as "intransitive in meaning"—"when he had risen" rather than "when he had been raised." Earlier books of the New Testament produce nineteen times where it "says that God the Father raised Jesus from the dead. But in the Fourth Gospel it has become clear that the Father's power is also Jesus' power (10:30)," and "John insists that Jesus rose by his own power (10:17–18)."[27]

Here sensitivity to the syntax of New Testament Greek led Brown to refer, albeit briefly and largely implicitly, to a theme of major theological significance. The final section of this article will show in detail the important theme that John 21:14 touches on and how it should be translated accordingly: "now this was the third time that Jesus appeared to the disciples after rising from the dead" (trans. mine). We should avoid a passive rendering, and recognize Jesus' active involvement in his resurrection coming from his divine identity.

Christ's Active Involvement in His Own Resurrection and that of Others

In what is widely agreed to be the earliest, surviving Christian document, the resurrection of Christ is presented as the action of the Father, "[the living God] who raised (*ēgeiren*) [Christ] from the dead" (1 Thess 1:10). The opening words of Galatians propose the same causality, speaking of "God the Father who raised (*egeirontos*) him [Jesus Christ] from the dead" (Gal 1:1). 1 Corinthians follows suit: "God raised (*ēgeiren*) the Lord [Jesus]" (6:14).

Christ's resurrection is also expressed in the passive, with the

---

[27] Brown, *The Gospel According to John*, vol. 1, 116.

agency being implied (the "by God" of the divine passive): "he [Christ] has been raised (*egēgertai*) on the third day" (1 Cor 15:4; see 15:12). Christ is the representative, "the first of those who have fallen asleep" and "will be made alive" again, it is implied "by God" (1 Cor 15:20–22). Romans speaks of those who "believe in [God] who raised (*egeironta*) Jesus our Lord from the dead," adding a famous description of redemption that incorporates two verbs in the passive: "he [Jesus] was handed over [by God] because of our sins and raised [by God] for the sake of our justification" (4:24–25).[28] Two chapters later, Paul writes of "Christ who has been raised (*egertheis*) from the dead" (Rom 6:9; see 7:4) and obviously implies that this came about through the action of God the Father. A few verses earlier, he had said that "Christ was raised (*egerthē*) from the dead by the glorious power of the Father" (Rom 6:4; REB). Repeatedly Paul connects God's raising Christ with the coming general resurrection: for instance, "the One who raised (*egeiras*) the Lord Jesus will also raise us with Jesus" (2 Cor 4:14).

Similar passages in Romans show how Paul describes God as the One who has raised Jesus from the dead; through the Holy Spirit, God will raise others to life with him (Rom 8:11). In the words of Douglas J. Moo, "it is typical of Paul to designate God as the One who raised Jesus."[29] To be wrong about this message of resurrection is to "give false witness" about God (1 Cor 15:15).

Leaving aside the Synoptic Gospels and other New Testament books written after Paul's seven clearly authentic letters (Romans, 1 and 2 Corinthians, Galatians, Philippians, 1 Thessalonians, and Philemon), we move to John's Gospel, one of the latest works of

---

[28] D. J. Moo, *The Epistle to the Romans* (Grand Rapids: Eerdmans, 1996), 289.
[29] Ibid., 287.

the New Testament. The language of resurrection enters this Gospel when Jesus cleanses the Temple in Jerusalem.

The claim of Jesus, that after the destruction of the Temple he will raise it up (*egerō*) in three days, are misunderstood by his audience. Their misunderstanding is concerned with the object of the raising, but not with Jesus being directly involved and effective in the action. That direct involvement is explicitly assumed in their question: "the building of the Temple has taken 46 years, and you are going to raise it up in three days?" Jesus was, however, speaking about raising his 'body (*sōma*)."[30] His disciples recalled his words after "he had risen (*ēgerthē*) from the dead" (John 2:19–22).

The Greek form (*ēgerthē*) here is an aorist passive but the context makes it obvious that the meaning is active (or middle). Schnackenburg remarks on the shift from earlier New Testament books (where Jesus' resurrection is the work of the Father) to John where that resurrection is directly attributed to Jesus.[31] Nevertheless, Schnackenburg's rendering involves a divine passive: "when, therefore, he was raised [by God] from the dead (als er nun von den Toten erweckt war)."[32] One would have expected Schnackenburg to have translated, "when he rose/had risen (auferstanden war) from the dead," or "after his resurrection" (REB).

In his subsequent figurative language, Jesus presents himself as the good/beautiful shepherd who is ready to lay down his life for his sheep. "This is why the Father loves me: because I lay down my life in order to take it up again…I lay it [my life] down of my own accord. I have power (*exousian*) to lay it down, and I have power

---

[30] This word will be used in John 19:31 of the three dead bodies (*sōmata*) on Calvary.
[31] Schnackenburg, *The Gospel according to St John*, trans. Kevin Smyth, vol. 1 (London: Burns & Oates, 1968), 352.
[32] Ibid., 353.

(*exousian*) to take it up again. This command I have received from my Father" (John 10:11, 15, 17–18). In "the bond of love that exists between the Father and the Son," the Father wills "that the death of Jesus should lead to resurrection and a return to Himself."[33]

Later in the same chapter, Jesus continues to speak of his uniquely close relationship with the Father, and even says: "the Father and I are one" (John 10:30). This discourse ends with Jesus' claim that he is performing the works of the Father (John 10:37–38). Brown highlights what is at stake here: "the unity that exists between Father and Son" was "one of power and operation." That is why "the works of Jesus can reveal this unity, for they are common works of [the] Father and Son."[34] It is not stated that it is through his own power and operation that Jesus has worked his own resurrection (and will work the final resurrection of others), or that such works are common to the Father and the Son. But we are not far from those convictions, given the earlier language about the good/beautiful shepherd who not only enjoys the love of the Father but also lays down his life and takes it up again.

A fully developed picture of Christ's active involvement in resurrection, his own and that of others, calls for reflection on many more passages in John's Gospel. Firstly, answering those who criticized his "working" on the Sabbath, Jesus linked himself with the Father in raising the dead (John 5:21; see 5:26). In a passage that anticipates the later resuscitation of Lazarus, Jesus speaks of those who hear the voice of the Son of God and come forth from their tombs (John 5:25, 28–29). The Father and the Son share the power of giving spiritual and physical life.

Second, in the discourse on the bread of life that Jesus twice

---

[33] Brown, *The Gospel According to John*, vol. 1, 399.
[34] Ibid., 412.

promises that "on the last day" he "will raise up (*anastēsō*)" those who believe in him (John 6:39–40). When the focus on the bread of life becomes more clearly a focus on the Eucharist, he teaches that those who eat his flesh and drink his blood "have eternal life and he will raise them up on the last day" (John 6:54).

Third, the revivification of Lazarus occasions Jesus' self-presentation: "I am the resurrection (*anastasis*)." Jesus announces that "those who believe in me, even if they die, will come to life (*zōē*)" (John 11:25). John's Gospel uses "life" 35 times, often qualifying it as "eternal" and reaching a climax when identifying it simply with Jesus: "I am the way and the truth and *the life*" (John 14:6). Apart from the passage just quoted, *anastasis* occurs only three times in John (5:29 twice; 11:24), with forms of the corresponding verb *anistēmi* turning up eight times (6:39; 6:40; 6:44; 6:54; 11:23; 11:24; 11:31; 20:9).[35] One of these occurrences refers simply to someone "rising to her feet" (11:31). In the New Testament the verb *egeirō*, as we saw in the case of Paul, is commonly used of Jesus' resurrection. This verb turns up 14 times in John's Gospel, but on five of these occasions it does not refer to resurrection (e.g., 5:8).

A fourth set of passages that imply the new life and activity (exercised with the Father) of the risen Jesus emerges in what he says at the Last Supper. He promises the disciples: "if I go and prepare a place for you, I shall come again and take you to myself, so that where I am, there you also may be" (John 14:3; trans. mine). This "coming back to you" (John 14:18) and seeing Jesus again "after a little while" (John 16:16) will entail his making a dwelling place, along with the Father, in believers (John 14:23; see 17:26). The verbs

---

[35] "*Anistēmi*," BDAG, 83.

anistēmi and *egeirō*, like the noun *anastasis*, are not to be found in Jesus' final discourse and prayer (Chs 13–17). Without using the explicit language for the resurrection, these chapters refer to the activity of the risen Jesus and how he will share his resurrection with those who believe in him and love him.

Conclusion

John's Gospel witnesses to a development from the earlier way of presenting the resurrection of Jesus that we find in Paul's letters, according to which it is the Father who raised the dead Jesus (or the dead Jesus was raised by the Father). Even though the earlier New Testament authors did not explicitly offer this justification, they correctly implied that, *inasmuch* as he was *human*, the dead Jesus could not be causally involved in his own resurrection.

John's Gospel, however, explicitly and variously highlighted the divinity of Christ. Without invoking this argument, it was correctly implied that, *inasmuch* as he was *divine*, he was causally involved in his own resurrection and in that of others. This involvement in overcoming death and giving himself and others new life required the divine causality that he shared with the Father and the Holy Spirit.

The Fourth Gospel joins the force of an inclusion (John 21:1–14) and the possibilities of Greek syntax to ensure that both the main verb and the participle in John 21:14, while passive in form, are active (or middle) in meaning: "this was the third time that Jesus revealed himself after rising from the dead."[36] In a gospel that em-

---

[36] Max Zerwick and Mary Grosvenor understand the aorist, passive participle *egertheis* in a middle sense ("having risen," "after rising" from the dead): *A Grammatical Analysis of the Greek New Testament* (Rome: Biblical Institute Press, 1981), 347. Daniel Wallace (*Greek Grammar*, 420), while noting difficulties in detecting the middle voice in New Testament Greek, seems open to the view of Zerwick and Grosvenor; he does not specifically discuss John 21:14.

phasized Christ's active engagement in his own resurrection and its aftermath in the Easter appearances, even to the point of identifying him as "the resurrection" (John 11:25), it would be strange to find the last two references to his resurrection framed in the passive: "this was the third time that Jesus was revealed [by God] to the disciples after he was raised [by God] from the dead."

Theologically something richly significant is at stake in the two ways of viewing Christ's resurrection—from the point of view either of his humanity (Paul) or of his divinity (John). Apart from Raymond Brown, none of the commentators on the Fourth Gospel seem to have taken account of Greek syntax; it raises no problems for those who read the two verbs in John 21:14 as having an active or middle meaning. If the commentators had paused to set out the relevant syntax and its possibilities, they might have encouraged more translators to avoid the passive and recognize the active (or middle) meaning of the final two references to resurrection in John's Gospel.

Pauline Correspondence

8

Does Philippians 2:6–11 present Christ as a Superior Angel?

A hymnic passage in Paul's Letter to the Philippians (2:6–11), an epistle probably written by the apostle from a Roman prison around 61 AD, expresses vividly the early Christian worship of the crucified, risen, and exalted Jesus. This passage has been cherished in liturgy, devotion, and theology since the beginning of Christianity.[1] It stood behind the Nicene-Constantinopolitan Creed of 381 which reaffirmed Nicea I's (325) doctrine of Christ's sharing "one being (*homoousios*) with the Father," and behind the teaching of Chalcedon (451) about the two natures (divine and human) of Christ.

The human nature or condition assumed by Christ is upheld in the language of Philippians: "he emptied himself, taking the form (*morphē*) of a slave." He was not only "born (*genomenos*)" in a complete "human likeness (*homoiōma*)" and came across as truly "human in appearance (*schema*)," but also died, "becoming obedient to the point of death, even death on a cross." The truth of "taking the

---

[1] On the place and date for the writing of Philippians, see Paul A. Holloway, *Philippians* (Minneapolis: Fortress Press, 2017), 19–24. Holloway argues persuasively for the literary integrity of canonical Philippians (ibid., 10–19) and for the Pauline provenance of our particular passage, a "piece of encomiastic prose composed by Paul himself specifically for the present letter" (ibid., 115). He also provides a valuable bibliography (ibid., 193–208); but see also George Hunsinger, *Philippians* (Grand Rapids: Brazos Press, 2020), 216–25, and, for non-English scholarship, Nunzio Capizzi, *L'uso di Fil 2,6–11 nella cristologia contemporanea (1965–1993)* (Rome: Gregorian University Press, 1997), 483–512.

form of a slave when he was born in human likeness" was clearly vindicated by his horrible, public death by crucifixion.²

What does Paul mean by Christ's being "in the form (*morphē*) of God," not thinking it an "*harpagmon* to be equal with God," being "highly exalted" in the aftermath of the crucifixion, and sharing the divine name "to the glory of God the Father"? This language and its origins have continued to provoke controversy.

Did and does Christ share a uniquely divine mode of being, an existence that makes him instrumental in creation and sovereign Lord of all things (see 1 Cor 8:6) and establishes his equality with God? Is that "equality with God" a reality that Christ eternally possesses, irrespective of any "before" or "after" of his incarnate state?

Does Paul's language of being "in the *morphē* of God" anticipate and support the later conciliar teaching of one divine *ousia* or substance—or even of the one divine *physis* or nature—shared by the trinitarian persons?

From Adam to Angel Christology

Adam Christology

In the late twentieth century, James Dunn detected an Adam Christology in the notion of Christ being in the "form (*morphē*) of God" (Phil 2:6). This was to be understood in the sense of Adam and Eve being made in the image and likeness (Gen 1:26–27) of God (*eikōn* and *homoiōma*). Adam and Eve wanted to become even more like God, whereas Christ in humility became human and mortal, to the point of dying like a slave on a cross.

---

² On crucifixion, see John Granger Cook, *Crucifixion in the Mediterranean World* (Tübingen: Mohr Siebeck; 2nd edn, 2019); Gerald O'Collins, 'Crucifixion', *Anchor Bible Dictionary*, vol. 1 (New York: Doubleday, 1992), 1207–10.

Unlike the Book of Genesis, Paul's encomium in Philippians neither mentions Adam by name, nor refers to his creation (out of earth) and his sin. Unlike Romans 5:12–21, no reference is made to the way in which Adam's sinful disobedience was more than countered by Christ's obedience. Nevertheless, Christ's pre-existence and an Adam Christology remain compatible. In his post-incarnation human state, Christ humbly plays the role of last Adam.[3]

The *morphē* or form of Philippians 2:6 is not synonymous with the *eikōn* or image of Genesis 1:26–27. That does not, however, necessarily rule out an Adam Christology in Philippians 2:6–7.[4] Some commentators entertain a link between Adam and the Philippians passage.

Angel Christology

Now we have from Paul Holloway the thesis that angel Christology and "a kind of metamorphosis" unlock the meaning of Philippians 2:6–11. Christ was "a mighty angel" who originally existed "in the form of God." "For the sake of humans and in obedience to the divine will, he took the form of a slave, changing himself into human likeness and appearance." After his death on a cross, "God restored him to his original angelic form, but now as the even

---

[3] See J. D. G. Dunn, *Christology in the Making*, 2nd edn (London: SCM Press, 1989), 113–21. See *eikōn* in W. Bauer, F. W. Danker, W. F. Arndt and W. Gingrich, *Greek-English Lexikon of the New Testament and other Early Christian Literature* (Chicago: The University of Chicago Press, 2000), 281–82; hereafter BDAG. See also "*morphē*," BDAG, 659; on "*homoiōma*," BDAG says: "it is probable that he [Paul in Phil 2:7] uses our word to bring out both that Jesus in his earthly career was similar to sinful humans and yet not totally like them" (707),

[4] J. D. G. Dunn, "Christology (New Testament)," *Anchor Bible Dictionary*, vol. 1 (New York: Doubleday, 1992), 983. On Dunn's thesis of an Adam Christology being the key to Phil 2:6–11, see Gordon D. Fee, *Pauline Christology* (Grand Rapids: Baker Academic, 2007), 275–91; Otfried Hofius, *Der Christushymnus: Philipper 2:6–11*, 2nd edn (Tübingen: Mohr Siebeck, 1991); Larry Hurtado, *Lord, Jesus, Christ: Devotion to Jesus in Earliest Christianity* (Grand Rapids: Eerdmans, 2005), 121–26.

more glorious ruling angel who bears the divine Name and shares the divine throne."[5] Holloway argues that an "emerging tradition of an exalted Name-bearing angel in contemporary Jewish apocalypticism" provides the background for a Pauline "allusion to Christ as the principal angel who now bears the divine Name."[6]

In the context of an angel Christology in Philippians 2:6–11, Holloway understands the language about "every knee bowing" and "every tongue confessing" as referring to Christ, promoted to being God's angelic vice-regent, now coming and sitting on God's throne as universal judge.[7] But does the apostle's encomium mention either the divine throne or the final judgment? As we shall see below, Paul quotes language from Isaiah 45:23, which refers to the universal dominion of God and not as such either to judgment or to an angelophany.[8]

When we turn to Paul's earlier letters, it is hard to find him developing anywhere an angel Christology by which we might assess the possibility of the encomium in Philippians also expressing such an angel Christology. The passage itself never refers to angels, nor does any other section of the letter. The apostle himself only occasionally refers to angels (in Romans, 1 Corinthians, Galatians, and 1 Thessalonians), and fails to show much enthusiasm for them (see Rom 8:38; 1 Cor 6:3; Gal 1:8; 3:19). He occasionally mentions bad angels or spiritual powers resistant to the divine will (e.g., 2 Cor 11:14). In a letter that may have been written by Paul himself from Rome and near the end of his life (and hence close to the time of the

---

[5] Holloway, *Philippians*, 49–50.
[6] Ibid., 127, 129.
[7] Ibid., 49–50.
[8] Ibid. Klaus Baltzer, *Deutero-Isaiah* (Minneapolis: Fortress Press, 2001), 250, interprets the passage as presenting a "theophany" and the appropriate human response to this divine appearance.

composition of Romans), the apostle takes his distance from the "worship of angels" (angelic worship of God?) (Col 2:18).

Romans 8:32 (see also 5:5–10 and Mark 1:11) stresses the unique love of the Father for the Son. Is there anything in Paul's letters, or, for that matter, in pre-Pauline, Jewish literature, where God expresses such love even for the highest angel?

While the background of Pauline thought itself hardly encourages reading Philippians 2:6–11 as expressing angel Christology, Holloway finds such a background in Jewish apocalypticism, above all in 1 Enoch.[9] Paul may share with this apocryphal work what we can call an apocalyptic outlook. But does he share its sustained interest in angels?

Holloway seems reluctant to countenance the possibility that the early Church had come to believe that Christ's relationship with God was unique. Having dropped this conviction, which flowered in classical Christian doctrine, did Holloway have to look elsewhere and light upon angel Christology?

But let us investigate directly Holloway's case. We can begin with the central message contained in Paul's encomium, and then move to specifics in Holloway's exegesis.

The Central Message of Philippians 2:6–11

The exegetical choice, as Holloway presents matters, involves either (a) the angelic Christ's *promotion/elevation* after a mission that he has accomplished (a kind of *per ardua ad astra* ("through difficulties to the stars")), or (b) the Father's *endorsing* the original status of Jesus Christ, which is his divine equality (as Son of "God

---

[9] An index contains nearly two columns of references to 1 Enoch: Holloway, *Philippians*, 210; see also ibid., 42–45.

the Father"). The Father and Jesus would then be identified with one another as sharing the divine name, and so existing together as the divine Lord (*Kurios*). Was this being "in the form of God," constituted and specified by "being equal to God," endorsed at the end of the passage as an implied Sonship that shares the very name of God?[10]

Holloway argues for (a): "God grants Christ a kind of celestial promotion." He suggests that Christ was understood to become "the principal Name-bearing angel."[11] But is it possible for a powerful angel to be promoted celestially to bear "the name above every name" and rule the entire creation (Phil 2:9–11)? Does the thesis sound impossible in itself—someone who is finite and created becoming the infinite Creator, a creature promoted to receive adoration from every being "in heaven and on earth and under the earth," and be confessed as divine "Lord" by "every tongue"?

The language of "every knee bowing" and "every tongue confessing" echoes Isaiah 45:23, as Holloway himself observes.[12] But he does not note that this language occurs in a classic Old Testament passage celebrating YHWH, the one and only true God of Israel and the whole world. The nations and Israel are invited to receive salvation by worshipping the one, true God and by submitting to his will. Through adopting such language in his Philippians encomium, Paul expresses his faith that the crucified and exalted Jesus enjoys lordship over everyone and everything. Jesus exercises an all-determining role, a universal divine sovereignty that dovetails with the "glory of God the Father" (Phil 2:11).

---

[10] Holloway puts the choice in a reverse order, restoration/endorsement or elevation/promotion: "a restoration of the crucified Christ to his preexistent glory, or his elevation to a status over and above what he initially enjoyed" (ibid., 126).

[11] Ibid., 125.

[12] Ibid., 129, n. 118.

Add too how in an earlier letter Paul split the classic Jewish confession of monotheism contained in the *Shema* (Deut 6:4–5), glossing "God" with "Father" and "Lord" with "Jesus Christ" to put Jesus as Lord alongside God the Father: "for us there is one God, the Father from whom are all things and for whom we exist, and one Lord, Jesus Christ, through whom are all things and through whom we exist" (1 Cor 8:6).[13] Paul recast his perception of God by introducing Jesus as "Lord" and redefining Jewish monotheism to include Christ.

Sharing in the eternal existence of the one Lord God, Christ shares instrumentally in an essential prerogative of God, the universal, creative power. If Christ belongs on the side of the universal Creator and infinite, divine Lord, how can he also be finite and infinitely less, a principal angel waiting to be awarded with "celestial promotion"? Does Paul renounce in Philippians what he has already taught in 1 Corinthians?

Specific Questions

The big picture does not appear to favor Holloway's exposition of Paul's encomium. What of the details? Verse 6 is vital for Holloway's thesis of the angelic Christ, a thesis which rejects the eternal divine status of Christ and his incarnation.

Form of God and Equality with God

When expounding "although existing in the form of God, he [Christ Jesus] did not regard equality with God" as an "*harpagmon*," Hol-

---

[13] Holloway *never* cites 1 Cor 8:6, which sheds significant light on Paul's understanding of Jesus. See Joseph A. Fitzmyer, *First Corinthians* (New Haven, CT: Yale University Press, 2008), 342–44; Anthony C. Thiselton, *The First Epistle to the Corinthians* (Grand Rapids: Eerdmans, 2000), 631–38; N. T. Wright, *The Climax of the Covenant* (Edinburgh: T. & T. Clark, 1991), 120–36.

loway follows many versions (e.g. the NRSV) by introducing a concessive "although" not found in the original Greek, rather than a causative "since" also not found in the Greek text. The "although" suggests that the behavior is not what you might expect from someone who "existed in the form (*morphē*) of God." Holloway's translation runs as follows: "who, although he [Christ Jesus] existed in the form of God, did not consider [his] equality with God a possession that he could not part with (*harpagmon*), but emptied himself, taking the form of a slave."[14]

When commenting on "the form of God" and "equality with God," Holloway has to face two questions. First, is Christ's being "in the form of God" (specified as "equality with God") to be understood in a way that falls short of full divine status?[15] Using 1 Enoch and other apocalyptic sources, Holloway claims that "to say that Christ existed in the form of God is *simply* to say that prior to his self-humbling metamorphosis, Christ enjoyed a luminous appearance of the sort a powerful angel might possess."[16]

But the ancient sources and modern commentaries quoted by Holloway on the very same page would suggest rather the conclusion: "to say that Christ existed in the form of God is to say *at least* that, prior to his self-humbling metamorphosis, Christ enjoyed a luminous appearance." Whether that *glory* (*doxa*) or luminous appearance is simply "a luminous appearance of the sort a powerful angel might possess" needs to be established. Again on the same

---

[14] Holloway, *Philippians*, 114. The NIV translates: "who, being in very nature God, did not consider equality to God something to be used to his own advantage; rather he made himself nothing by taking the nature of a servant." This version weakens the force of *doulos* by proposing "servant" rather than "slave," but "used to his own advantage" improves on "a possession he could not part with."

[15] On "*isos*," see BDAG, 480–81.

[16] Holloway, *Philippians*, 118.

page, Holloway quotes 1 Enoch on God being identified by 1 Enoch as "the Great Glory." Could it be that Christ enjoyed a luminous appearance because he showed his full divine status through his unique way of sharing in the "glory of God the Father"?

Second, is being equal with God a possession that one could part with, even if Christ did not do so? What would have counted as "parting" with this possession? How would that have been possible?

Holloway observes that Christ's equality with God "must be taken in a qualified sense."[17] Innumerable philosophers and theologians would agree, since every statement that concerns God must be qualified. The question remains: in what sense should this equality with God be understood and qualified? Should one say that Christ's equality with God entails a unique relationship, a sharing as Son in the divine existence that reveals "the glory of God the Father" (Phil 2:11)?

Selectivity and Silence

As regards the meaning of *harpagmos*, Holloway excludes the view of Ray Hoover that Christ possessed equality with God but did not regard it as a situation to exploit, a view endorsed by the NRSV ("something to be exploited") and NIV ("used to his own advantage"). Some readers may (mistakenly) wonder why Holloway does not discuss the recent defense of Hoover by Michael Martin: "*Harpagmos* Revisited: A Philological Reexamination of the New Testament's 'Most Difficult Word.'"[18] This 2016 article presumably appeared after Holloway's commentary had gone to press.

In a review Nijay K. Gupta finds Holloway "very selective in his dialogue partners"; this selectivity has produced some "glaring

---

[17] Ibid., 120.
[18] *Journal of Biblical Literature* 135 (2016), 175–94.

omissions." Richard Bauckham, Larry Hurtado, and N. T. Wright are ignored. They differ significantly from Holloway by understanding Paul's hymnic passage to attribute to Christ an eternal preexistence and an incarnation.[19] Yet Holloway never mentions them with reference to Paul's understanding of *harpagmos* or anything else in Philippians.

Theology and Philosophy

Holloway disqualifies "a host of religiously conservative commentators whose conclusions one cannot help suspect have been determined by theological commitments as well as historical judgments." His corresponding footnote yields examples of these suspects: Gerald F. Hawthorne, Ralph P. Martin, Peter T. O'Brien, Moises Silva, Gordon D. Fee, Marcus Bockmuehl, and Ben Witherington. The footnote ends by admitting that "there are, of course, many fine exegetical observations in some [which?] of these commentaries."[20]

Being blessed years ago by attending lectures on Romans given at the University of Tübingen by Ernst Käsemann, I remain convinced by his advice that exegesis needs to be theological (and philosophical) as well as historical. In a review of Holloway's *Philippians*, Gerald W. Peterman admits an "area of concern": "sadly" there is "little or no theological reflection," "At times" the author "strikes a condescending tone regarding theology," and asserts (see above) that "there is a host of religiously conservative commentators whose views are skewed by their theological commitments."[21]

---

[19] *Interpretation: A Journal of Bible and Theology* 73 (2019), 401.
[20] Holloway, *Philippians*, 10, and 10, n. 81.
[21] Peterman, a review of Holloway, *Philippians*, in *Journal of the Evangelical Theological Society*, 62 (2019), 182.

Nevertheless, what Holloway himself writes about "the angelic Christ"[22] calls for theological and philosophical probing. When, for instance, we read that Christ "retains his angelic identity throughout the metamorphosis of vv. 6–8," we might well ask: What counts as identity, angelic or otherwise? And what counts as this identity being retained in a situation of metamorphosis? Holloway rightly insists that Christ's "exaltation must be more than a simple restoration."[23] We are left with the question: What will make an exaltation more than a simple restoration? Over and over again, Holloway's language calls for theological and philosophical explanation. He appears to distance himself from theology (and philosophy) but he cannot avoid them.

Conclusions

Will the angel Christology developed by Paul Holloway to explain Philippians 2:6–11 succeed? It is a scheme that remains unsupported by the passage itself; it never calls Christ an "angel" who is promoted to sit on the divine "throne." Verses 10–11 apply to the exalted Christ the language of Isaiah 45:23 about the adoration of the one, true God (and not of some principal angel). The scheme cannot appeal to other letters of Paul, since the apostle remains elsewhere unenthusiastic about angels and never develops an angel Christology. Holloway shows disdain towards the role of theology (and philosophy) in exegesis. But his claims raise theological and philosophical questions that are not aired and answered.

---

[22] Holloway, *Philippians*, 126.
[23] Ibid., 126, n. 91.

9

Revisiting Angel Christology in Philippians 2:6–11

In the *Expository Times* I challenged the angel Christology which Paul A. Holloway developed in his commentary on that Pauline letter for the *Hermeneia* series.[1] This thesis proposed that an angelic Christ changed himself into human form, and, after his crucifixion, was highly elevated in his angelic status to bear the divine Name and share the very throne of God. But we do not find in the passage itself the language of angels and thrones that Holloway's thesis required. Nor had Paul developed elsewhere an Angel Christology which would support the proposal. Philippians 2:6–11 used Isaiah's language of adoring the one, true God, not the terminology of some principal angel.

In a response, "Ideology and Exegesis," Holloway expressed his "disdain" (275) for my critical view of his thesis. "At several points" (left unspecified) my essay was allegedly written "with a barely concealed *odium theologicum* characteristic of a previous age" (278, n. 14).[2] I reply to Holloway in this hitherto unpublished essay by first taking up some specific details and then moving to the heart of the matter, general issues of biblical interpretation where we converge more than might be expected.

---

[1] P. A. Holloway. *Philippians* (Minneapolis: Fortress Press, 2017).
[2] G. O'Collins, 'Does Philippians 2:6–11 present Christ as a superior angel?', *Expository Times* 233 (2022), 269–74; P. A. Holloway, "Ideology and Exegesis: A Response to Gerald O'Collins," ibid., 275–83. References to these two articles will be given within the text.

Seven Details in the Debate over Angel Christology

First, Holloway criticizes me for ignoring "a crucial text for Paul's evolving understanding of Christ" (276). The apostle praises the Galatians for "having welcomed me as an angel of God, as Christ Jesus" (4:14). Despite the supposedly crucial nature of this verse, Holloway himself ignored it completely in his entire commentary and not merely in his discussion of Philippians 2:6–11! In his response to me, he does not clearly explain why this verse is "crucial." He seems to do so because it is the only place where Paul apparently identifies Christ as an angel, albeit "a very important one" (276). Does this identification stand up? What do other commentators say?

Being cited by Holloway in fourteen footnotes, an earlier commentary (on Galatians and in the *Hermeneia* series) by Hans Dieter Betz appears to win his approval, But Betz does not identify Christ as an angel when translating the verse: "you welcomed me as if I were an angel of God, as you might have welcomed Jesus Christ himself." Betz explains: "The *hōs* ('as if') expresses a distinction [not an identification], since Paul does not intend to say that he [Paul] actually came as an angel." As "the apostle and imitator of Christ," Paul represents Christ, and has been welcomed by the Galatians as if he were Christ himself. Paul is making statements about himself and the welcome he received, not about Christ, and certainly not about Christ as an angel, superior or otherwise.[3]

In his Anchor Bible commentary on Galatians, J. Louis Martyn writes of a "correspondence" and not of an identification: "The odiously sick, apparently demonic figure [Paul] was seen, then, to be in fact an angel sent from God, just as the legally executed

---

[3] H. D. Betz, *Galatians* (Minneapolis: Fortress Press, 1079), 226.

criminal [Jesus] was seen to be in fact God's own Son. That correspondence caused the Galatians to welcome Paul, and that correspondence caused their attachment to Paul to be an attachment to Christ."[4] In Galatians 4:14 (as in Gal 1:8), Paul seems for once to take a reasonably high view of angels, but he does not propose an angelic *identification* of Jesus Christ.

Second, inevitably matters of authorship came up in the debate with Holloway. The *New Oxford Annotated Bible* notes the scholarly diversity about the authorship of the Letter to the Colossians: it was either written by Paul himself or by one of his disciples.[5] To respect the diversity of opinion, I wrote that this letter, which distances itself from the worship of angels, "*may* have been written by Paul himself" (271). "May have been written" is not the equivalent of "was written." Holloway denounces my "careless and shoddy argument," and "for starters" rejects what I never wrote of Colossians being "almost certainly written by the apostle" (276).

Third, Holloway agrees that Philippians 2:10–11 applies to Christ language (about "every knee bowing" and "every tongue confessing") originally attributed to God (Isa 45:23). Holloway alleges that I claim to find "Nicene trinitarianism" in Paul's reference to Isaiah (276), ignoring the fact that I never mention the Holy Spirit in this context and am interested only in the attribution to Christ of Old Testament language used about God.

Holloway also rejects what I never claimed: that Paul read Isaiah 45:23 "with a view to its historical meaning" (278) as if the apostle "were a modern historical critic" (279). Paul did not ask:

---

[4] J. L. Martyn, *Galatians* (New York: Doubleday, 1997), 421. Holloway describes correctly and even more vividly the odiously sick condition of Paul (277).

[5] Ed. Michael D. Coogan et al.; 5th edn. (New York: Oxford University Press, 2018), 2105.

What were the author(s) of Isaiah 45:23 intending to convey when they used the words they did? The apostle's interest concerned something different—the application to Jesus Christ of language attributed originally to God.

Philippians 2:10–11 echoes the language of Isaiah 45:23, without adding a reference to "the judgment seat of God." But Romans 14:10–11 does so: "we must all stand before the judgment seat of God, for it is written: 'As I live, says the Lord, every knee shall bow to me and every tongue confess to God.'"

In Romans 14:10–11, Paul adds a reference to "the judgement seat," but without mentioning any angels. Yet Holloway wants to recognize "a great angel tradition" as somehow present in those verses and *also* in both Philippians 2:10–11 and Isaiah 45:23: "an exalted angel not only sits on Yahweh's throne and executes judgment on Yahweh's behalf, but [also] bears Yahweh's name as well" (278).

Romans 14:10–11 does not provide genuine (historical?) evidence for the presence of "a great angel tradition" to be detected in Philippians 2 and Isaiah 45. Rather those verses in Romans 14:10–11 illustrate the truth of Holloway's statement about the freedom of Paul in his choice of biblical quotations and their interpretation: "apocalyptic Jews like Paul cared little for historical meaning in their quotations of Scripture. The Qumran *pesharim* are a parade example of this" (278). Beyond question, "Paul did *not read* Isaiah 45:23 with an eye to its historical meaning" (278, ital. orig.) and historical context, as contemporary scholars would deem "historical."

That said, it would look like "eisegesis" on the part of Holloway to allege that in the passages from Philippians, Isaiah, and Romans Paul refers to or implies any "exalted angel" who "not only sits on Yahweh's throne," "executes judgment on Yahweh's behalf", but "bears Yahweh's name as well," What do leading commentators say?

In discussing Philippians 2:6–11, Gordon D. Fee knows nothing of exalted angels and divine thrones.[6] Klaus Baltzer does not discover anything of "a great angel tradition" in Isaiah 45:23.[7] Likewise, Joseph Fitzmyer never introduces anything of such a tradition when he expounds Romans 14:10–11 in terms of the love owed by "strong" (probably Gentile members of the Roman community) to "weak" (probably Jewish members of the same community).[8]

Fourth, here and there Holloway's essay introduces what should be described as exaggerated language. He claims "myriad flaws" in my argument (276). Can it be the case that my essay of less than six pages literally contains countless flaws that are extremely great in number? I would have needed hundreds or, really, thousands of flaws per page to justify the charge of "myriad."

Fifth, here and there Holloway introduces precise and valuable expressions and descriptions. He revives, for example, a useful but widely forgotten term, "prepositional metaphysics" to summarize what we read in 1 Corinthians 8:6: "for us [Christians] there is one God, the Father, *from whom* are all things and *for* whom we

---

[6] (Grand Rapids: Eerdmans, 1995). We likewise find nothing about angels and thrones in Morna Hooker, "The Letter to the Philippians," in *The New Interpreter's* Bible, vol. xi (Nashville: Abingdon Press, 2000), 469–549; on the Christological "hymn" 500–10, at 509–10.

[7] Klaus Baltzer, *Deutero-Isaiah*, trans. Margaret Kohl (Minneapolis: Fortress Press, 2001), 250, interprets Isa 45:23 as presenting a "theophany" and the appropriate human response to this divine appearance,

[8] J. A. Fitzmyer, *Romans* (New York: Doubleday, 1993), 687, 692.

exist, and one Lord Jesus Christ *through* whom are all things and *through* whom we exist" (279).

But recognizing here Paul's version of "prepositional metaphysics" means hearing him adapt in a Christological direction the Jewish confession of monotheism, and so producing "a binitarian pattern of Christianity" and "the origin of the worship of Christ, who is reverenced along with the God of Judaism."[9]

Sixth, apropos of 1 Corinthians 8:6, Holloway appeals to the NRSV translation to support his detection of mere henotheism in Deuteronomy 6: "the proper translation of Deut 6:4 is not 'Yahweh our god, Yahweh is one' but 'Yahweh is our god, Yahweh alone" (see NRSV)' (279). We should note that, while the NRSV chooses a translation ("The Lord is our God, the Lord alone") that actually differs from the one favoured and reported by Holloway, the NRSV also recognizes three alternative renderings: "The Lord our God is one Lord"; or "The Lord our God, the Lord is one"; or "The Lord is our God, the Lord is one."

Seventh, before leaving 1 Corinthians 8:6, let me note how Holloway understands that Paul imagines Christ as "a divine craftsman through whom the sensible world was created." But that does not exclude also imagining the eternal existence of the one *Lord* God, the Kyrios of Paul's confession (280). We face here, not an either/or but a both/and. Joseph Fitzmyer quotes with approval Andreas Lindemann's comment about Paul presenting Christ the Lord as "the preexistent mediator of creation."[10]

---

[9] J. A. Fitzmyer, *First Corinthians* (New Haven, CT: Yale University Press, 2008), 343. See also Wolfgang Schrage, *Unterwegs zur Einzigkeit und Einheit Gottes: zum Monotheismus des Paulus und seiner alttestamentlich-frühjudischen Tradition* (Neukirchen-Vluyn: Neukirchener Verlag, 2002); Anthony C. Thiselton, *The First Epistle to the Corinthians* (Grand Rapids: Eerdmans, 2000), 628–38.

[10] Fitzmyer, *First Corinthians*, 343; the quotation comes from A. Lindemann, *Der erste Korintherbrief* (Tübingen: Mohr Siebeck. 2000), 193.

Biblical Interpretation as Uncovering the Meaning of Ancient Authors

By entitling his response to me "Ideology and Exegesis," Holloway seemed to hint that, over against my "ideology," he championed acceptable (historical) "exegesis." What he saw as a mistake to be challenged was "the imposition of anachronistic religious biases" on "ancient" authors (274). We need to reflect on what is at stake when he excludes "biases" from exegetical practice.

Is Holloway opposed to *all religious* biases? In that case he would represent exegesis as being a simply non-religious activity. To engage in it, exegetes should lay aside all their religious questions and convictions and attempt to interpret in a non-religious fashion the unquestionably religious texts of the Bible. At first glance this would seem to involve a mismatch—between the hermeneutical method (what excludes everything religious or concerned with God) and the texts it expounds (eminently religious and concerned with God). But, as we shall see, Holloway describes his exegetical work as that of a "cultural historian," and culture includes religion.

Holloway seems to exclude from exegetical practice only what he calls "anachronistic" religious biases. Other (non-anachronistic) religious biases could be allowed to come into play when practicing biblical exegesis. If that is the case, what is deemed non-anachronistic would have to be carefully distinguished from the anachronistic.

Holloway may wish to proscribe all religious biases, especially *all* religious questions and convictions that emerged after the writing of the Bible was completed and that could (or do) affect the exegesis of scriptural texts. If so, that pits himself against, for example, a notable contribution to the *Hermeneia* series, the commentary on Matthew by Ulrich Luz.[11]

In the preface to the first edition, which first appeared in the Continental Commentary series and was then reworked in the *Hermeneia* series, Luz expressed his conviction that a commentary which "not only explains biblical texts but also aids in their understanding is not permitted simply to remain in the past, it must also draw lines into the present." He added: "I am convinced that the history of the text's influence can make a significant contribution here. After the text itself, I am probably most indebted to the church fathers and to the Protestant and Catholic exegesis of the sixteenth through the eighteenth centuries."[12]

Holloway, however, seems to want "to remain in the past" and not "draw lines" from the biblical texts, right down from the present. Far from making any "significant contribution" towards understanding Matthew, Paul, and other Scriptures, the "theological interpretation" of ancient church fathers and later exegetes is largely avoided by Holloway. It can only "do violence" to the "historical meaning" (282).

Luz himself makes it clear in his preface for the *Hermeneia* edition that he wishes to "integrate various methodological approaches." He wants to introduce fully "the history of the text's influence (*Wirkungsgeschichte*)" or "all of the reflections on and receptions and actualizations of the gospel in new historical situations." And that includes reading the meaning of the biblical texts in the context of "art history."[13] In short, the full work of exegesis should also involves examining meanings that have emerged in the wide reception history of the Bible.

---

[11] U. Luz, *Matthew 1–7*, trans. James E. Crouch (Minneapolis: Fortress Press, 2007.
[12] Ibid., xv.
[13] Ibid., xvii.

Holloway supports his limited view of exegesis by appealing to the editors' foreword for every Hermeneia volume (275). Clearly these editors, no matter what they intended, did not prevent Luz from attending to the full scope of the *Wirkungsgeschichte*. That work introduces some items that the four volumes of *The New Cambridge History of the Bible* (2012) report about the interpretation of biblical texts, right down to the modern world. In the *Hermeneia* series we find another major contribution, François Bovon's three-volume commentary on Luke's Gospel, also citing theological interpretations and actualizations of the biblical texts provided by the fathers of the church and later scholars and teachers.[14]

Second, Holloway cites from the general editors' language about the need to "*lay bare* the ancient meaning" of biblical works (275; italics mine). This sounds a little like imagining biblical interpretation as a kind of archeology. We are meant to remove a subsequent theological overlay that hides the real meaning of the text. One hears here an echo of some notable exponents of the nineteenth-century quest for the historical Jesus. They stripped away dogmatic implications and expressions to conclude through his words and deeds he was only a very notable prophetic, non-eschatological preacher. Albert Schweitzer, who was at least sensitive to the eschatological material, told the misguided story brilliantly in *The Quest of the Historical Jesus*.[15]

Third, Holloway agrees that his aim is not to offer any "constructive theological interpretation of Philippians" (282). This statement expresses a non-controversial meaning that should be

---

[14] *Luke: A Commentary*, trans. Donald S. Deer et al., 3 vols (Minneapolis: Fortress Press, 2012).

[15] Trans. W. Montgomery; 2nd edn (London: A. & A. Black, 1936; German orig. 1906).

widely accepted: his profession as a scriptural exegete does not call on him to join systematic theologians in constructing a full-blooded theological scheme in the light of Philippians 2:6–11. But what have the theologians themselves succeeded in constructing? Holloway reports his experience of the wide-spread failure of such theologians to incorporate biblical witness in their work: "I have yet to see a constructive theological reading of a New Testament document that does not do violence to its historical meaning" (282).

Here my own experience converges somewhat, but not universally, with that of Holloway. Often enough theologians and exegetes read biblical texts in ways that do violence to their historical meaning. Over and over again, since publishing *The Easter Jesus*[16], I have taken issue with some doing such violence to Easter texts of the New Testament. I have also insisted that theologians become as familiar as possible with the Scriptures (an uncontroversial recommendation) and interpret them responsibly (according to principles that, at least in part, can only remain controversial).[17]

At the Gregorian University in Rome I directed a doctoral dissertation on Philippians 2:6–11 which illustrated the truth of Holloway's assertion: "theological exegesis [read 'the exegesis practiced by theologians'] tends strongly toward theological eisegesis" (282). After Pauline studies at the Biblical Institute in Rome, Nunzio Capizzi examined the use of Philippians 2:6–11 by a number of French, German, and Italian theologians who had published substantial volumes in Christology. He showed how some of them indulged a regrettable tendency to consult only one or

---

[16] G. O'Collins, *The Easter Jesus* (London: Darton, Longman & Todd, 1973).

[17] G. O'Collins, "Ten Principles for Theologians Interpreting the Scriptures," in O'Collins, *Inspiration: Towards a Christian Interpretation of Biblical Interpretation* (Oxford: Oxford University Press, 2018), 166–94.

two biblical scholars and naively adopt their views. Worse than that, unmistakable examples of eisegesis turned up: for instance, reading the Holy Spirit into Paul's verses, and so detecting there an emerging *trinitarian* faith.[18]

Fourth, Holloway describes himself as "an unapologetic cultural historian" (276). A wide term, culture, should be recognized as involving religion and hence incorporating biblical texts, the field for exegetical activity.[19] Through being generated in the historical realm the texts involve a triple relationship to history: development in the past, creation in the present, and being read, re-read, and actualized in the future.

While challenging the specific angel Christology that Holloway attributes to Paul, I find a triple relationship to history respected in his treatment of Philippians 2:6–11. He recognizes, for instance, the past origins of Philippians 2:10–11 in Isaiah 43:23. He pays major attention to what Paul intends in his encomium to Jesus. The subsequent reading and interpretation are not lacking in Holloway's exegesis. He introduces and values, for instance, what the third-century father of the Church, Origen, contributes to our understanding of the passage from Paul (281–82).

Holloway's vision of the work of a "cultural historian" does not allege the possibility of an exegesis that purports to refrain from all presuppositions. He pictures himself as "a finite human being with a limited perspective and unconscious biases" (283, n. 34). He ends this note by presenting "objectivity" as his aim, albeit "a stubbornly elusive goal." This goal remains, however, a little ob-

---

[18] N. Capizzi, *L'uso di Fil. 2,6–11 nella cristologia contemporanea (1965-93)* (Rome: Gregorian University Press, 1997).

[19] On "culture," its overlap with, and its difference from "tradition," see G. O'Collins, *Tradition: Understanding Christian Tradition* (Oxford: Oxford University Press, 2018), 53–55.

scure. While it is characterized as "stubbornly elusive," does this way of putting responsible exegetical activity risk implying that "my" exegesis has an objective goal, even a purely objective one, freed from all subjectivity? That would be to forget that all knowledge is personal and subjective, and that, while subjectivity and objectivity may be distinguished, they continue to be inseparable. "Purely objective" exegesis remains an impossible dream.

Conclusion

I was grateful to Holloway for taking time to respond to my article. Yet, as should be clear, too many specific details in his case for reading an angel Christology in Philippians 2 remain unconvincing. At the same time, however, his general view of biblical exegesis as the work of a cultural historian is not totally alien to the way I would conceive such work.

Holloway supports a certain uniqueness of Christ and does so in terms of his angel hypothesis: "in Jewish apocalyptic myth and thus in Paul's Christ myth the relationship between the Name-bearing angel and God was also 'unique'" (279). Many Pauline scholars locate that uniqueness in Christ being not only preexistent but also the "Father's own Son" (Rom 5:8–10; 8:3, 32; Gal 4:4).

10

Collaborators of the Apostles and Vatican Reform

In "The Roman Curia at and after Vatican II: Legal-Rational or Theological Reform," Massimo Faggioli ended by pleading for the recovery of theological traditions concerned with the Church's institutions, and looking, in particular, for some ancient, perhaps biblical, traditions that might inspire and shape the reform of the present Roman Curia.[1] Do we have much data, for instance, about Peter's collaborators that would support an analogy between their ministry and that of the contemporary Roman Curia which works with and under the pope? Or do we need to turn to Paul's letters which testify to a variety of "co-workers" who might provide a vision illuminating the functions of the Curia and its reform?

Where might we find some precedents, or at least some ancient analogies for reforming theologically the Roman Curia, and going beyond a merely legal and bureaucratic restructuring that simply promises to make the Curia more efficient, transparent, representative, and honest? The obligation to prepare budgets, the thorough sifting of expenditure, the appointment of lay members, serious decentralization of decision-making, are further items are obviously desirable—from a legal and rational point of view. But what biblical tradition(s) could throw light on and inspire the overall function of the Curia with and under the pope?

---

[1] M. Faggioli, "The Roman Curia at and after Vatican II: Legal-Rational or Theological Reform?," *Theological Studies* 76 (2015), 550–71.

Apostolic Leaders and their Collaborators

The letters of St Paul, the Acts of the Apostles, and further New Testament sources report how Peter, Paul, and others exercised leadership in the very early church. Peter himself left Jerusalem to preach, for instance, in Lydda and Joppa (Acts 9:32–43), but we know little of his missionary activity outside Palestine.[2] His visit to Antioch prompted a famous clash with Paul (Gal 2:11–21); he was traditionally said to have become the head ("bishop") of the church of Antioch. He may have visited Corinth (1 Cor 1:12). There is a possible reference to Peter's ministry in Rome (Rom 15:20), and he was martyred there, probably in AD 64. It is only from years after his martyrdom (apparently by crucifixion) that we have clear and convincing evidence of the existence of a monarchical Bishop of Rome.[3] He may have written 1 Peter, a circular letter (encyclical?) sent from Rome (1 Pet 5:13) to Christian communities in five Roman provinces (1 Pet 1:1). The ancient tradition about Peter's being associated with Mark in writing the second Gospel has been recently defended vigorously by Richard Bauckham.[4] The Acts of the Apostles, right up to the Council of Jerusalem in Acts 15 provide many details about Peter acting collegially with John, Paul, and other apostles. But, apart from a tan-

---

[2] Peter (along with John) also visited Samaria (Acts 8:14–25) and was in Caesarea for his important meeting with Cornelius (Acts 10:24; see 12:19). On Peter and his activity, see Raymond E. Brown, Karl P. Donfried, and John Reumann (eds), *Peter in the New Testament: A Collaborative Assessment by Protestant and Roman Catholic Scholars* (Minneapolis: Augsburg, 1973); Markus Bockmuehl, *The Remembered Peter: In Ancient Reception and Modern Debate* (Tübingen: Mohr Siebeck, 2010); Martin Hengel, *Saint Peter: the Underestimated Apostle*, trans. Thomas H. Trapp (Grand Rapids: Eerdmans, 2010).

[3] Peter Lampe, *From Paul to Valentinus: Christians at Rome in the First Two Centuries*, trans. Michael Steinhauser (Minneapolis: Fortress, 2003).

[4] R. Bauckham, *Jesus and the Eyewitnesses: The Gospels as Eyewitness Testimony*, 2nd edn (Grand Rapids: Eerdmans, 2017),155–82.

talizing reference to Silvanus and Mark (1 Pet 5:12–13) and to "six brothers" who accompanied Peter on his visit to Cornelius (Acts 10:23, 45; 11:12), the New Testament yields little direct evidence about non-apostles who collaborated closely with Peter and could be understood to prefigure the members of the Roman Curia, the contemporary administrative arm of the Bishop of Rome.

For Paul, however, the other outstanding apostolic leader who like Peter was martyred in Rome and who continues to be celebrated as the co-founder of its church, we have some indications of his immediate collaborators, albeit collaborators not so much in leading some settled community but rather in his travelling ministry as missionary apostle. Could that collaboration with Paul provide some vision and inspiration for the kind of theological reform of the Roman Curia that Faggioli looks for?

Timothy as Collaborator of Paul

To examine thoroughly a limited amount of data, I propose restricting myself largely to the seven letters that by general agreement were directly composed by Paul and so constitute the earliest body of Christian literature: Romans, 1 and 2 Corinthians, Galatians, Philippians, 1 Thessalonians, and Philemon. We can begin by investigating three collaborators of the apostle: Timothy, Titus, and Epaphroditus.[5]

After recommending Phoebe (Rom 16:1–2) and sending his own greetings to many people in the Christian community of

---

[5] For the New Testament data on these three Christians, see John Gillman. "Epaphroditus," in David Noel Freedman (ed.), *Anchor Bible Dictionary*, vol. 2 (New York: Doubleday, 1992), 533–34; Gillman, "Timothy," ABD, vol. 6. 558–60; Gillman, "Titus," ABD, vol. 6, 581–82. See also F. F. Bruce, *The Pauline Circle* (Grand Rapids: Eerdmans, 1985); Wolf-Henning Ollrog, *Paulus und seine Mitarbeiter* (Neukirchen-Vluyn: Neukirchener, 1979).

Rome (Rom 16:3–15), Paul adds a general greeting from "all the churches of Christ" (Rom 16:16), a warning against those who cause dissent (Rom 16:17–20a), and a concluding blessing (Rom 16:20b). He then sends greetings from eight companions, starting with Timothy, his "co-worker" (Rom 16:21–23). Presumably Timothy is with the apostle when he dictates the letter. Should we also presume that Timothy is known to some or even many of the Christians in Rome?[6]

Timothy's being named, sometimes without explanation, in other letters suggests that he was widely known in various, scattered Christian communities. In Paul's earliest extant writing he is mentioned as sending the letter with the apostle: "Paul, Silvanus, and Timothy, to the church of the Thessalonians in God the Father and the Lord Jesus Christ: grace to you and peace" (1 Thes 1:1).[7] Later in the same letter the apostle recalls how at the time of persecution he had dispatched Timothy to the Thessalonian Christians: "we sent Timothy our brother and co-worker for God in proclaiming the gospel of Christ, to strengthen and encourage you for the sake of your faith, so that no one would be shaken by these persecutions" (1 Thes 3:2). Paul is an apostle of Christ Jesus,[8] but he associates Timothy with him when corresponding with the church of Corinth: "Paul an apostle of Christ Jesus by the will of God and Timothy our brother to the church of God that

---

[6] Although some scholars still disagree, many hold that Rom 16 belongs to Paul's original letter: see Brendan Byrne, *Romans* (Collegeville, MN: Liturgical Press, 1996), 29; Joseph A. Fitzmyer, *Romans* (New York: Doubleday, 1992), 49–50; Robert Jewett, *Romans* (Minneapolis: Fortress, 2007), 8–9; Douglas J. Moo, *The Epistle to the Romans* (Grand Rapids: Eerdmans, 1996), 5–9, 912.

[7] Sylvanus is the Latin form of Silas, whom Acts mentions as a travelling companion of Paul (Acts 15:22–18:5), and whom Paul names as being with him at the founding of the Corinthian church (2 Cor 1:19).

[8] In 1 Thes 2:7, the phrase "apostles of Christ" may be meant to include Timothy along with Paul (and Silvanus).

is in Corinth" (2 Cor 1:1). (We will see below how Timothy is no stranger to the Corinthian Corinthians.⁹) Paul is in prison awaiting trial (Phil 1:12–26) when he and Timothy. "slaves of Christ Jesus" (Phil 1:1) send a letter to the Philippians. (Below we will see how Timothy is known also to the Christians in Philippi, a Roman colony and a major city in Macedonia.) Without clarification, Timothy joins with Paul in a personal and public appeal to Philemon, Apphia, and Archippus, as well as to the church that meets in one of their homes: "Paul, a prisoner of Christ Jesus, a prisoner of Christ Jesus, and Timothy, brother, to Philemon, our dear friend and co-worker, to Apphia our sister [a fellow Christian and probably Philemon's wife], to Archippus, our fellow soldier, and to the church in your house: grace and peace to you and peace from God our Father and the Lord Jesus Christ' (Philemon 1–3).[10] In short, Timothy is no anonymous companion of the apostle Paul but someone widely known in the young Christian communities.[11]

What is Timothy known for and what motivates Paul in calling him "my co-worker" and brother? The story of three communities fills out an answer. First, Paul obviously has great affection for the

---

[9] Since Paul wrote 1 Cor from Ephesus (1 Cor 16:10) and sent Timothy from that city to Corinth (1 Cor 4:17; 16:8–11), we can presume that Timothy was also known at least to some Ephesian Christians. According to 1 Tim 1:3, he would be urged to remain in Ephesus and correct misleading teaching that was being disseminated there.

[10] See James D. G. Dunn, *The Epistles to Colossians and Philemon* (Grand Rapids: Eerdmans, 1996), 311–13.

[11] Other New Testament sources yield further evidence that Timothy was widely known. In Col 1:1, 1 Thes 1:1 and 2 Thes 1:1, he is presented as co-sender of the three letters; according to Acts 16:3, he was a companion of Paul. In the practical greetings and instructions which make up the final chapter of Hebrews, we read: "I want you to know that our brother Timothy has been set free' and if he comes in time, he will be with me when I visit you' (Heb 13:23); see H, Koester, *Hebrews* (New York: Doubleday, 2001), 580–81. Finally, whatever we hold about the authorship of 1 and 2 Tim, the fact that two letters attributed to Paul are addressed to Timothy suggests the latter's known standing as a co-worker of the apostle, at least among other Christians.

congregation he founded in Thessalonica, the capital of the Roman province of Macedonia: "you are our glory and joy" (1 Thes 2:20). Separated from them and worried about them, the apostle sent Timothy to "strengthen and encourage them" (1 Thes 3:2).

Second, Timothy worked with Paul when they proclaimed "the Son of God, Jesus Christ" in Corinth and so became a co-founder of the church there (2 Cor 1:19; see Acts 18:5). Later, when troubles break out in that community, Timothy acts as Paul's representative (1 Cor 4:17; 16:10–11; see Acts 19:22). What Timothy has done encourages the apostle to name him not merely with respect as "our brother" (2 Cor 1:1) but also as "my beloved and faithful child in the Lord" (1 Cor 4:17). This latter passage and its context call for close attention as they show how Timothy's mission has gone to the very heart of Paul's existence as apostle of Christ.

Paul presents that mission in this way: "in Christ Jesus I became your father through the gospel. I appeal to you, then, be imitators of me. For this reason I sent you Timothy, who is my beloved and faithful child in the Lord to remind you of my ways in Christ Jesus, as I teach them everywhere in every church" (1 Cor 4:15–17).[12] Having reminded the Corinthian Christians that he is their one and only "father" because he brought them to birth in Christ Jesus through the gospel, Paul draws the conclusion: "The picture is one of a father who has instructed his children in proper behavior by his own example. They are to be 'like father, like children.'"[13] By modelling their lives on Paul's example and teaching, his "ways in Christ," the Corinthians will in fact be imitating Christ himself. Later in the same letter Paul says just that: "Be imitators of me, as I am of Christ" (1 Cor 11:1; see 1 Thess 1:6).

---

[12] See Fitzmyer, *First Corinthians*, 221–24.

[13] Gordon D. Fee, *The First Epistle to the Corinthians* (Grand Rapids: Eerdmans, 2014), 186.

Since he comes in the place of Paul, Timothy should be regarded by the Corinthians "as though Paul himself were present among them."[14] By helping the Corinthian community to remember Paul's "ways in Christ Jesus," Timothy is entrusted with mediating to them nothing less than the imitation of Christ, which they had seen modelled by the apostle Paul himself. This is a delicate and profound mission that goes to the heart of Christian existence. One can understand why in this context the apostle is not content to describe Timothy simply as a "co-worker," "brother," or "fellow slave," but characterizes him tenderly as "my beloved and faithful child." Here "faithful" indicates that Timothy is worthy of the trust Paul places in him. Timothy displays the faithfulness God requires of his servants (1 Cor 4:2).

Third, it is as "son" that Paul represents Timothy when writing from prison to the Philippians—a letter to a third community that fills out the apostle's picture of Timothy:

> I hope in the Lord Jesus to send Timothy to you soon, so that I may be cheered by news
>
> of you. I have no one else like him (*isopsychos*) who will be generously concerned for
>
> your welfare. All of them are seeking their own interests, not those of Jesus Christ. But
>
> Timothy's worth you know, how like a son with a father he has served/slaved with me
>
> in the work of the gospel. I hope therefore to send him as soon as I see how things go
>
> with me, and I trust in the Lord that I will also come soon (Phil 2:19–24).

---

[14] Ibid., 188.

Here we have Paul's fullest and finest tribute to Timothy. Timothy is obviously not to be aligned with those who "are seeking their own interests, not those of Jesus Christ." Rather he is "equal" or "like soul (*isopsychos*)" with Paul (and with the Philippians?). someone who "sees things as we do." Like a son with his father, he has slaved with/for Paul "in the work of the gospel." More than simply being a "co-worker," Timothy has served like a son with his father,[15] as if he were in the family business of spreading the good news. The Christians of Corinth, evidently from previous contacts (see Acts 16), are acquainted with his worth. Timothy's record and character are known to them. Moreover, he will be "genuinely concerned" for their "welfare." He shares in what Paul calls elsewhere "my anxiety for all the churches" (2 Cor 11:28). Since Timothy shows all these qualities, he is obviously the right person to be sent by the imprisoned apostle as his delegate or emissary to the community of Philippi.

The seven authentic letters of Paul yield a picture of Timothy and his relationship with the apostle that suggests what should be expected from members of the Curia in their relationship with the pope. In all that Paul says about Timothy, no hint of careerism comes through; Timothy is not an upwardly mobile church official, ambitiously "seeking his own interest," carefully planning for higher office, and not "genuinely concerned" with the "welfare" of other Christians around the world. No faceless bureaucrat, he is widely known for having proclaimed the gospel in Corinth and having "with and under" Paul co-founded the church there. Other Christians, such as those who make up the communities in Rome, Thessalonica, Philippi, or who are associated with Philemon, have met Timothy or at least are aware of him. He is a missionary of

---
[15] See John Reumann, *Philippians* (New Haven, CT: Yale University Press, 2008), 422.

proven worth, totally trusted by Paul as a "brother," "son," and "fellow slave" of Jesus Christ, and a faithful servant of God. He sees things as Paul does and helps Christians to model their lives on Paul's teaching and example and so promotes the "imitation" of Christ himself.

The standard descriptions of Timothy as Paul's "travelling companion," "envoy," "delegate," or "representative" fall short of the mark. They can mask the full reality of how Timothy "slaved" away with the apostle. Even the term "co-worker" fails to summarize all that Paul says about being on mission with Timothy. The full account of Timothy supplies a challenging narrative for those called to collaborate with the pope in the Roman Curia. This holds true also of Titus, especially in the area of handling money.

Titus as Collaborator of Paul

Gentile ("Greek") by birth, Titus may have been personally converted and baptized by Paul himself. He joined the apostle on a visit to the Christian leaders and community in Jerusalem.[16] Some Jewish Christian held that conversion to the practices of Judaism formed the precondition for entry into Christianity, and required the circumcision of Titus—a concession that Paul vigorously rejected. Titus provided a test case for accepting uncircumcised Jews into the church and not imposing on them other prescriptions of the Torah. Peter, John, and James (the relation of Jesus and not one of the Twelve) agreed with Paul's continuing his mission among the uncircumcised Gentiles. They "asked only one thing," that Paul "remember the poor" Christian community in Jerusalem—something that he was in any case "eager to do" (Gal 2:1–10). In fact, he organized among the churches he had founded a

---

[16] See J. Louis Martyn, *Galatians* (New York: Doubleday, 1998), 187–228.

collection on behalf of the church in Jerusalem. It was a project of financial assistance in which, as we shall see at once, Titus played a central role.[17]

Like Timothy and Silvanus (2 Cor 1:1, 19), Titus was involved in Paul's relations with the Christian community in Corinth. He probably carried there the apostle's "letter of tears" (2 Cor 2:3–4, 7–8). He brought back to Paul, who had travelled to Macedonia (2 Cor 2:13), the welcome news that this letter had been favorably received by the Corinthians: "God who consoles the downcast consoled us by the arrival of Titus, and not only by his coming but also by the consolation with which he was consoled about you, as he told us of your longing, your mourning, your zeal for me, so that I rejoiced even more" (2 Cor 7:6–7). Having already alerted the Corinthians to "the consolation with which he [Titus] was consoled about you," Paul underlined the joy of Titus himself over the happy outcome of his mission that firmly re-established the community's obedience to Paul, the apostle who had founded their church:

> In addition to our own consolation, we rejoiced still more at the joy of Titus, because his
>
> mind has been set at rest by all of you. For if I have been somewhat boastful about you to
>
> him, I was not disgraced. But as everything we said to you was true, so our boasting to

---

[17] Barnabas also joined Paul on that visit to Jerusalem, and was obviously involved with him in the mission to the Gentiles (Gal 2:1, 9). When Paul confronted Peter in Antioch, he feared that Peter was leading Barnabas astray in compelling Gentile Christians to live like Jews (Gal 2:13). In another letter, Paul mentions the way he and Barnabas did not press their right to be supported financially by the communities (1 Cor 9:6). Yet in Paul's seven certainly authentic letters, he says little about Barnabas, a central figure in Acts 4–15, and never names him even as his "co-worker."

> Titus has proved true as well. And his heart goes out all the more to you, as he remembers
>
> the obedience of all of you, and how you welcomed him with fear and trembling (2 Cor 7:13–15).

After helping to put things right in Corinth, Titus rejoiced to recall how things worked out in Corinth, just as Paul had promised. At once we learn of Titus being pressed into service for another project.

Paul appealed to the Corinthians to complete their contribution to a collection for the Christian community in Jerusalem, a collection intended not only to relieve its economic poverty but also to express its union with the relatively well-off and largely Gentile churches around the Mediterranean.[18] Paul had started this collection in Corinth and among other churches (1 Cor 16:1–4; Rom 15:25–27), and now he wanted Titus to "complete this generous undertaking" among the Corinthians (2 Cor 8:6). The apostle was astonished at the spontaneous response of Titus, whom he called "my partner and co-worker in your service" (2 Cor 8:23): "thanks be to God who put into the heart of Titus the same eagerness for you that I have. For he not only accepted our appeal but also, since he is more eager than ever, he is going to you of his own accord" (2 Cor 8:16–17).

Before 2 Corinthians ends, we learn that Paul needed to answer charges that he and Titus had taken advantage of the community in Corinth to enrich themselves. Some Corinthians accused Paul and Titus of skimming the collection funds—a charge that Paul vigorously denied (2 Cor 12:14–18). He mentions one or

---

[18] See Stephan J. Joubert, "Collection, The," in Katharine Doob Sakenfeld (ed.), *The New Interpreter's Dictionary of the Bible*, vol. 1, 698–99; Keith F. Nickle, *The Collection: A Study in Paul's Strategy* (London: SCM Press, 1966).

two anonymous "brothers" sent with Titus to Corinth, who could witness to the honesty of the proceedings (2 Cor 8:18, 22–23; 9:5; 12:18). At the risk of becoming anachronistic, one might see the accusations concerning the collection foreshadowing fictitious or well-founded accusations of financial wrongdoing involving members of the Roman Curia.

All in all, on his two visits Titus resolved grave difficulties over Paul's missionary activity (which provoked the apostle's "letter of tears" to the Corinthian community) and promoted the collection for the church in Jerusalem (which occasioned the charge of financial irregularities). Paul was obviously and deeply grateful for the generous and successful collaboration Titus offered on both occasions.[19]

Even though the apostle very likely never wrote these words, his sentiments were reflected when, according to the Letter to Titus, he called Titus a "loyal child in the faith" (Tit 1:4). Paul's known, even widely known, regard for this collaborator provided plausibility for this letter encouraging Titus to complete a mission on the island of Crete (Tit 1:5).

Epaphroditus as Collaborator of Paul

It is only in Philippians 2:25–30 and 4:18 that Paul mentions Epaphroditus.[20] He brought gifts to the apostle from Philippi. When he returned, he was most likely the courier who carried Paul's Letter to the Philippians. Those are the headlines; let us now see the small print.

---

[19] The two visits may have taken place in reverse order, with Titus first visiting Corinth to administer the collection for the church in Jerusalem and returning later to negotiate a reconciliation between Paul and the Corinthians. They had come to doubt the apostle's legitimacy and financial reliability.

[20] See Reumann, *Philippians*, 423–34, 438–39, 442–50, 666–70.

As regards the Philippians, Epaphroditus is their "messenger and minister." For Paul, he is "my brother, co-worker, fellow soldier" and "minister (*leitourgos*) to my need" (Phil 2:25). Paul reaches for cultic language to describe the gifts that have come at the hands of this *leitourgos*: "I have received from Epaphroditus the gifts you sent, a fragrant offering, a sacrifice acceptable and pleasing to God" (Phil 4:18). The apostle's language about Epaphroditus being his "co-worker and fellow soldier" seems to imply someone arriving with gifts from a Christian community and then returning home with a letter for that community. But Paul offers no details about any ongoing collaboration that would further justify speaking about Epaphroditus as sharing with him the "work" and "battle" of missionary activity.

Epaphroditus risked his life to visit Paul, fell ill, and almost died. In describing what happened, the apostle evoked his own feelings, as well as those of his visitor and his community, as being longing, distress, sorrow, eagerness, rejoicing, and anxiety:

> He has been longing for all of you, and has been distressed because you heard that he was
>
> ill. He was indeed so ill that he almost died. But God had mercy on him, and not only on him
>
> but also on me, so that I would not have one sorrow after another. I am the more eager to
>
> send him, in order that you may rejoice at seeing him again, and that I may be less
>
> anxious. Welcome him then in the Lord with all joy, and honor such people, because he
>
> came close to death for the work of Christ, risking his life to make up for those services
>
> that you could not give me (Phil 2:26–30).

To sum up. Epaphroditus symbolizes a wonderful blend of material and spiritual collaboration with an apostolic leader. He brings to Paul financial support, and then takes home to the community at Philippi an affectionate, very joyful, and utterly Christ-centered letter.

Further Collaborators of Paul

Any list of Paul's co-workers should take in Phoebe, Prisca, Aquila, and Urbanus—all mentioned in the final chapter of Romans. Phoebe brought Paul's letter to the Christians of Rome.[21] Paul spoke of Phoebe as "our sister" and "a deacon of the church at Cenchreae."[22] The Cenchreae in question was a port serving the nearby city of Corinth, from which Paul wrote to the Roman Christians. As "our sister," Phoebe was a fellow Christian of the Corinthian community with whom Paul was then staying. The apostle asked the church in Rome to welcome and help her "in whatever way she may require from you," as "is fitting" for a fellow Christian, one of "the saints" (Rom 16:1–2). But Phoebe was not merely a Christian who acted as a courier for Paul.

"She has been," the apostle wrote, "a patroness (*prostatis*) of many here and of myself too" (Rom 16:2). While many commentators have understood the title figuratively as helper or benefactor, Fitzmyer points out that, like the Latin *patrona*, it "denoted a person of prominence in the ancient Greco-Roman world." So Paul is

---

[21] On Phoebe, see Byrne, *Romans*, 447–48; Fitzmyer, *Romans*, 728–33; Florence Morgan Gillman, ABD, vol. 5, 348–49.

[22] Fitzmyer comments: "*Diakonos* may designate her generically as an 'assistant' or 'minister' in the church or specifically as a 'deacon,' a member of special group in the church. There is no way of saying whether the term refers at this time to the diaconate, an 'order' which clearly emerged in the church by the time of Ignatius of Antioch" (*Romans*, 729).

acknowledging "the public service that this prominent woman has given to many Christians at Cenchreae," as a leader of their community. Fitzmyer comments: "she probably owned a house there and, as a wealthy, influential person involved in commerce, was in a position to assist missionaries and other Christians who travelled to and from Corinth. We can only speculate about the kind of assistance she gave: hospitality? Championing their cause before secular authorities? Furnishing funds for journeys? Paul also "acknowledges the debt he owes Phoebe. She perhaps played hostess to him when he visited Cenchrae at times during his three-month stay in Corinth."[23]

Unlike Phoebe, who seems to have been a Gentile Christian, Prisca (sometimes called by the diminutive "Priscilla") and Aquila were a Jewish-Christian couple who, around 49 AD, had been banished from Rome by an edict of the Emperor Claudius (Acts 18:2).[24] They created a church community in their home (1 Cor 16:19) and become fellow workers" of Paul (Rom 16:3), sharing in his mission of evangelization both at Corinth (Acts 18:3) and at Ephesus (1 Cor 16:19; Acts 18:26). It is plausible to think with Fitzmyer that, when Nero permitted Jews (and Jewish Christians) to return to Rome, "it was Paul who urged them [Prisca and Aquila] to return to Rome as a 'vanguard' to assemble a house church and prepare for his arrival." They were "undoubtedly Paul's source of information about the contemporary situation in the Roman community ."[25]

As well as having been "co-workers," Prisca and Aquila had "risked their necks" for Paul (Rom 16:4). Fitzmyer comments:

---

[23] Fitzmyer, *Romans*, 731.
[24] Peter Lampe, "Prisca," ABD, vol. 5. 487–88.
[25] Fitzmyer, *Romans*, 735.

> Paul gratefully recalls some intervention of Prisca and Aquila on his behalf which endangered them as well, either at Ephesus (perhaps at the riot of the silversmiths, Acts 19:23 or during some imprisonment to which Paul may refer in 1 Cor 15:32 and 2 Cor 1:8–9). They may have attempted to use some of the influence that their wealth and social position gave them.[26]

In the course of his greetings to the Roman Christians, Paul also saluted "Urbanus, our co-worker in Christ" (Rom 16:9), but added no details about the place and nature of their collaboration. When dealing with the rivalry that the ministry of Apollos had triggered in Corinth, Paul wrote: "we are God's servants, working together" (1 Cor 3:9). Thus Urbanus and Apollos belong with Timothy, Titus, Epaphroditus, Aquila, and Clement (see below) among Paul's treasured "co-workers." The group also included Phoebe and Prisca and, as we shall see, some other women—a reminder that, if the contemporary Roman Curia is to be modelled on those who also collaborated with the apostolic founders of Christianity. It must also include an appropriate number of women.

Two women leaders among the Christians of Philippi, Euodia and Syntyche, may well have been heads of house churches and so belonged among the "overseers and helpers," to whom Paul and Timothy addressed the Letter to the Philippians (Phil 1:1).[27] Paul recognized how these women "have struggled beside me in the work of the gospel, together with Clement and the rest of my co-workers" (Phil 4:2–3). This language recalls Paul's earlier

---

[26] Fitzmyer, *Romans*, 735.
[27] See Florence Morgan Gillman, "Euodia," ABD, vol, 2, 670–71; Gillman, "Syntyche," ABD, vol 6, 270; Reumann, *Philippians*, 607–11; 625–33.

injunctions about "struggling side by side for the faith of the gospel," and not becoming "intimidated by your opponents." (Phil 1:27–30).

Some disagreement had broken out between Euodia and Syntyche, and was having a bad impact on church life in Philippi. Paul asked "my loyal companion," an unknown but obviously influential person to mediate between the two women.[28] But the current difficulty took nothing away from the apostle's esteem for Euodia and Syntyche, his co-workers, "whose names are in the book of life" (Phil 4:3).

In their closing greetings to Philemon, Paul and Timothy refer to "co-workers," who also send greetings: Mark, Aristarchus, Demas, and Luke (see Col 4:10–14). But nothing further is indicated, at least here, about the collaboration of these four in the mission of the apostle (Philemon 24).

Conclusion

Concentrating on seven certainly authentic letters of Paul, we can see how some of his collaborators were men and some women; some were Gentile Christians (e.g. Titus) and some Jewish Christians (e.g., Prisca and Aquila); some were closely associated for a long time with Paul's ministry (Timothy), while with others (Urbanus) we have no information about such details. How the collaborators were recruited to share in Paul's apostolic ministry remains, for the most part, obscure. Even in the case of Timothy, we do not learn from Paul himself but only from Acts 16:2–3 that the apostle chose Timothy because of his "good reputation." Even then, we are not told what this reputation was based on.

---

[28] The Greek word for "companion" could be translated as a proper name, Syzygus.

Nevertheless, Paul does let us see what these collaborators whom he called his "co-workers" did. We can draw three conclusions about them.

Firstly, their mission covered a range of activities: from co-founding a new church community (Timothy) to acting as couriers for Paul's letters (Epaphroditus and Phoebe); from resolving difficulties for the apostle (Titus) to bringing him financial support (Epaphroditus); from being co-senders of Paul's letters (Timothy) to making their home into a house church (Prisca and Aquila); from promoting the imitation of Paul (and so of Christ) (Timothy) to fund-raising for the Jerusalem church (Titus); from being a "patroness" of Paul and others (Phoebe) to "working for the gospel" (Euodia and Syntyche); from "risking their neck" for Paul (Prisca and Aquila) to bringing him good news (Titus); from fulfilling a local, residential ministry (Euodia and Syntyche in Philippi and Phoebe in Cenchreae) to being itinerant missionaries with Paul (Timothy and Titus).

The collaborators of Paul gave themselves to a variety of missions, working with an apostle who was to become through martyrdom the co-founder of the church of Rome. They can be seen as prefiguring the many tasks assigned in our times to the members of the pope's curia.

Second, for most of his co-workers, Paul has nothing but praise. In the case of Euodia and Syntyche there are personal conflicts to deal with. Paul values them highly and has no doubts about inscribing them in God's "book of life." They remind us that his collaborators could also have to struggle with personal and interpersonal issues.

Third, from what Paul indicates about his co-workers, no hint comes through of their seeking their own personal interests and wanting to make a "successful" career of apostolic collaboration. Here they diverge sharply from some in the Roman Curia who have evidently looked for power, privilege, and financial gain,

The apostolic collaborators presented by Paul represent inspiring models for reforming the Roman Curia. Many particular administrative decisions will necessarily shape that reform. But Pope Francis, his "co-workers" and, indeed, the Catholic Church at large need an overall (spiritual and theological) vision of what the Vatican Curia could become. Apostolic pointers to reform can be retrieved from the New Testament and serve usefully in the context of the twenty-first century.

As head of the worldwide episcopal college, Pope Francis is the successor of Peter, the head of the apostolic college. He is also the Bishop of Rome, the church founded on the martyrdom of Peter *and Paul.* As regards Peter, we have little news about his "co-workers," the collaborators who might inspire a spiritual reform of the Roman Curia. But in the case of Paul we enjoy a relatively rich picture of his "co-workers," those men and women who engaged in a ministry analogous to that of the Vatican Curia and can serve as biblical models for that group's radical conversion.

Massimo Faggioli looked for some early tradition that could inspire a conversion of the Roman Curia that goes beyond mere administrative restructuring. Such a tradition could be retrieved. I submit, from the New Testament and, specifically, from what the Paul, the great apostle of Jesus Christ, writes about his co-workers.

11

THE FAITH OF JESUS (HEBREWS 12:2A)

Hebrews 11:1–12:2 is the longest passage in the New Testament that deals with "faith (*pistis*)," using this noun 25 times and citing numerous heroes and heroines of faith. Some are named like Abel (Heb 11:4) and Sarah (Heb 11:11) and others left anonymous in the "cloud of witnesses" (Heb 12:1). This encomium of faith reaches its high point in verse 12:2a, which writes of "*ton tēs pisteōs archēgon kai teleiōtēn Iēsoun.*" Does "the faith" refer to Christian faith which believes in the crucified and risen Jesus (*objective* genitive) or does it refer to the perfect faith that Jesus himself exercised from the beginning to the end of his earthly existence (*subjective* genitive)? The identification of the faith which the author of Hebrews primarily has in mind here will affect how we understand calling Jesus the *archēgos* and *teleiōtēs* (pioneer and perfector) of faith. Was he the *archēgos* and *teleiōtēs* of our faith or of his own faith?

Contemporary commentaries on Hebrews have regularly opted for a subjective genitive, whereas translators have normally accepted an objective genitive—often by qualifying faith as "our faith," even though there is no corresponding "our" in the Greek text. Let us see the details by sampling major translations and leading modern commentators.

Translators of Hebrews 12:2a

Responsible for the first complete translation of the Bible into English, William Tyndale (d. 1536) left his mark on subsequent English versions. His rendering of the relevant words in Hebrews 12:2a (with spelling adjusted to modern usage) ran as follows: "looking unto Jesus the auctor and finisher of our faith."[1] The 1611 King James Version (also called the Authorized Version), followed suit ("looking to Jesus the pioneer and perfecter of our faith"), but substituted "pioneer and perfecter" for "auctor and finisher." Tyndale had drawn the Latin "*auctor*" from the (Latin) Vulgate that went back the translation of Jerome: "*aspicientes in auctorem fidei et consummatorem Iesum*." Both Tyndale and King James' team of translators knew that neither the original Greek nor the longstanding Vulgate translation read "our (*hēmeterēs/ nostrae*)" to specify whose faith was in question.[2] Yet they felt free to add "our," in order to clarify what they took to be the meaning. In doing so, were Tyndale and King James' team moving beyond the work of translation to introduce commentary and explanation?

The Douai-Reims Bible translation (New Testament 1582), which was allegedly made from the Vulgate Latin and not from the original languages, remained faithful to the Vulgate (and, behind that, to the original Greek): "looking on Jesus, the author and finisher of faith." The DRB team of translators, like Tyndale and King James' team, moved "Jesus" up to follow immediately

---

[1] In his translation of Heb 12:2a, John Wycliffe (d. 1384) did not gratuitously qualify faith as "our": "beholding unto Jesus the maker of faith, and the perfect enderer." Nor did the 1535 Miles Coverdale Bible: "looking unto Jesus ye auctor and finisher of faith."

[2] The possessive adjective *hēmeteros* is in any case rare in the entire New Testament, appearing only about nine times (Robert W. Funk, *A Greek Grammar of the New Testament* (Chicago: University of Chicago Press, 1961), 149).

upon "looking on," but, unlike them, left open the reference of "faith." In the revision of the DRB made in 1749–50 by Richard Challoner, the translation of Hebrews 12:2a remained unchanged. Was it a question of Jesus' own faith? Or was it rather a matter of our faith directed towards him, "who leads us in our faith and brings it to perfection" (the Jerusalem Bible (JB) of 1966 and the New Jerusalem Bible (NJB) of 1985? I return below to the Jerusalem Bible and its revisions.

During the first half of the twentieth century, a translation of the Bible by James Moffatt appeared in various editions. The Complete Moffatt Bible of 1935 rendered Hebrews 12:2a as follows: "our eyes fixed upon Jesus as the pioneer and perfection of faith." Several later translations picked up "our eyes fixed upon Jesus." Apropos of the issue raised by this chapter, Moffatt was one of the few modern translators who refrained from inserting "our" to qualify "faith."

In his 1945 translation Ronald Knox supported Moffatt's choice of "fixing our eyes": "Let us fix our eyes on Jesus, the origin and crown of all faith." Where Moffatt had turned only the second of the two personal nouns *archēgos* and *teleiōtēs* into impersonal nouns ("pioneer and perfection"), Knox made them both impersonal, "origin and crown.". His "origin and crown of all faith" implied that it is not the faith exercised by Jesus which is intended, but rather the faith of all those who believe in him (or, perhaps, the origin and crown of faith wherever it is found).

Placed in the tradition of the King James Bible, the Revised Standard Version of 1946 simply repeated the former's version of Hebrews 12:2a: "looking to Jesus the pioneer and perfecter of our faith." Once again "our" was read into the text.

In 1966 the Good News for Modern Man, later renamed Good News Bible, produced a fairly readable rendering. But it continued to import an "our," not to be found in the original Greek: "Keep our eyes fixed on Jesus, on whom *our* faith depends from beginning to end" (italics added).

The 1966 Jerusalem Bible translated Hebrews 12:2a as follows: "let us not lose sight of Jesus, who leads us in our faith and brings it to perfection." In the 1985 *New Jerusalem Bible*, for which Henry Wansbrough had become general editor, the first half of the translation now took over the language of Moffatt (1935) and Knox (1945),[3] while the second half maintained the wording of the JB: "let us keep our eyes fixed on Jesus, who leads us in our faith and brings it to perfection." Wansbrough remained in charge for the 2019 *Revised New Jerusalem Bible*. Here the second half of the translation was also changed: "keeping our eyes fixed on Jesus, the pioneer and perfecter of our faith." To translate as "the pioneer and perfecter of our faith" brought the RNJB into line with the KJB, RSV, and NRSV, and like them qualified "faith" with an "our" not found in the original Greek.[4]

The New English Bible of 1970 produced a notably literary translation. The translators of the New Testament, led by C. H. Dodd, made it quite clear that they still interpreted "faith" as the faith exercised by Christians: "let us keep our eyes fixed on Jesus, on whom faith depends from start to finish." The revision of this

---

[3] NAB (1970), NEB (1970), and Phillips (1972) would also adopt the language of "fixing our eyes on Jesus."

[4] The 1956 *La Bible de Jérusalem* on which the 1966 JB was based also qualified "faith" as "our faith": "fixant nos yeux sur le chef de *notre* foi, qui la mène à la perfection, Jésus" (italics mine). Note that, by changing to "let us keep our eyes fixed on Jesus" (in the 1985 NJB), Wansbrough brought the translation closer to the original *Bible de Jerusalem*.

translation, the Revised English Bible of 1989, restored "pioneer and perfecter" but, unlike Tyndale, the KJB, and the RSV, did not explicitly qualify the faith in question as our faith and left matters open: "our eyes fixed on Jesus, the pioneer and perfecter of faith."

In 1970 the New American Bible (NAB), later known after its revisions as NABR (New American Bible Revised), sided with the majority when translating Hebrews 12:2a: "let us keep our eyes fixed on Jesus, who inspires and perfects our faith." In the revisions of 1986 and 2011, however, "our" as describing "faith" was dropped: "keeping our eyes fixed on Jesus, the leader and perfecter of faith."

John Phillips in his 1972 Modern English translation rendered Hebrews 12:2a as "our eyes fixed on Jesus the source and the goal of our faith." "Our eyes fixed on" is already found in the 1935 Moffatt Bible (as well as in Knox of 1945, and in the NAB and NEB, both of 1970), but "source and goal" seem unique to Phillips's translation. Identifying faith by introducing "our" agreed with English translators since Tyndale, except for Coverdale, the DRB and Moffatt. But another translation soon joined this small minority.

In 1978 the New International Version replaced "looking to Jesus" by "our eyes fixed on Jesus." But it did not follow the tradition of Tyndale and KJB by implying that there was a question of "our faith." It rendered Hebrews 12: 2a: "fixing our eyes on Jesus, the pioneer and perfecter of faith."

Appearing in 1989, the New Revised Standard Version simply repeated the translation that went back through the RSV to Tyndale and the KJB: "looking to Jesus the pioneer and perfecter of our faith." However, when the NRSV was published in an ecumenical study edition, *The New Oxford Annotated Bible*, the notes on Hebrews 12:2a raised questions about the translation on which they were commenting.[5] We will return to this below.

To sum up this sample of English translations of Hebrews 12:2a: Tyndale, KJB, Knox, RSV, JB (to be followed by the NJB and RNJB), Good News Bible, NAB, NEB, Phillips, and NRSV all primarily understand the faith of Hebrews 12:2a as "our faith" in the crucified and exalted/risen Jesus. We could add five other English translations that did the same: the 1959 Modern Language Bible ('with our eyes on Jesus the cause and completer of our faith'); the 1995 The New Testament and Psalms: An Inclusive Version ('looking to Jesus, the pioneer and perfecter of our faith'); the 1996 New Living Translation ('keeping our eyes on Jesus the champion who initiates and perfects our faith'; the 2001 English Standard Version ('looking to Jesus, the founder and perfecter of our faith'); and the 2015 American Standard Version, which coyly introduces brackets ('looking unto Jesus the author and perfecter of {our} faith'). We can add here Nicholas King's 2004 translation, *The New Testament,* which renders Hebrews 12:2a: "we should fix our eyes on Jesus, our pacemaker and trainer in faith." This is equivalent to saying, "Jesus the pacemaker and trainer of our faith."

That makes seventeen translations which favor qualifying faith as "our" faith.[6] I could find only five English translations, DRB, Moffatt, NIV, NABR, and the REB, which did not insert "our," and left it open to understand the faith in Hebrews 12:2a as the faith exercised perfectly by Jesus himself.

---

[5] This happened with the 1991, 2007, and 2018 editions of *The New Oxford Annotated Bible* (New York: Oxford University Press).

[6] Is this an example of a "translator" being a "traitor"?

The Commentators

New Oxford Annotated Bible

Before launching into major commentators on Hebrews, we look at the brief notes that accompany Hebrews 12:2a in *The New Oxford Annotated Bible* of the edition of 1991 edited by Bruce M. Metzger and Roland E. Murphy in which Metzger and Pheme Perkins annotated Hebrews; then in the edition of 2007 edited by Michael D. Coogan (with Marc Z. Brettler, Carol A. Newsom, and Pheme Perkins as associate editors) in which Cynthia Briggs Kittredge annotated Hebrews; then in the edition of 2018 (edited by the same 2007 team) in which David A. deSilva annotated Hebrews.

In the 1991 edition, Metzger and Perkins observed that "literally" the original Greek of Hebrews 12:2a read "the faith" and not "our faith."[7] The notes by Kittredge for the 2007 edition went further in rejecting the NRSV's translation ("Jesus, the pioneer and perfecter of our faith") by calling Jesus "the ultimate example of faith," "the supreme example of faith in God and an example for those who follow him." As Kittredge recognized, Jesus was such an example for those who follow him because they see that the way in which he exercised his faith in God provides an ultimate and supreme example. He exemplified faith in its highest form and proved the perfect model to be imitated.

In his 2018 annotations deSilva noted how the Greek text of Hebrews 12:2a does not identify faith as "our faith." He continued: "the author presents Jesus here as the ultimate example of faith, who has gone farther in and more completely demonstrated that virtue than anyone else." DeSilva was chosen to compose the

---

[7] *The New Oxford Annotated Bible* (1991 ed.), 328.

annotations after publishing *Perseverance in Gratitude: A Socio-Rhetorical Commentary on the Epistle "to the Hebrews"*.[8]

Commentaries: Spicq, Westcott, Vanhoye, Michel, Hughes[9]

Turning now to regular and fuller commentators, we begin in 1953 with Ceslas Spicq. He understood Hebrews 12:2a to indicate that Christ confers on *our faith* his full achievements and eventually a heavenly reward. All Christian life and faith depend on Christ. Hebrews represents him as guiding his disciples in the race of faith and guaranteeing their final victory.[10] This commentary would support, for instance, the translation by Nicholas King that came half a century later: "we should fix our eyes on Jesus, our pacemaker and trainer in faith" (see above).

But a generation before Spicq's commentary appeared, another leading scholar wrote to interpret *Christ's faith* as the primary reference of Hebrews 12:2a: Brooke Foss Westcott. He proposed that the faith invoked by the author of Hebrews is of the absolute type traced under the Old Covenant (Heb 11:1–12:1). In Jesus we have the perfect example of that faith which we are to imitate. Jesus exhibited faith in the highest form. As the head of a great army of heroes and heroines of faith, he carried faith, "the source of their strength, to its most complete perfection and to its loftiest triumph." Westcott adds: "this ascription of faith to the Lord is of the highest importance for the realization of his perfect humanity."[11]

---

[8] Grand Rapids: Eerdmans, 2000.

[9] Christopher A. Richardson provides a valuable bibliography of 53 commentators on Hebrews, from John Chrysostom, through Thomas Aquinas, Martin Luther, John Calvin down to the twenty-first century (*Pioneer and Perfecter of Faith: Jesus' Faith as the Climax of Israel's History in the Epistle to the Hebrews* (Tübingen: Mohr Siebeck, 2012), 229–31).

[10] C. Spicq, *L'Épître aux Hébreux*, vol. 2 (Paris: Gabalda, 1953), 386.

[11] W. F. Westcott, *The Epistle to the Hebrews* (Grand Rapids: Eerdmans, 1920; reprinted 1965), 395.

In two earlier studies, Albert (later Cardinal) Vanhoye converged with Westcott. First, he refrained from specifying "our faith" when translating Hebrews 12:2a: "gazing at the leader and fulfiller of the faith."[12] Second, he explained that Jesus is the model of those whom God takes to be his children.[13] But then in a book-length commentary on Hebrews, he joined Spicq in interpreting Hebrews 12:2a: "in the depths of his being Jesus was not a mere [sic] believer, he was the Son united to the Father". Vanhoye added: 'Jesus is the source [*archēgos*] of faith in the sense that, by his paschal mystery, he gave faith the perfect foundation which is needed...he carries faith to its goal (*teleiōtēs*), because he gives the believer entry into God's intimacy forever."[14] We will discuss below Vanhoye's reasons for supporting this interpretation of the verse. Here we list him as the other major commentator along with Spicq, who expound Hebrews 12:2a in terms of our faith rather than the faith of Jesus.

Westcott's language of exemplar or model (*Vorbild*) turned up in a 1966 commentary on Hebrews by Otto Michel: "Weil Jesus in der schwersten Anfechtung den Glauben bewahrt und ihn damit auf die Stufe höchster Vollendung erhoben hat, geht er allen anderen im Glauben voran und ermöglicht ihnen, seinem Vorbild zu folgen (since Jesus has kept the faith in the most difficult temptation and by doing so has lifted it to the level of the highest per-

---

[12] A. Vanhoye, *A Structural Translation of the Epistle to the Hebrews* (Rome: Pontifical Biblical Institute, 1964), 32.

[13] A. Vanhoye, *La Structure Littéraire de L'Épître aux Hébreux* (Paris: Desclée, 1963), 196. This was translated as *Structure and Message of the Epistle to the Hebrews* (Rome: Biblical Institute, 1989). Myles Bourke picked up the idea of Jesus as model of faith: "The Epistle to the Hebrews," in Raymond E. Brown, Joseph A. Fitzmyer and Roland E. Murphy (eds), *New Jerome Biblical Commentary* (London: Geoffrey Chapman, 1989), 940.

[14] A. Vanhoye, *L'Épître aux Hébreux*, in *Les dernières épîtres* (Paris: Bayard, 1997), 7–108, at 91–92.

fection, he precedes everyone else in faith and enables them to follow his model)."[15]

A little over ten years later Graham Hughes questioned whether Jesus, as presented in Hebrews 12:2a, is the *source* of faith or its greatest *exemplar*.[16] He noted how English translations regularly opted for the former interpretation. Hughes suspected that the translators have suffered from a subconscious reluctance to see Jesus as both a (supreme) participant in faith and the object of faith. But, he continued, the context brings Jesus into direct continuity with the suffering readers. This passage can only mean: "here Jesus is understood, as in his humanity he stands before the dark uncertainty of his impending death, to be repudiating the possibility of unbelief and on the contrary allowing that threatening present to be illuminated by his confidence in the future." In this way Jesus "becomes a perfect *model* for the Christian readers."[17] The author of Hebrews, Hughes argued, grasped the fact that Jesus had a faith of his own as among the clearest implications of incarnation. This was neither an inappropriate nor an unwelcome aspect of Jesus' being pioneer and model of our Christian faith.[18]

Attridge, Hamm, Koester, and *Richardson*

The index of modern authors for Harold W. Attridge's *The Epistle to the Hebrews*[19] revealed the respect he held for Spicq and

---

[15] O. Michel, *Der Brief an die Hebräer* (Göttingen: Vandenhoeck und Ruprecht, 1966), 434.
[16] G. Hughes, *Hebrews and Hermeneutics* (New York: Cambridge University Press, 1979), 80.
[17] Ibid.
[18] Ibid., 86.
[19] (Philadelphia: Fortress Press, 1989), 436, 437.

Vanhoye. With Michel, they are the two most quoted commentators on Hebrews. Nevertheless, from his introduction Attridge showed that he followed Westcott and Michel by arguing that Hebrews 12:2a refers to the supreme example of Christ's faith.[20] When expounding in detail "the initiator and perfecter of faith," Attridge explained "the two polyvalent epithets." He commented: "it is precisely as the one who perfectly embodies faith that he serves as the ground of its possibility in others (*archēgos/aitios*) and the model they are to follow (*archēgos/prodromos*)." In short, Christ "provides the perfectly adequate model" for a life of faith.[21]

At the start of the nineties Dennis Hamm lined up with those like Westcott, Michel, and Hughes who, with minor differences of nuance, understand Hebrews 12:2a to portray Jesus as model and exemplar of faith and hence as enabler and facilitator of faith.[22] Hamm insists that Hebrews 12:1–2 may not be considered apart from Hebrews 11:1–40; this underlines the parallel between the faith race of Jesus and the faith race to which disciples are called. Hamm directs us to other passages in Hebrews which indicate how Jesus, being "like" us "in every respect" except sin (Heb 2:17; 4:15), exercised faith, albeit a faith that was lived in an utterly exemplary way. As high priest in the service of God, Jesus was "*pistos*," trustworthy and faithful (Heb 2:17; 3:2). In his suffering Jesus exhibited "*eulabeia*," that faithful obedience to God despite temptation (Heb 2:17–18; 4:15) which serves as a model for Christian believers (Heb 5:7–8; 10:5–10).[23]

In 2002, commenting on Hebrews 12: 2a, Craig R. Koester had

---

[20] Ibid., 27.
[21] Ibid., 356–57.
[22] D. Hamm, "Faith in the Epistle to the Hebrews: The Jesus Factor," *Catholic Biblical Quarterly* 52 (1990), 270–91.
[23] Ibid., 284–85.

much the same to say. He wrote: "Jesus is [the] pioneer [of faith] because he takes faith to its goal, going where others have not yet gone. He is the source and model of faith for others."[24]

In 2012, Christopher A. Richardson, while not publishing a commentary on Hebrews, in a doctoral thesis drew on the entire epistle to present Jesus as the superlative example of faith (Heb 3:1–6), tested and true (Heb 4:15), and typologically anticipated by "the ancestors of Israel's history."[25] Richardson summed up the meaning of being "pioneer and perfecter of faith": "Jesus exercised perfect faith for the sake of God's people, even unto death on a cross."[26] In conclusion, Richardson proposed that Hebrews 11:1–12:3 is, ultimately, an encomium not to the Old Testament examples of faith, but to Jesus, who is portrayed as the perfect example of *pistis*.

Conclusion

We could examine other contemporary writers on Hebrews, like Paul Ellingworth (1931–2018) who published a commentary on Hebrews in 1991 and later examined Richardson's dissertation. But the sample already offered illustrates how a strong majority of commentators interpret "pistis" in Hebrews 12:2a as the faith exemplified pre-eminently by Jesus himself when faced with death. That is the view of Attridge, deSilva, Hamm, Hughes, Kittredge, Koester, Michel, Richardson, and Westcott. Spicq and Vanhoye stand out in solitary fashion as two modern commentators who understand faith in this context as our faith in Jesus.

We might risk identifying the background for the explanation

---

24 C. R. Koester, *Hebrews* (New York: Doubleday, 2002), 523.
25 Richardson, *Pioneer and Perfecter of Faith*, 10, 49–74, 109–224.
26 Ibid., 95–107.

offered by Spicq and Vanhoye. Their early theological education endorsed a view going back to Thomas Aquinas, according to which the earthly Jesus lived by a complexity of knowledge, which included the beatific vision, an immediate vision of God enjoyed by the saints in their heavenly existence. Setting aside any intricacies of argument, we could say that if Jesus in his human mind during the years of his historical existence shared such a beatific vision of God, he knew God in the highest possible way; his knowledge *of* God ruled out faith *in* God. The opinion of Aquinas about the earthly Jesus enjoying the beatific vision lived on for centuries. Vanhoye died in 2021, long after Spicq died in 1992. In their basic theological training, they had both learned Aquinas's view about Jesus and the beatific vision. During their lifetime, however, leading Catholic theologians quietly abandoned Thomas Aquinas' view, as did the official International Theological Commission. The post-Vatican II *Catholic Catechism* of 1992 ignored talk of Jesus' having the beatific vision during his life on earth. It may be impertinent for me to speculate about any motivation at work on Spicq (a Dominican like Aquinas) and Vanhoye. But we do face at least one possibility. In their youth they learned from Aquinas that Jesus knew God in the beatific vision. This made them permanently inhibited about understanding Hebrews 12:2a in terms of Jesus' own faith.

When we turn to ask why the overwhelming majority of those who *translated* the New Testament into English have opted for a translation that reads "our faith" into Hebrews 12:2a, explanations seem more hazardous. Could it be that these translators are more traditional than commentators? Here and elsewhere, the influence of Tyndale, the KJB, the RSV and the NRSV has lived on down to the twenty-first century, One thing, at least, is clear:

those who continue to translate Hebrews 12:2a as "our faith" in the crucified Jesus have not consulted and followed the clear majority of contemporary commentaries. Otherwise they would have expounded the text in terms of the Jesus, the supreme model and exemplar for a life of faith.

12

TRANSLATING HEBREWS

As John Barton remarks, "in the twentieth century translations of the Bible into English proliferated and the flood continues to this day."[1] When comparing and contrasting such translations, one needs to include particular examples. This article samples four passages from six English versions of the Letter to the Hebrews—by William Tyndale (1534, TYN), Douay Bible (1582, Douay), King James Version (1611, KJV), Revised English Bible (1989, REB, a revision of the New English Bible of 1970), New Revised Standard Version (1989, NRSV, a revision of the Revised Standard Bible of 1946), and the Revised New Jerusalem Bible (2022, RNJB, a second revision of the Jerusalem Bible of 1966). Do these passages render the original Greek accurately, and in acceptable English? The traditional principles of fidelity (or remaining true to the original meaning and message) and intelligibility (or being usable for worship, prayer and study), while interpreted in somewhat different ways, still sum up the major objectives for translators.

Ultimately at stake is the English rendering of an exceptional New Testament book. Strikingly Christ-centred, Hebrews takes its inspiration from the high priesthood exercised by Jesus, "the high priest according to the order of Melchizedek."

To what extent do the three modern translations (REB, NRSV, and RNJB) take over the language of their classical predecessors?

---

[1] J. Barton, *The Word: On the Translation of the Bible* (London: Penguin, 2022), 19.

Apropos of two of those versions (Douay and KJV), do they display influence from TYN? These and other questions arise naturally from analysing passages from the six translations.

Some may rightly prefer, when assessing translations, to enlist the help of experts in interlinguistic communication and their theories.[2] I draw and rely more on a lifetime's experience of translating (into English) Greek and Latin texts (from the age of twelve), and, later, French, German, Italian, and Spanish texts. Over many years I have both translated prose and poetry (1) *from* those ancient and modern languages and translated (2) *into* them—attempting to (1) render accurately (in English) texts composed in those other languages, and to (2) conform at least to the basic grammatical rules of those languages, even if I fell short of writing truly elegant French, German, Italian, or Spanish, not to mention Greek and Latin. For nearly thirty years (1968–2006) my main languages for teaching were English and Italian. That I have a reasonably good grasp of my own native language could be established by my authoring or co-authoring so far over 80 books in English; 17 of these were published by Oxford University Press. In collaboration with international publishing houses, I have produced over 50 books in foreign languages. They include Arabic, French, German, Italian, Korean, Norwegian, Polish, Portuguese, and Russian. Occasionally, above all with the Italian versions, I was asked to check the translation.

A lifetime of being engaged with translations shapes my reflections on the work of translators. As a contemporary receptor of English translations of New Testament, I remain grateful for a

---

[2] Eugene A. Nida, "Theories of Translation," *Anchor Bible Dictionary*, vol. 6 (New York: Doubleday, 1992), 512–15; for a valuable bibliography on this topic, see Barton, *The Word*, 265–76.

rich, lifelong preparation that can underpin useful observations about the fidelity (understood primarily as meaning for meaning and not as word for word) and the intelligibility of translations (normally proposed for the distinct yet related goals of worship, prayer, and study).[3]

Hebrews 1:3a

The four passages from Hebrews deal, respectively, with divine revelation through Christ (1:3a), human faith (11:1), the faith of Jesus (12:2a), and sacrifices pleasing to God (13:16).[4] Modernizing the spelling and punctuation of TYN, Douay, and the KJV, we begin with a verse from the prologue of Hebrews:

"which Son being the brightness of his [God's] glory and the very image of his substance" (TYN);

"Who being the brightness of his glory and the figure of his substance" (Douay);

"Who being the brightness of his glory and the express image of his person" (KJV);

"He is the radiance of God's glory, the stamp of God's very being" (REB);

"He is the reflection of God's glory and the exact imprint of God's very being" (NRSV);

"He is the radiant light of God's glory and the perfect copy of his nature" (RNJB).

---

[3] On these twin goals of translation, see G. O'Collins with John Wilkins, *Lost in Translation* (Collegeville, MN: Liturgical Press. 2017), 20–31.

[4] On these and other verses in Hebrews, see Harold W. Attridge, *The Epistle to the Hebrews* (Philadelphia: Fortress Press, 1989); and Craig R. Koester, *Hebrews* (New York: Doubleday, 2001).

Here four nouns structure the Greek text: *apaugasma*, *doxa*, *charaktēr*, and *hypostasis*—in that order.

When rendering *doxa*, the six versions prove unanimous in choosing "glory."[5] They differ, however, in specifying what kind of glory is intended. The Douay and KJV follow Tyndale in translating *apaugasma* as "brightness" and so suggesting the active condition of that glory, or brightness from a source."[6] In himself, Christ is the brightness of God's glory. A similar active implication comes through two other translations: Christ is the very "radiance" (REB) or "radiant light" (RNJB) of the divine glory. "Reflecting" God's glory (NRSV) seems less active by implying divine glory that bears on Christ and lets him "give back" the divine glory he has received, a case of "brightness shining back."[7]

BDAG refrains from pronouncing on the meaning here of "*apaugasma*": active or passive? Radiance or reflection? This magisterial lexicon does, however, include a unanimous list of Greek fathers of the church who favour the active sense, and so find scriptural warrant for the credal "light from light (*phōs ek phōtos*)".[8] According to this interpretation, Christ, as Koester puts matters, "actively radiates divine glory." Yet, as he points out, "the

---

[5] Walter Bauer, Frederick William Danker, William F. Arndt, and F. Wilbur Gingrich, *A Greek-English Lexicon of the New Testament and other Early Christian Literature*, 3rd edn (Chicago: University of Chicago Press, 2000; hereafter BDAG) opens its entry on "*doxa*" by naming it as "the condition of being bright or shining, brightness, splendour, radiance" (257). Nida warns that "the meaning of words and sentences cannot be defined *merely* by what is to be found in dictionaries and grammars" ("Theories of Translation," 514; emphasis added). True, a mere reference to the BDAG is not enough. At the same time its accounts of NT usage remain an indispensable help for translators.

[6] "*Apaugasma*," BDAG, 99.

[7] Ibid.

[8] Ibid.

text does not deal primarily with God's relationship to the Son, but with the way God communicates through the Son." [9]

When translating the third noun (*"character"*), each of the six versions more or less goes its own way: "the very image" (TYN)[10], "the figure" (Douay), "the stamp" (REB), "the exact imprint" (NRSV),[11] and "the perfect copy" (RNJB). By rendering *"charaktēr"* as "the express image", the KJV concurs with Tyndale's choice of an English equivalent. We are still left with five, non-synonymous options provided by the six versions. Despite its absence in the Greek text, Tyndale added "very" (in "the very image"). Three of the other versions insert adjectives, which as such do not occur in the New Testament text: "the *express* image" (KJV); "the *exact* imprint" (NRSV); and "the *perfect* copy" (RNJB). Were they encouraged to do so by Tyndale's precedent in underlining the noun by adding "very"?

Do any of these translations approximate to the rendering of Hebrews 1:3a (*charaktēr tēs hypostaseōs*) offered by BDAG: "an exact representation of God's real being"?[12] An "image" (TYN and KJV) is always in some sense a "representation," although not necessarily "an exact representation' (BDAG) or "exact imprint" (NRSV), still less a "perfect copy" (RNJB). However we assess "the exact imprint" (NRSV) and "the stamp" (REB), those translations remind readers of the ordinary, secular origins of *"charaktēr"* conveyed by "impression" and "reproduction." Hebrews invokes

---

[9] Koester, *Hebrews*, 179, 180.
[10] Koester observes: *charactēr* is "similar to image (*eikōn*), which can be used for the way that Christ made God known" (180).
[11] Koester comments: "calling the Son an impress [why not "imprint"?] emphasizes that God and the Son are congruent without explaining how they are alike"; "Jesus is God's 'impress' because he reveals God's power, presence and faithfulness" (*Hebrews*, 180).
[12] *"Charaktēr,"* BDAG, 1978.

"*charaktēr*" in an extended, metaphorical sense, as do the English terms used in translation, "stamp" and "imprint."

Literally the Son of God is not a stamp or imprint. But the truth about him (and his sharing in the divinity, understood here as being in charge of the created universe) is expressed by naming him that way.

In early Christianity the fourth noun, *hypostasis*, conveyed meanings that can be summed up as basic, "underlying structure"—what BDAG calls "substantial nature, essence, [or] actual being."[13] Four of our translations exemplify, except for "essence," the use of such language: "the very image of his *substance*" (TYN), "the figure of his *substance*" (Douay), "the perfect copy of his *nature*" (RNJB), and "God's very *being*" (REB and NRSV). "Substance," "nature," and "being" speak of *what* Christ is. "Being" has become familiar to many contemporary Christians through the creedal translation of "*homoousios*," "of one being with the Father."

By choosing "the express image of his *person*," the KJV opted for a meaning that would be attached to *hypostasis* only in the late fourth century CE when the Cappadocians and others standardized the terminology used of the Trinity as three divine *hypostaseis* ("individual realities" or "persons") sharing one divine *ousia* (being, essence or nature).[14] The Nicene Council of 325 had used "*hypostasis*" and "*ousia*" as equivalents, but not the Cappadocians and the 451 Council of Chalcedon. It was to give official approval to the Cappadocian language. The BDAG does not find in the New Testament or the literature of early Christianity examples to cite of *hypostasis* understood in some sense as "person" (identifying *who*

---

[13] "*Hypostasis*," BDAG, 1040.
[14] "*Hypostasis*," Andrew Louth (ed.), *The Oxford Dictionary of the Christian Church*, 4th edn (Oxford: Oxford University Press, 2022), I, 941; hereafter ODCC.

Christ is).¹⁵ The KJV is misleading. Hebrews was written in the second half of the first century, a time when *hypostasis* was not yet used as "person" in some identifiable meaning.

"The figure of his substance" shows the Douay version following the traditional Latin translation (the Vulgate): "*figura substantiae eius.*" Tyndale had adopted in part this translation: "the very image *of his substance.*" The suggestion of BDAG about "*substantial* nature"—an adjective ("substantial") rather than the related noun ("substance")—associates it with Tyndale and Douay.

BDAG listed "nature" with possible translations of "*hypostasis*" as in "substantial nature," thus supporting the RNJB in its rendering, "the perfect copy of his *nature.*" But "perfect copy," unlike "image," "figure," "stamp," and "imprint" may say too much. Are there in existence two divine natures: the original one and its perfect copy? Or are we to recognize here an extended, metaphorical use of language: a "copy" which is so perfect that it is identical with the reality itself?

Hebrews 11:1

The second passage to be examined opens the longest account of faith (*pistis*) found in the New Testament (Hebrews 11:1–12:3):¹⁶

"Faith is a sure confidence of things which are hoped for and a certainty of things which are not seen" (TYN);

"And faith is the substance of things to be hoped for, the argument of things not appearing" (Douay);

---

¹⁵ See "*hypostasis*," BDAG, 1041–42.
¹⁶ See "*pistis*," BDAG, 818–20; "*elenchos*," BDAG, 315. On faith in Hebrews, see Erich Dautzenberg, "Der Glaube im Hebräerbrief," *Biblische Zeitschrift* 17 (1973), 161–77; Erich Grässer, Der *Glaube* im *Hebräerbrief* (Marburg: Elwert Verlag, 1965); Koester, *Hebrews*, 468–521.

"Now faith is the substance of things hoped for, the evidence of things not seen" (KJV);

"Faith gives substance to our hopes and convinces us of realities we do not see" (REB):

"Now faith is the assurance of things hoped for, the conviction of things not seen" (NRSV);

"Only faith can guarantee the blessings, or prove the existence of the realities that at present remain unseen" (RNJB).

Given the carefully constructed encomium of faith in Hebrews 11, the chapter opens unsurprisingly with an attempt to define what faith is—proving itself to be the only passage of the New Testament that attempts such a definition: "faith gives substance (*hypostasis*) to the realities we hope for, and provides evidence (*elenchos*) for things we do not see" (my trans.). Faith allows us to perceive realities we hope for, even if they are so far not apparent to the senses; it puts us in touch with what is most real, yet hidden,

Convergences between the translations stand out: all but one of the six versions use "hoped for" (TYN, Douay, KJV, and NRSV) or "hopes" (REB). By translating "*ou blepomenōn*" as "things not *appearing*," the Douay Bible differs from the other five versions which prefer "things *not seen*" (TYN, KJV, and NRSV), or "realities we do not *see*" (REB), or "the realities that at present remain *unseen*" (RNJB). "Things not appearing" shifts attention from what we "see" or "do not yet see" to those "things" (that is to say, heavenly realities) which "appear," that is to say, somehow make themselves seen or show themselves.

Some have favoured translating the whole opening account of faith with an eye on the subjective, and so follow Tyndale: "faith is a sure *confidence* of things which are hoped for and a *certainty* of things which are not seen." By rendering "*hypostasis*" as "assurance." The NRSV takes advantage of the two possibilities this English word offers: "*objectively* it is a pledge or guarantee and *subjectively* it is a personal state of certainty," hope, or expectation.[17] In this interpretation, the objective assurance of faith *comes from* what is hoped for, just as the firm, personal assurance of faith *concerns what* is hoped for. Through faith we are bonded with "things unseen"—in this context, bonded with the unseen God. The "unseen realities of God give proof of their existence by their power to evoke faith."[18]

Sensitive to the first-century, possible meanings of a noun (*hypostasis*) that points to the basis for this confidence, others take *hypostasis* as the objective reality ("substance" in Douay, KJV, and REB) of the good things ("the unseen realities" which constitute the heavenly world) that are hoped for.[19] *Elenchos* is then understood as the objective proof ("prove" in RNJB) or at least "guarantee" (RNJB) of what so far remains unseen (the heavenly world), with its "evidence" (KJV) or "argument" (Douay) that produces "certainty" (TYN) or "conviction" (NRSV; see "convince" in REB).

Where the original Greek text remains impersonal and laconic, the REB, by adding "our," "us," and "we," makes the passage warmly personal: "Faith gives substance to *our* hopes and convinces *us* of realities *we* do not see." Some might consider this equivalent to distorting the original meaning by specifying a personal meaning.

---

[17] Koester, *Hebrews*, 172; emphasis added.
[18] Ibid., 473.
[19] With "*hypostasis*" the lead noun in this verse, "realities" (as in "realities we do not see") look preferable to "things." On "*hypostasis*," the ODCC remarks that "in popular language it was used originally for 'objective *reality*' as opposed to illusion," and rightly judges: "this seems to be roughly its meaning at Heb 1:3" (I, 941; emphasis added).

By using "substance" in the idiomatic expression about "giving substance to," the REB remains traditional by drawing on the language of the Douay and KJV about "the substance of things."

Taking 18 words to translate nine in the original Greek, the RNJB risks becoming a paraphrase. It introduces language for which there is seemingly no basis in the Greek ("only" as in "only faith"; "can"; "the existence of the realities"; and "at present"). In a sense, "only" and "can" cancel each other out. Since "only faith," to the exclusion of every other agency, "can guarantee the blessings," why not say simply: "faith guarantees the blessings"? Some readers may find that "only faith" sounds like Luther's "*sola fide* (by faith alone)" awkwardly inserted into the argument of Hebrews—"faith alone and not works" guarantee the blessings of heaven.

Some may worry about "guaranteeing the blessings" (also RNJB) as translating "faith being the substance of things hoped for." Hoping for implies human expectations, whereas "blessings" come from God and may go far beyond what we expect (1 Cor 2:9). Moreover, Hebrews refrains from distinguishing between the sheer *existence* and the *nature* of "the realities that at present remain unseen" (RNJB). Should translations refrain from entering into particulars by distinguishing between existence and nature?

Essentially the RNJB shapes its rendering by legitimately turning two Greek nouns into verbs (*hypostasis* into the verb "guarantee," and *elenchos* into the verb "prove"). The translation might, accordingly, have been trimmed down and converged with the REB and NRSV: "faith guarantees for us things hoped for, and proves for us realities not yet seen."

Hebrews 12:2a

The third passage which supplies the translations to be compared comes at the close of the section on faith (12:2a):

"looking (*aphorōntes*) unto Jesus the auctor (*archēgos*) and finisher (*teleiōtēs*) of our faith" (TYN);

"looking on the author of faith, and the consummator" (Douay);

"Looking unto Jesus the author and finisher of our faith" (KJV);

"our eyes fixed on Jesus, the pioneer and perfector of faith" (REB);

"looking to Jesus, the pioneer and perfecter of our faith" (NRSV);

"Let us not lose sight of Jesus, who leads us in our faith and brings it to perfection" (RNJB).

Tyndale and the Douay version reflect their Latin predecessor by each including one word from the Vulgate: "auctor" in TYN and "consummator" in Douay. With the KJV, the two nouns became "author" and "finisher." The REB and NRSV introduces an attractive alliteration between two nouns: "the pioneer and perfector." They become verbs in the RNJB: "who leads us in our faith and brings it to perfection."

In the KJV an "our" was inserted for which the Greek original offers no equivalent: "the author and finisher of our faith." This addition or its equivalent shows up in the NRSV and many other translations into English (for example, Knox 1945; Modern Language Bible 1959; Good News for Modern Man 1966; Jerusalem Bible 1966 (to be followed by the NJB and RNJB); New English Bible 1970; New American Bible 1970; Phillips 1972; New Testament and Psalms: An Inclusive Version 1995; New Living Translation 1996; English Standard Version 2001; King, The New Testament 2004; and American Standard Version 2015.

This makes at least seventeen translations which favour qualifying "faith" as "our" faith. I could find only five English translations (the Douay 1582; Moffatt 1935; New International Version 1978; New American Bible Revised 1986; and the REB 1989), which did not add and insert "our." They rightly left it open to interpret faith in Hebrews 12:2a not as "our faith' but as the faith exercised perfectly by Jesus himself. The overwhelming majority of contemporary commentators on Hebrews agree: the text is describing the perfect faith exemplified, from the start of his life to its finish, by Jesus himself, "the paradigm of faithful endurance."[20]

Adding "our" to faith suggests a doctrinal inhibition that fails to grasp an implication of the incarnation: Jesus came as the shining example of perfect faith which Hebrews has been elaborating in Chapter 11. He is the supreme model for lives of faith.[21]

Tyndale, who launched the addition of "our" and so altered the meaning intended by Hebrews, also left a legacy with his choice of words in "looking unto Jesus." Other translations followed his choice: "looking on" (Douay), "looking unto Jesus" (KJV), and "looking to Jesus" (NRSV).

Favouring the REB ("our eyes fixed on Jesus"), BDAG also proposes something stronger than merely looking: "to direct one's attention without distraction, fix one's eyes trustingly."[22] "Fixing eyes trustingly" was already found in its 1957 predeces-

---

[20] Attridge, *Hebrews*, 354.
[21] For full documentation on translating Hebrews 12:2a and the different interpretations taken by scholarly commentaries, see the previous chapter.
[22] BDAG, 158.

sor and may well have encouraged the REB to use "our eyes fixed on Jesus," albeit without adding the spirit in which this is done ("trustingly").[23]

Once again we find the RNJB opting for verbs instead of maintaining two nouns (*archēgos* and *teleiōtēs*): [Jesus] "leads us in our faith and brings it to perfection." Once again there is also a hint of *paraphrase*: the Greek text included nine words, but the RNJB takes 18 words to translate it: "let us not lose sight of Jesus, who leads us in our faith and brings it to perfection."

Where the REB excels by choosing "our eyes fixed on Jesus," the RNJB does not appear to gain anything by rendering matters in the negative: "let us not lose sight of Jesus." "Our eyes fixed on Jesus" hints at a warm, interpersonal relationships—something "losing sight of" does not always do. Newspapers report how the police lost sight of fleeing criminals, or how clouds involved losing sight of some unidentified drone.

The passages translated from Hebrews according to six versions rarely reveal an outright "winner." They seem to do so, however, in the case of 12:2a. Here the REB stands out: "our eyes fixed on Jesus, the pioneer and perfector of faith."

Hebrews 13:16

The fourth and final passage comes from the closing exhortations of Hebrews:

"To do good and to distribute forget not; for with such sacrifices God is pleased" (TYN);

"And beneficence and communication do not forget, for with such hostes [sic!] God is promerited" (Douay);

---

[23] "*Aphoraō*," ibid., 127.

"But to do good and to communicate forget not; for with such sacrifices God is well pleased" (KJV);

"Never neglect to show kindness and to share what you have with others; for such are the sacrifices which God approves" (REB);

"Do not neglect to do good and to share what you have, for such sacrifices are pleasing to God" (NRSV);

"Keep doing good works and sharing your resources, for these are sacrifices that please God" (RNJB).

Two strings of verbs and two of nouns offer links between these translations. First, "*mē epilanthanesthe*" yielded "forget not" in TYN, Douay, and KJV. This is the first and somewhat more frequent meaning listed for the verb in BDAG and adopted by three classical translations. But BDAG also lists "be inattentive to," "neglect," "overlook," and "care nothing about" as a possible meaning. "Never neglect" and "do not neglect" occur in REB and NRSV, respectively.

The RNJB expresses matters positively and so can dispense with the verb which others have translated as "do not forget" or "neglect": "keep doing good works and sharing your resources." This move may seem to be simply a case of expressing the same meaning positively (the RNJB) rather than negatively (REB and NRSV). One misses, however, the hint of value systems that "never neglect" and "do not neglect" can communicate. BDAG thought it correct to list alongside "neglect" several roughly synonymous equivalents: "be inattentive to," "overlook," and "care nothing about." Being inattentive to, overlooking, and caring nothing about all indicate, albeit indirectly, that the exhortation is directed towards those for whom doing good and sharing their resources do not rank high among the values which they wish to put into practice.

Another verb ("*euaresteitai*") recommends the "sacrifices (*thysiae*)" with which God *is pleased*' (TYN). This language, strengthened by adding "well" for which the Greek text yields no equivalent, returns in the KJV ("with such sacrifices God is *well pleased*"). The NRSV ("such sacrifices *are pleasing* to God") and the RNJB ("these are sacrifices that *please* God") converge with Tyndale rather than the KJV.

Here the REB ("the sacrifices which God *approves*") remains within striking distance of these other four translations. "I approve of what you are doing" corresponds substantially with "I am pleased with what you are doing."

The Douay version, however, went it alone by following the Vulgate: "with such hostes God is promerited." The Vulgate could translate "*thysia*" as "*sacrificium*" (e.g.. Phil 2:17) but preferred "*hostia*" (e.g., Rom 12:1; Phil 4:18; and Heb 13:15; which expressed the sense of "sacrificial offerings" or "sacrifices"). In 1 Peter 2:5 the Vulgate writes of offering "spiritual sacrifices" (*spiritales hostias,* for *pneumatikas thysias*) to God. The Douay choice of the Latinized "hostes," while denoting "sacrificial offerings" or "sacrifices," had no future and "sacrifices" prevailed as the widely preferred translation. Those who practise "beneficence and communication," in the Douay version, deserve or win ("promerit") God's favour. This verb, which has become obsolete, embodied Catholic notions of "merit," and grated on the religious sensibilities of some Protestants.

So too could RNJB's language about "keep doing good *works.*" The Greek text includes no equivalent of "works," which might stir again controversy over the role of "works (*erga*)" in salvation. "Keep doing good" (see NRSV) would be enough to translate satisfactorily what the Greek original says.

Four translations (KJV, REB, NRSV, and RNJB) followed Tyndale in 13:16 by rendering "*thysiae*" as "sacrifices." The translators most probably thought—not literally of "sacrificial offerings"—but figuratively of "spiritual sacrifices," as do BDAG[24] and such New Testament passages as Philippians 4:18 and 1 Peter 2:5.

After "*thysia*," there remains two other nouns in Hebrews 13:16 to examine: "*eupoia*" and "*koinōnia*." Tyndale began the habit of translating the first as "doing good" (KJV, NRSV, and RNJB). The Douay version uses the English equivalent ("beneficence") in deference to the Latin Vulgate (*beneficientia*). BDAG chimes in with "well-being".[25] The REB ("show kindness") takes the step of specifying slightly a particular form taken by doing good. All showing kindness entails doing good. But not all doing good can be classified as showing kindness; it may be much too discreet to allow us to speak of something being "shown." We may do good by overpowering some evil that threatens others: for instance, by delivering a group of teenagers from the ugly schemes of a serious sex abuser. It would seem trivial to describe such an intervention as merely "showing kindness."

The other noun (*koinōnia*), so BDAG proposes, denotes here "generosity, fellow-feeling [or] altruism," which can be paraphrased as an "attitude of good will that manifests an interest in a close relationship."[26] Back in the sixteenth century, Tyndale spoke of a readiness "to distribute," an attitude that would later shape

---

[24] "*Thysia*," BDAG, 462–63.
[25] "*Eupoia*," BDAG, 410.
[26] "*Koinōnia*," BDAG, 552–53, at 553.

the 19th-century economic theory of distributism, according to which the world's productive assets should be widely owned and not concentrated. The Douay version and the KJV switched to the language of "communication" and "communicate." Recent years have seen translators turn the noun into the verb "share" and adding to what they read in the Greek text: "to share *what you have with others*" (REB); "to share *what you have*" (NRSV); and "sharing *your resources*" (RNJB) (emphases added). It would be enough to write "do not neglect to share"; obviously it can only be a matter of sharing what we have or sharing our "resources"; we cannot share what we do not have and what does not belong among our resources.

Conclusions

First, our sample of English translations shows how later translators read and at times followed earlier ones. The (direct or indirect) impact of Tyndale on Douay and KJV, and through them on later versions is hard to miss. When translating Hebrews 1:3a, all the other five translation, albeit not surprisingly, fall into line with TYN and translate "*doxa*" as "glory."

Four out of five versions agree with TYN's choice of "sacrifices" for "*thysiae*" in Hebrews 13:16.

Occasionally Douay ("the figure of his substance" in Heb 1:3a; 13:16) and even TYN ("his substance" in Heb 1:3a) seem to hearken back to the Latin translation in Jerome's Vulgate ("*figura substantiae eius*").

Second, at least twice the RNJB turns nouns into verbs, and so produces a lighter, more vigorous English (Heb 11:1; 12:2a). This same version is also ready to use *metaphors*, language that in an extended sense is true (and puts us in touch with reality) but is untrue in a literal sense: for instance, "copy" in Hebrews 1:3a. Far from being mere illustrations or examples of second-rate language, appropriate metaphors can establish themselves as lively, first-rate English, even if they frequently end up becoming dead metaphors.

Third, we detected a couple of times a tendency to wordiness verging on paraphrase in the RNJB (Heb 11:1; 12:2a). This version could employ twice as many words to translate the original, Greek text. But we noted other examples of translations adding words (e.g., REB and NRSV to Heb 13:16) in order, presumably, to bring out meaning. The boundary between what the Greek words say and what they are understood to mean can easily be breached.

Fourth, this examination also brought up particular and general examples of meaning being changed through the addition of words that have no counterpart in the original Greek. The REB's introducing "our," "us," and "we" when translating Hebrews 11:1 makes the meaning more personal. The original Greek left the sense more general.

The most serious case of meaning being modified comes through Tyndale adding "our" to "faith" and encouraging many (but not all) subsequent translations to interpret wrongly Hebrews 12:2. As the vast majority of commentators have made clear, Hebrews does not directly address our faith, but the faith of Jesus, the supreme model for a life of faith.

Translations may accidentally introduce associations that they might otherwise consider undesirable. Thus the Douay version of Hebrews 13:16 could bring up bogeys about human merits by choosing the (now obsolete) verb "promerited." The RNJB unwittingly associates itself with Catholic-Lutheran debates by featuring "only faith (*sola fide?*)" in its rendering of Hebrews 11:1.

Sixth and finally, we should note how some of these versions deal with difficulties by adding notes. Thus contributors to *The New Oxford Annotated Bible*, when they came to Hebrews 12:2a in the NRSV on which they comment, raised the appropriate objections against adding "our" to "faith" and insisted, ever more clearly, that the Greek text presents Jesus as the supreme example of a faith that was his own.

Having published (now in the last chapter) an essay on translating Hebrews 12:2a, I thought it worthwhile returning to Hebrews and filling out the picture by examining some major translations of three further passages from the same New Testament book.

Jesus Questions

13

JESUS BETWEEN POETRY AND PHILOSOPHY

Back in the 1970s I attended a lecture at the Goethe Institute Rome delivered by Hans-Georg Gadamer (a retired professor of philosophy from Heidelberg University) on the relation between philosophers and poets. Gadamer mused on the ups and downs of, the loves and hates, the convergences and divergences of that relationship. It runs all the way from Plato to the later Heidegger. Plato called the poets' stories of the gods "theologies." His ideal republic, he believed, would be better off if it severely controlled this kind of theology and even banished the poets. Plato refused to accept that his own master in philosophy, Socrates, had corrupted the youth of Athens, but he clearly believed that poets could be corrupting influences. Other philosophers have proved much kinder to poets. In the last century Martin Heidegger turned from his earlier work and drew from poetry the material for his later philosophical reflections.

All in all, it was a brilliant lecture by Gadamer. It set a number of questions buzzing in my head. Would a period that was high on poetic imagination prove likely to be low on philosophical thought? Do poetry and philosophy represent completely different ways of approaching reality, with neither matching and not even having much to do with the other? Does philosophy train us to think, while poetry trains us to see? And what of Dante whose poetic genius ruled in and not out the philosophy he had on offer?

And then came the question, which eventually gave rise to this chapter. Would reflection on some of the ways poets and philosophers work throw light on the mind and imagination behind the preaching of Jesus? Let us first explore the last group and learn what philosophers might suggest.

Philosophers

First of all, philosophers and their revolutions. Some philosophers like Ludwig Wittgenstein have, in effect, stood back from their culture, surveyed centuries of intellectual history, and quite consciously tried to take philosophy and, in general, human thought in new directions. In their own way such philosophers could appropriate the saying of Jesus. "of old such and such was said to you. But I say to you" (Matt 5:21–22). Beyond question, some poets have attempted a similar form of revolution. William Wordsworth and T. S. Eliot creatively examined poetic language, rejected standard traditions, and initiated new styles of poetry. But, on balance, more philosophers than poets have attempted such revolutionary changes.

When they made radical breaks with the past, philosophers employed general formulae. The generalizations offered by Aristotle, Descartes, and Kant separate them from Jesus. He expressed himself in concrete language, not generalizations. He often delivered his message in the form of parables. His instructions and invitation could take very specific forms: "Go, sell what you have and give to the poor. Then come, follow me" (Mark 10:21). Nevertheless, not all philosophers have indulged in generalizations, lofty or otherwise. Wittgenstein could introduce specific cases with a strong imaginative impact. Plato himself gave myths a key place in several of his major dialogues. But, after allowing for some exceptions, we can risk a generalization. The vernacular vigor and earthy directness of Jesus' language sets him apart from most philosophers and their talk.

Jesus resembles the philosophers in their passion for truth. At the same time, he differs from them on two scores. Firstly, he is not interested in clear thinking, exciting speculation, or accurate speaking for their own sake. His preaching aims at presenting the truth which will set his hearers free to live as genuine sons and daughters of God. Second, Jesus does not spend time clarifying concepts or hunting down ultimate truth through Socratic dialogues with lake-side listeners—let alone arguing matters out with close attention to logic. He already knows how things are and bluntly confronts his audience with a true vision of reality.

Like a poet Jesus presents a vision—a vision of the Father who "makes his sun rise on the evil and on the good and sends rain on the righteous and the unrighteous" (Matt 5:45). He presents that vision of things as poets might, and does not argue for it as philosophers do. Philosophers may try to turn human thought in new directions and declare: "Of old such and such was said to you. But I say to you." Yet they do not merely communicate their vision; they add their arguments. Jesus, however, simply confronts us with his insights. He does not lead us through a set of arguments.

Any comparison between the preaching of Jesus and the work of philosophers fails to yield very much. Normally philosophers have dealt with concepts, made speculation their medium, and reached for generalizing principles.

At times Jesus shares a certain "philosophical" concern for logic. Is healing on a sabbath always to be avoided as forbidden work? Jesus handles that issue by appealing to a calculus of values. "I ask you, is it lawful to do good or to do harm on the sabbath, to save life or to destroy it?" (Luke 6:9). Doing good by restoring the sick or disabled to full human health takes precedence over seeking at all costs to observe the prohibition against work on a sabbath. For the most part, however, Jesus appeals to logic less frequently and clearly than the philosophers. His style of preaching does not make him a latter-day Socrates, or some first-century, Middle-Eastern anticipation of Kant or Wittgenstein.

Poets

What of poets? Can we sort out and relate some ways in which Jesus and the poets might match each other? His commitment to language suggests a significant point of similarity. He shows a striking respect for words and will not tolerate their misuse. "On the day of judgment you will have to give an account for every careless word you utter; for by your words you will be justified; and by your words you will be condemned" (Matt 12:36–37). Jesus uses language with care, creates concise, unforgettable parables, and like most poets speaks of what we see, hear, taste, touch, and smell. "Dogs came and licked" the sores of Lazarus" (Luke 16:21). The crowds who listened to John the Baptist did not go out into the desert to see "a reed shaken by the wind" (Matt 11:7). The disciples of the Baptist are told to go and tell him what had heard and seen (Matt 11:4).

Furthermore, Jesus resembles most poets by talking as a man committed. Here poetry differs from philosophy. What philosophy accomplishes in the world of thought need not directly project how philosophers behave. But poems, like deeds, tend to reveal the standards and personality of their makers. Not always, of course. Not every poet speaks with his or her own voice. Only feeble sentiment and faint experience may back up what he or she says. Yet frequently poems express keen feeling and intense experience. We do not expect such strong emotion from the philosophers, but only rational clarity.

Under the headings of language and experience, we can spot some analogy between the preaching of Jesus and the practice of poets. But we would let ourselves off too easily if we slipped over the differences. Poets as poets depend on language far more than philosophers and even more than Jesus himself. His ministry extends beyond his preaching to his miracles and symbolic actions. He eats and drinks with sinners. He thus offers them divine pardon, and conveys the promise that they will share in the great party that God will throw at the end of time. If Jesus depends on his chosen language more than philosophers, he depends on it less than poets. Language in its sound, meaning, music, and overtones is all the poets have.

Poets use expressive language to order and interpret their experience. Strong experience and deep commitment may back up what they write. Nevertheless, once they publish their poetry, they leave it to speak for itself. Their texts take over from them. But we never hear of any impulse from Jesus to write and publish. He betrays no interest in getting his message down on papyrus. Nor does he seem attracted by the challenge as such of wrestling with words. Language for its own sake fails to preoccupy him.

A few words of summary may now be in order. The question triggered off by Gadamer's lecture on poetry and philosophy seems to have led me nowhere. We can sort out carefully and list some resemblances between the preaching of Jesus and the work of poets and philosophers. But we run the risk of making strained and artificial comparisons. Jesus was neither a poet nor a philosopher, but a wandering rabbi martyred like John the Baptist and other prophets before him. Yet that is not quite that. By discussing the language of philosophers and poets, Gadamer ultimately left this question in my mind. Does the language of Jesus give us a clue to his imagination and sensibility? I would like to spend the rest of this chapter tackling that question. Does the language used by Jesus suggest anything about the way his (human) imagination worked?

Three Disclaimers

Before exploring the imagery of Jesus, let me introduce three disclaimers. Firstly, I am not dealing with, let alone exploring, his divine identity. Of course, any appeal to his status as Word of God made flesh will tell us nothing significant about the actual way his human imagination functioned. We may get some clue about that from the material in the gospels. Second, the historical method—as developed in form criticism, redaction criticism, and other techniques—has indicated that the gospels do not provide exact transcriptions of what Jesus said during his ministry. We simply cannot take the preaching, even as found in the Synoptic Gospels, as an unmodified version straight from the lips of Jesus. However, in appealing to Matthew, Mark, and Luke, I will select and use *only those sayings* which—at least in their substance—seem to derive from the preaching of Jesus.[1]

---

[1] In discerning the sayings that derive, at least substantially, from Jesus himself, Richard Bauckham (for Mark and John), François Bovon (for Luke), Joseph A. Fitzmyer (for Luke), Ulrich Luz (for Matthew), Rudolf Schnackenburg (for John), and (across the Gospels) Raymond E. Brown and (in part) John P. Meier have persistently proved helpful.

My third disclaimer is perhaps the most important. Obviously, Jesus used much expressive language which others had provided. He inherited the Old Testament and extra-canonical traditions—a rich and diverse storehouse which he could adopt and creatively employ. This imagery drawn from the past, for example, striking language from the Psalms and Daniel, may have helped liberate his originality and serve his strongly individual style of preaching. Nevertheless, in this chapter I am not assessing his degree of originality. The question is *not*: How uniquely inventive did Jesus show himself in his language? Rather my question is: What do the imagery and language that Jesus used suggest about his imagination and sensibility?

Three Features of Preaching

Let me single out three features of Jesus' preaching. The first thing we may note is this. He shows himself aware of and responsive to many forms of human activity. suffering and happiness. He observes what happens when farmers sow crops, sees how they may need to build extra barns to house the proceeds of a bumper harvest (Luke 12:16–21), and recalls their methods for forecasting the weather: "When you see a cloud rising in the west, you immediately say, 'it is going to rain,' and so it happens. And when you see the south wind blowing, you say: 'there will he scorching heat,' and it happens" (Luke 12:54–55). Jesus has watched how people put patches on torn cloaks (Mark 2:21) and use fresh wine skins for new wine (Mark 2:22). Jesus speaks of financial loans, taxation, the role of stewards in large households, the work of shepherds in guarding their flocks, the soft clothing of the wealthy (Luke 16:19), dogs waiting for scraps to fall from the table, travelers turning up late at night and looking for food, the administration of the law, the current price of sparrows, and much else besides. Jesus' eye sweeps over a wide range of human activity. If we put together his images, we would have a fairly adequate picture of daily life in ancient Galilee.

Jesus does not flinch from facing human suffering. One of his most memorable stories features a traveler who is robbed, beaten up, and left half-dead on a country roadside. He points to the greed of rich men which allows them to overindulge, although sick and starving beggars may be lying in the streets outside. He recalls the calculations made by princes before they lead their armies into war. But human happiness does not pass Jesus by: the joy of a father whose renegade son returns (Luke 15:11–32), the celebrations at weddings (Luke 5:34), and a housewife delighted to have recovered some missing money (Luke 15:8–9).

Jesus reveals an imagination sensitively aware of what is going on in his world. Nevertheless, there some gaps in the picture; and this is my *second* point about his preaching. He delights in children, but has next to nothing to say about the mother-child relationship. At times he glances at the father-child relationship: "What father among you, if his son asks him for a fish, will instead of a fish give him a serpent, or if he asks him for an egg, will give him a scorpion" (Luke 11:11–12). Somehow Jesus finds his way around the mother-child relationship almost without pausing to notice it. When his eye runs forward to the troubles to come. He sympathizes over the sufferings that will afflict pregnant women and nursing mothers: "Alas for women with child in those days, and for those who have children at the breast" (Mark 13:17). Apart from a few such tangential remarks, Jesus bypasses the mother-child relationship. Nothing turns up about the joy of women when their sons returned safe from military service. Did he have such an utterly untroubled relationship with his own mother that this intimate area of human living produced nothing for his language? Or was there such a deep and pervasive tradition against a rabbi using such imagery, that in this regard Jesus had no ready storehouse of language to draw on? Whatever the reason(s), his preaching hardly draws imagery from the mother-child relationship.

Almost as remarkable is his silence about the husband-wife relationship. He defends married life by rejecting divorce, and insisting that even in their minds men should not go lusting after other men's wives. But nothing survives from his preaching about the loving and caring life together of married people. To illustrate the nature of persistent prayer, Jesus tells a story about troubling one's neighbor at midnight to borrow some food:

> Suppose one of you has a friend and you go to him at midnight and say to him, 'Friend,
>
> lend me three loaves of bread, for a friend of mine has arrived, and I have nothing to set
>
> before him.' And he answers from within, 'Do not bother me; the door has already been
>
> locked, and my children are with me in bed; and I cannot get up and give you
>
> anything.' I tell you, even though he will not get up and give you anything, because he
>
> is his friend, at least because of his persistence, he will get up and give him whatever he needs (Luke 11:5–8).

We might have expected the story to run: "Do not bother me. The door is now shut, and my wife and children are with me in bed."

But Jesus has the man say only, "my children are with me in bed." Was the man a widower? Had his wife gone away on a trip?

Besides the mother-child and husband-wife relationships, other facets of human life fail to be reflected much or even reflected at all in the language and imagery of Jesus. Despite his reference to the ravens and the lilies, he shows little delight in nature and natural beauty (Luke 12:24, 27). We have, of course, from Homer the language of "the wine-dark sea" and "the rosy-fingered dawn." But few in the ancient world shared the delight such language may imply.

Jesus does not indulge much pathos at the transience of things. He is so busy urging his audience to live like genuine children of God, that he has no time to gratify any wistful sadness over the world—still less, disillusionment with it. He could never make his own Virgil's feeling; "human affairs make us weep, and mortal things touch the mind/heart (*sunt lacrimae rerum et mentem mortalia tangunt*)." Admittedly Jesus weeps over Jerusalem and shakes his head sadly: "Jerusalem, Jerusalem, the city that kills the prophets and stones those who are sent to it! How often have I desired to gather your children together as a hen gathers her brood under her wings, and you were not willing" (Luke 13:34). But, by and large, Jesus says little about his own failures and perplexities.

Finally, images drawn from non-religious literature, history, and current world affairs hardly surface in the preaching of Jesus. There is a hereness and a nowness about his language, a preoccupation with the scene right in front of him. He recalls, of course, a few episodes from biblical history or a myth like the story of the flood and the destruction of Sodom. All in all, Jesus betrays little interest in the past. The Maccabean revolt, the Hasmonean period, the capture of Jerusalem by Pompey, the switch of Jewish allegiance to Julius Caesar, the reign of Herod the Great (37–4 BC) and other crowded events of recent history never even get a passing nod in Jesus' preaching. The larger world of politics fails to come into sight. Apart from a brief remark about paying taxes to Caesar (Mark 12:13–17) and a comment on some victims of Pilate's brutality (Luke 13:1–2), Jesus hardly hints that he is living under Roman rule.

Jesus once draws a lesson from a military build-up—the king with 10,000 troops deciding not to risk war against a king with 20,000 troops. But Jesus names no specific king nor any particular, cold-war situation in the Mediterranean world of the first century. Another time he speaks vaguely of a "nobleman" who "went into a far country to receive kingly power and then return" (Luke 19:12). But he mentions no historical figure as the peg on which he hangs the parable of the pounds that follows. Jesus' mind reaches out to the immediate situation here and now. He neither scans history, not even the most recent history, nor lets his eye run around the Roman Empire for images and examples that he could press into service.

In short, the language of Jesus did not represent the whole of the world in which he lived. One might postulate that his preaching introduced historical references, included much imagery drawn from the mother-child relationship, and so forth. But the early church censored out nearly all this material. One could only respond that there are no compelling, or even plausible reasons for believing that such censorship took place. In general, we do best to work with what we have rather than speculate about missing material.

Thirdly, we would neglect at our peril the earthy particularity of Jesus' language. Characteristically, he answers general questions like "who is my neighbor?" (Luke 10:29–37) with a parabolic example. Of course, other rabbis did that to some extent, both before and after Jesus. But the fact that they can also display this habit does not make it any less his. He thinks from below, not by way of deduction from above. He offers cases from which his audience can draw general principles. Even his generalizing remarks stay close to the earth: "no one after drinking old wine desires new" (Luke 5:39). There is a common teaching in the proverbial sayings he cites: "doubtless you will quote to me this proverb 'Physician, heal yourself'" (Luke 4: 23). He invites his hearers to perceive the particular things around them. His imagery is attuned to the earthy wisdom of ordinary people. All of this makes Jesus the supreme preacher with the common touch. He speaks with us and to us, not merely at us.

To sum up. The imagery and language that Jesus employs suggest at least three conclusions. First, a wide range of things in his immediate environment catches his eye. If he is intensely aware of God, he is also intensely aware of what he experiences on the human scene. Second, there are some seemingly surprising gaps in what he appears to notice. Third, his mind works from below— from the concrete cases. In his own unique way he reveals the earthy wisdom of ordinary people.

Conclusion

Such then is the yield from the question triggered off by Hans Georg Gadamer's lecture. I might have persevered with the task of comparing and contrasting Jesus with poets and philosophers. Plenty of further points spring to mind. (1) Jesus could weep over Jerusalem. On occasions poets too can shed tears. But how many weeping philosophers have emerged on the world scene?

(2) By and large poets and philosophers have not proved men and women of action. Admittedly, Plato tried to put into practice his theory of philosopher-kings. Dante was deeply involved in the affairs of Florence and other city-states. But most poets and philosophers have dealt in words. Was Jesus a man of action? And in what sense? He showed himself supremely concerned with what people did and left undone. (3) At the end Jesus went into action and died for his cause. How many poets have done that? One Greek philosopher died for the sake of truth. But no one has ever claimed that the virtuous acts of Socrates remain with us in the sense that the virtuous acts of Jesus are believed to remain with us. Belief in Jesus and beliefs about Jesus create Christology, the area of theological thought concerned with who he is in himself—not to mention what he has done for us. But there is no Socratology.

Comparisons with the most talented poets and the noblest philosophers fail to take us very far in understanding Jesus. All the same, poets and philosophers may lead us to reflect on language. The imagery that Jesus used gives clues to the ways his imagination and perception of the world worked. To move through his language to some insights into his sensibility can only be a real gain,

14

THE FREEDOM OF EASTER FAITH

In *De Spectaculis* (nr 30), the early Christian writer Tertullian mentions a theory which had been advanced to rebut the resurrection of the crucified Jesus and which built on a detail found in the passion narrative of John's Gospel. There "was a garden in the place" where Jesus was crucified; and he was buried in a new tomb in that garden (John 19:41–42). According to this counter-resurrection theory, the local gardener, fearing that many visitors would come and trample on his vegetables, removed the corpse of Jesus from the tomb before the women arrived on Easter Sunday morning. On finding the tomb to be empty, they and then the other disciples wrongly concluded that resurrection had taken place. The gardener was supposed to have said nothing to disturb their good faith.

Down to modern times, similar theories have been advanced to explain away the emptiness of Jesus' tomb. A British writer Malcolm Muggeridge (1903–90) proposed the theory that, hearing of Jesus' kingship and hoping for some gain, grave robbers stole the corpse.[1]

The New Testament, as well as reporting the discovery of the empty tomb, also recalls that the risen Jesus appeared to such individuals as Mary Magdalene (John 20:11–18) and Simon Peter (Luke 24:34) and to such groups as "the Twelve" (e.g., 1 Corinthians 15:5). A second-century philosopher, Celsus, addressed

---
[1] M. Muggeridge, *Jesus Rediscovered* (London: Collins, 1969), 50–51.

Christian believers and dismissed such reports. The alleged witnesses to these appearances of Jesus were either hysterical, hallucinated, or else ambitious liars:

> When he was alive he did not help himself, but after death he rose again and showed the marks of his punishment and how his hands had been pierced. But who saw this? A hysterical female, as you say, and perhaps some other one [Peter] of those who were deluded by the same sorcery, who either dreamt in a certain state of mind and through wishful thinking had a hallucination due to some mistaken notion (an experience that has happened to thousands), or, which is more likely, wanted to impress the others by telling this fantastic tale, and so by his cock-and-bull story to provide a chance for other beggars (II.55).[2]

By branding Mary Magdalene as a hysterical woman, Celsus began a long tradition of gratuitously alleging that the disciples of Jesus, both female and male, were temperamental, even unbalanced by character and prone to visions. They have been depicted this way, even though there is not a shred of evidence that they were more disposed to be hallucinated than anyone else.

In recent years some writers have continued to propose hallucination to account for the post-resurrection appearances reported by Paul and the evangelists. Thus Dale C. Allison considers it plausible to describe these appearances as hallucinatory visions.[3] Let us take up some arguments concerning Jesus' empty tomb and his Easter appearances.

---

[2] Celsus, *True Discourse* (about 178 AD), quoted by Origen, *Contra Celsum*, trans. Henry Chadwick, *Origen: Contra Celsum* (Cambridge: Cambridge University Press, 1953; repr. 1980), 109.

[3] For details of Allison's argument, see Matthew Levering, *Did Jesus Rise from the Dead?: Historical and Theological Reflections* (Oxford: Oxford University Press, 2018), 40–47.

The Discovery of the Empty Tomb

Rejecting the reliable historicity of the oldest report about three women discovering Jesus' tomb to be open and empty (Mark 16:1–8; followed by Matthew and Luke) may take the form of alleging that the empty tomb story (a) was never intended by Mark himself to be an historical account and (b) was simply a creation of the evangelist himself.

(a) Willi Marxsen, for instance, notoriously maintained that "the earliest story of the empty tomb" (coming from Mark) was not "intended to be an historical account."[4] But how did Marxsen know that Mark did not intend to offer a story that was to be understood historically, as well as theologically? Or did Marxsen hold that an historical event could not *also* be theologically significant? Such a view is quite unconvincing and can be easily rejected. The crucifixion of Jesus is a widely accepted historical event. As St Augustine of Hippo remarked, not only Christians but also "the pagans believe" that Jesus died on a cross (*Expositions of the Psalms*, 101.7; 120.6). For the followers of Jesus, the crucifixion is *also* highly significant theologically. Some historical events can carry a rich load of theological meaning.

Or did Marxsen consider that the story of the empty tomb, like the parables of Jesus, was simply intended to convey a theological meaning and truth, but not to report some historical event? In that case, Matthew (28:1–8) and Luke (24:1–10) made a bad mistake. Most scholars rightly hold that they used Mark 16:1–8 as a major source in composing their Easter narratives. Matthew and Luke repeated the substance of Mark's story about the discovery

---

[4] W. Marxsen, 'The Resurrection of Jesus as a Historical and Theological Problem', in C. F. D. Moule (ed.), *The Significance of the Resurrection for Faith in Jesus Christ* (London: SCM Press, 1968), 15–50, at 25.

of the empty tomb as if it were a factual narrative. Did they misunderstand Mark and read as history what was intended only as imaginative fiction about the apotheosis of Jesus? Can a modern biblical scholar presume to evaluate better than those two evangelists the factual status of their main source?

(b) A few writers have maintained that Mark 16:1–8 was simply the creation of the evangelist himself—in other words, that prior to the composition of this gospel there was simply no empty tomb story at all. In *Immortality or Extinction?* Paul and Linda Badham do so because of the way they interpret Mark's closing verse: "they [the women] said nothing to anyone about it [the empty tomb], for they were afraid." "This comment" by the evangelist, according to the Badhams, "implies that the empty tomb story formed no part of the generally received oral traditions about Jesus which circulated before the Gospels were written. It would be manifestly absurd for Mark to write that the women said nothing about it to anyone, if the story of their finding the empty tomb were generally known. The comment," they argue, "*only* makes sense if Mark was conscious that he was adding a new element to the generally received traditions about Jesus, an element which was not known prior to the publication of his Gospel, and which he therefore had to account for by claiming that his sources had hitherto kept this knowledge secret out of fear." In short, "the story of the empty tomb was unknown before the appearance of Mark's Gospel." The evangelist simply invented the whole story himself.[5]

Many scholars, however, explain Mark's closing comment in ways that make good sense of it, without claiming, as did the Badhams, that the evangelist was consciously "adding a new element

---

[5] P. and L. Badham, *Immortality or Extinction?* (London: SPCK, 1984), pp. 23–24; emphasis added.

to the generally received [historical] traditions." The women's silence was temporary; they said nothing to anyone until they found the appropriate persons. Their fearful astonishment was an authentic response to divine revelation—here the astonishing revelation of Jesus' resurrection from the dead.

Despite the theological insights that modern commentators have detected in the Gospel of Mark, he does not seem to have been very creative from a literary point of view. It is hardly to be expected that he would invent out of nothing not only an entire episode (the discovery of the empty tomb) but also an episode that concerned something of supreme importance, the resurrection of Jesus from the dead. Joel Marcus, who has published the best contemporary commentary on Mark's Gospel, while allowing for some editorial additions made by the evangelist (for example, Mark 16:7), holds that Mark has incorporated "an existing narrative" into his final chapter. Marcus also draws attention to the independent witness of John 20: 1–2. It "tells the same basic story, and in a way that is in some respects more primitive (e.g., one woman rather than three, no angelic interpreter)."[6]

Eyewitnesses and the Role of Women

In recent years Richard Bauckham's work on the sources for the Gospels has provided more credibility for the role of eyewitnesses.[7] The period between the end of the earthly history of Jesus (crucified around 30 AD) and the final composition of Mark's Gospel (late 60s) was spanned by the continual presence and testimony of those who had participated as eyewitnesses in the human

---

[6] J. Marcus, *Mark 8–16* (New Haven, CT: Yale University Press, 2009), 1083.
[7] For details on the contribution of Bauckham, see Levering, *Did Jesus Rise from the Dead?*, 66–81.

history of Jesus. Mark's closing chapter mentions several of those witnesses: (1) the women at the tomb, namely, Mary Magdalene, Mary the mother of James (this James being presumably "James the younger" or "James the small" mentioned by Mark 15:40 and Luke 24:10), and Salome; and (2) those who were directed to Galilee (Mark 16:7)—Peter and other disciples. These female and male followers of Jesus played a significant role in transmitting traditions about him; some, or even many of them were still alive in the 60s. They would not have tolerated such a major innovation as a purely fictional story about three women discovering Jesus' open and empty tomb on the third day. It is hard to imagine that Mark would have exposed himself to such an easy rebuttal of his fiction by putting a number of named eyewitnesses into his new, non-historical story.

Even before Bauckham inspired a return to an eye-witness approach, apologists for the historicity of the empty tomb have frequently argued from the central place of women in the tomb narratives. If Mark or early Christians before him had simply created a legend about the discovery of the empty tomb, they would presumably have attributed the discovery of the empty tomb to male disciples rather than to women. In first-century Palestine, women and slaves were, for all intents and purposes, disqualified as valid witnesses. In his *Antiquities*, the Jewish historian Josephus says of courtroom procedure: "From women let no evidence be accepted, because of the levity and temerity of their sex" (4.219). The natural thing for someone making up a story about the empty tomb would have been to have ascribed the discovery to men and not to women. Legend makers do not normally invent positively unhelpful material. Why would anyone at that time and in that culture attribute to women the key testimony to the empty tomb unless that was actually the case?

Buried by His Enemies

Another, quite different argument against the historicity of the empty tomb has come from those who appeal to the Acts of the Apostles and St Paul's major address in Pisidian Antioch (Acts 13:16b–41). Paul spoke of "the residents of Jerusalem and their leaders" failing to recognize Jesus and "condemning him. Even though they found no cause for a sentence of death, they asked Pilate to have him killed. When they had carried out everything that was written about him, they took him down from the tree and laid him in a tomb. But God raised him from the dead, and for many days he appeared to those who came up with him from Galilee to Jerusalem and they are now his witnesses to the people" (Acts 13:27–31).

When we compare this account with what Luke himself had already written in the passion narrative of his Gospel, it seems to differ over the disposal of Jesus' body. According to Luke 23:50–56, Joseph of Arimathea, who played no role in the crucifixion, asked Pilate for permission to take the dead Jesus down from the cross, before wrapping him in shroud, and burying him in a new tomb in which no one had yet been buried. Mark 15:42–47 and Matthew 27:57–61 tell more or less the same story of Jesus' burial, while John adds that Joseph was generously and courageously helped by Nicodemus (John 19: 38–42). But should we discount the burial stories in the four Gospels, on the grounds that Acts 13 suggests an old tradition about Jesus being buried by his enemies—which could well mean burial in an unknown grave?

This objection should be met by recognizing in Acts 13, not an historical tradition that would in any case contradict what Luke had already recorded in his passion narrative, but rather a summary, in which the evangelist contrasted the divine reversal of resurrection with the human sentence that brought Jesus to his death and burial. Luke used a generalizing plural ("they"), concerned less with naming the precise agents and more with four actions (condemnation, crucifixion, deposition from the cross, and burial in a tomb), with a reference to the Easter appearances and proclamation appended to this four-part summary.[8]

All in all, difficulties can be met and a reasonable case be mounted for acknowledging the historical character of the discovery of the empty tomb. Even so, that conclusion by itself remains well short of accepting in faith the resurrection of Jesus. The New Testament itself warns against exaggerating the value of the empty tomb. According to Mark 16:1–8, the three women who find the tomb to be open and empty need to hear the resurrection message ("He has been raised; he is not here") before they come to believe. The reality of the resurrection is proclaimed ("he has been raised") before the body's absence is noted ("Look, there is the place where they laid him"). The explanation of resurrection is not deduced from the physical fact of an empty tomb. Mark has no particular apologetic for the empty tomb, nor does it assign it any independent status for proclamation. The message that the three women are to carry back to the disciples is not "come and see the empty tomb," but rather "he is going ahead of you to Galilee. There you will see him."

The fourth evangelist acknowledges that the sheer fact of an

---

[8] For further details, see G. O'Collins, "Buried by His Enemies? Acts 13:28–31?," *Expository Times* 130 (2019), 399–403; repr. O'Collins, *Illuminating the New Testament: The Gospels, Acts, and Paul* (Mahwah, NJ: Paulist Press, 2022), 139–45.

empty tomb remains ambiguous (John 20:2, 13–15). He puts into the mouth of a devoted follower of Jesus an objection, which would be repeated by non-believers down through the centuries. Grave robbers have been at work: "they have taken the Lord out of the tomb, and we do not know where they have laid him." It took an appearance of the risen Lord to set the ambiguity aside and bring Mary Magdalene to Easter faith.

The Appearances of the Risen Lord

St Paul led the way in reporting, in summary form, the appearances of the crucified and risen Lord to named individuals (e.g., Simon Peter and Paul himself) and groups (above all, the Twelve) (1 Corinthians 15:3–8). From the time of Celsus in the second century and down to Dale Allison in the twenty-first century, objections have come from those who claim that the disciples were hallucinated. Feverishly expecting to see Jesus victorious over death, they fell victims to their own imagination and "saw" him, but they were deceiving themselves. Like bereaved people who have been scientifically studied in recent years, they suffered from hallucinations.

Those committed to making a case for the reliability of the post-resurrection appearances of Christ face various objections. (1) Were Peter, Paul, Mary Magdalene, and the other disciples who claimed to have seen Jesus risen from the dead simply suffering from hallucinations? (2) When faced with the crucifixion of Jesus, what in fact were the expectations of the first disciples? (3) Do the bereavement experiences that have been studied repeatedly since the initial study by Dr Dewi Rees[9] in fact provide close

---

[9] D. Rees, "The Hallucinations of Widowhood," *British Medical Journal*, 2 October 1971, 37–41.

and convincing analogies to the post-Easter visions? (4) In any case how should we judge the method of analogy that has often been practised in discussions of the resurrection of Jesus?

(1) In somewhat different ways, Allison, Gerd Lüdemann,[10] and others have judged the Easter appearances to be the experiences of hallucinated persons who, after Jesus' death and burial, expected to meet him again and, through a kind of chain reaction, mistakenly imagined that they saw him present to them. They wrongly attributed to an external source what they had produced themselves: "the presence" of the risen Christ. The post-resurrection appearances would then be totally internal, psychological events that took place in the minds of the first disciples and were not produced by any external stimulus. In short, those so-called appearances were purely subjective visions, with no external reality corresponding to them.

The evidence that we have from the four gospels does not, however, support any picture of Jesus' disciples excitedly expecting to meet him risen from the dead. Instead of persuading themselves into thinking that they saw him, they had to be persuaded that he was gloriously alive again (e.g., Matthew 28:16–18; Luke 24:36–43; John 20:24 –25). What the gospels record seems credible: the crisis of Jesus' arrest and disgraceful death on a cross left the disciples crushed. Only by ignoring the evidence can we picture them anxiously awaiting his return from the dead and out of their imagination hallucinating his appearances.

The thesis of an ecstatic group hallucination might be more plausible if the New Testament had reported only one appearance and that to a particular group on a particular day. Instead, it wit-

---

[10] See G. Lüdemann, *The Resurrection of Jesus: History, Experience, Theology*, trans. J. Bowden (London: SCM Press, 1994), 79–84.

nesses to appearances taking place over a period of time and to different groups, as well as to different individuals (e.g., 1 Corinthians 15:5–8). As regards the groups to whom Jesus appeared, the New Testament testimony presents us with at least six distinct groups: the Twelve (1 Corinthians 15:5); "all the apostles" (1 Corinthians15:7, who in Paul's list seem to be a larger group than the Twelve); Simon Peter and six others (John 21:1–14); "more than five hundred believers" (1 Corinthians 15:6); Cleopas and his companion (Luke 24:13–35); and Mary Magdalene and "the other Mary" (Matthew 28:9–10). The variety of these traditions makes it quite unconvincing to reduce the six groups to one group, who, on a particular occasion and by a kind of chain reaction, imagined one after another that they saw Jesus.

A psychiatrist, Joseph W. Bergeron, joined forces with a New Testament scholar, Gary Habermas, to produce a landmark article on the hallucination hypothesis. Bergeron supplied technical, clinical considerations about the "complex and varied psychiatric and neurophysical milieu required for hallucinations to occur," naively ignored by those who indulge hypotheses about the disciples hallucinating the presence of the risen Jesus. Such hypotheses are "unlikely and at odds with current medical understanding"; in particular, they offer "no acceptable explanation for the simultaneous group encounters of the disciples with the resurrected Jesus," but "prove to be unconvincing and clinically implausible."[11]

(2) The hallucination hypothesis depends on what the disciples already believed and expected before Jesus died. This hypothesis cannot account for two remarkably new things the disciples began to proclaim.

---

11 J. W. Bergeron and G. Habermas, "The Resurrection of Jesus: A Clinical Review of Psychiatric Hypotheses for the Story of Easter," *Irish Theological Quarterly* 80 (2015), 157–72.

First of all, what options were available to the disciples after Jesus was executed as a messianic pretender and blasphemer? Could they have modified their incipient messianic belief in Jesus and claimed him to be another martyred prophet, like John the Baptist? Hardly, it seems to me. To be crucified meant not only to suffer an utterly cruel and humiliating form of execution but also to die under a religious curse (Gal 3:13) and "outside the camp" of God's people (Heb 13:12–13). In other words, crucifixion was seen as the death of a criminal and godless man who perished away from God's presence and in the place and company of irreligious persons.

In fact, the disciples began preaching the crucified Jesus as the divinely endorsed Messiah risen from the dead to bring salvation to the whole world. The notion of a messiah who failed, suffered, was crucified, and then rose from the grave was simply foreign to pre-Christian Judaism, and hence could not have shaped any alleged hallucinations on the part of the disciples.[12] Since their previous religious beliefs could not have prompted them into making such startlingly new claims about Jesus, what triggered this religious novelty? Where did it come from, if not from the resurrection of Jesus himself, now made known, primarily, through his appearances and, secondarily, through the discovery of his empty tomb?

The second novelty concerned a striking shift in religious expectations. By the time of Jesus, some or even many Jews cherished a hope that a resurrection of all the dead and a general judgement would bring an end to human history. But no one imagined that one individual would be raised to a new, transformed existence

---

[12] The Servant of Isaiah 53 suffered to atone for the sins of others. But he was neither presented as a Messianic figure nor said to have been crucified and raised from the dead.

in anticipation of the last day. But then the followers of Jesus began proclaiming that one individual had already been raised to a glorious existence which anticipated the end of all history. What prompted this remarkable change in expectations that had no precedent in Jewish faith and hope, and so could not have fed into alleged hallucinations experienced by the disciples? Once again the most plausible cause can only be the actual resurrection of Jesus, followed by his Easter appearances.[13]

(3) Some like Allison and Lüdemann have also challenged the Easter appearances by pointing to the cases of bereaved persons who experience their beloved dead. Lüdemann alleged that the Easter appearances were nothing more than ancient episodes in the psycho-biographies of bereaved persons.

Lüdemann and others quietly ignore decisive differences between the experiences of bereaved people and those of Jesus' disciples shortly after his death and burial. The bereaved, studied by Dewi Rees and subsequent researchers, experienced (through visions and in other ways) their dear ones who had died but never claimed that they had been resurrected from the dead.

Undoubtedly, we can make some positive comparisons between the experiences of (a) the widows and widowers studied by Rees and his successors, and (b) the experiences of Jesus' disciples after his death and burial. In both cases we learn of contact with the beloved dead, and it is contact that is life-giving. In both cases those who remain behind had experienced grief, even shattering grief, then followed by an unexpected, generally reassuring contact with the dead.

---

[13] This argument is developed by N. T. Wright, *The Resurrection of the Son of God* (Minneapolis: Fortress Press, 2003); see G. O'Collins, *Believing in the Resurrection* (Mahwah, NJ: Paulist Press, 2012), 3.

The analogy between (a) and (b) turns out, however, not to be that close and illuminating. In my *Believing in the Resurrection: The Meaning and Promise of the Risen Jesus*, I drew attention to seven points of dissimilarity, the one just mentioned (about the absence of any resurrection claim) and five others[14] First, that major Easter witness, St Paul, cannot be credited with a bereavement experience. He never seems to have known Jesus during the time of the public ministry, still less become a close and loving disciple. He met Jesus outside Damascus as a hostile persecutor, not as a grief-stricken follower. Second, the manner of death in cases of (a) never included a case of death by public execution, still less a horrible and shameful death on a cross. The 293 widows and widowers studied by Rees lost their beloved ones through accidents or death from natural causes. Rees did not report any suicides or homicides, still less any executions. Third. apropos of the place of the spouses' deaths, 270 died at home (161 cases) or in hospital (109 cases). The manner and place of death in the cases examined by Rees do not parallel what the Gospels report about the dramatic and terrible death that took Jesus away in the prime of life. A fourth reason for differentiating between the Easter experiences of the disciples and those of Rees' widows and widowers emerges from the New Testament reports of appearances to groups, as well as to individuals. But the pioneering study by Rees reported only individuals who saw, heard, spoke to, or even felt touched by their dead spouses. The individual nature of these experiences moved them away from the resurrection witness in the New Testament, for which appearances of the risen Christ to groups are at least as significant as the appearances to individuals. A fifth dissimilarity arises when we notice that around 40% of Rees' widows and wid-

---

[14] O'Collins, *Believing in the Resurrection*, 175–92.

owers continued to experience their deceased spouses for many years. But the appearances of the risen Christ to individuals or groups took place over a limited period of time, and did not continue for many years. Readers who are interested can consult my exposition of a full list of dissimilarities and of Rees' research.[15] It is enough to illustrate here some of the major dissimilarities between the experiences of Rees' bereaved widows and widowers and the Easter experiences of Jesus' disciples.

(4) Attempts to press the analogy of bereavement experiences bring up the issue of using analogy in historical investigations. In 1898, Ernst Troeltsch left a lasting legacy when he argued that a "basic postulate of the historical method" is that "agreement with normal, customary, or at least frequently attested happenings and conditions as we have experienced them, is the criterion of probability for all events that historical criticism can recognize as having actually or possibly happened."[16] In the twentieth century Troeltsch's principle of analogy dominated much understanding of history and, for many writers, rendered questionable the historicity of the resurrection and events pointing to the resurrection: for instance, alleged appearances of the risen Christ. As we have seen, these appearances have been explained away as ancient examples of bereavement experiences, "frequently attested happenings" that modern historical criticism can acknowledge.

In his now famous *Theology of Hope: On the Ground and Implications of Christian Eschatology*, Jürgen Moltmann enunciated Troeltsch's principle:

---

[15] Ibid., 175–91.
[16] E. Troeltsch, "Historical and Dogmatic Method in Theology," in Troeltsch, *Religion in History*, trans. James Luther Adams and Walter F. Bense (Edinburgh: T. & T. Clark, 1991), 11–32, at 13–14.

It is generally acknowledged that historical understanding nowadays is always analogical understanding and must therefore remain within the realm of what is understandable in terms of analogy. The omnipotence thus attaching to analogy implies ... the basic similarity of all historical events ... [This] presupposes that there is always a common core of similarity, on the basis of which the differences can be sensed and perceived.

Moltmann realized that the "presupposition of a fundamental similarity underlying all events" raised serious difficulties when we come to Christ's resurrection and the Easter appearances, events that are strikingly new and even unique. But Moltmann briefly insisted that dissimilarity forms "the other side of the analogical process." Hence, absolutely speaking, analogical understanding does not exclude the resurrection and subsequent appearances.[17]

This insight must be developed. When analogies for the resurrection of Christ and his Easter appearances are offered—and they have been offered since the origins of Christianity—we deal with comparisons between things that are both like *and unlike*. We face, for instance, both similarities *and dissimilarities*, when St Paul appeals to the Festival of the Weeks (Deut 16:9–12) and the first fruits of the harvest being presented at a central sanctuary. He names the risen Jesus as "the first fruits of those who have died" (1 Cor 15:20, 23), whose resurrection inaugurated the final resurrection of the dead to which Christians looked forward in hope. Analogies have their undoubted place in the historical and Christian understanding of Christ's resurrection and events associated with it, provided we reckon up the similarities and dissimilarities. Does *this* analogy enjoy enough similarities to make it a close and illuminating comparison? Or is it characterized by

---

[17] Trans. James W. Leitch (London: SCM Press, 1967), 175–78.

too many dissimilarities, so that it is neither close nor really illuminating? Sadly, such an explicit calculus of dissimilarities and similarities is something that rarely, if ever, happens in studies of Christ's resurrection.

Easter Faith Remains Free

So far this chapter has treated questions of an historical character, and has set itself, above all, to show how there is a reasonable case to be made for the reliability of the discovery of the empty tomb and the appearances of the risen Jesus. When probed, opposing arguments and theories (e.g., about the disciples hallucinating the personal presence of Christ) prove unconvincing. But this does not mean that believing in Christ risen from the dead is simply the probable or even highly probable conclusion of an historical argument that only unreasonable or "bad" people would deny. To be sure, important human decisions are often made on the basis of some conclusion being proved to be "beyond reasonable doubt." In courts of law, judges and juries are constantly reaching verdicts when they convict or acquit accused persons on evidence that produces a conclusion which is "beyond reasonable doubt" but not necessarily utterly certain. Easter faith, however, goes beyond any such conclusion, which is simply based on historical probabilities.

In his apology for Easter faith, a now emeritus Oxford University philosopher, Richard Swinburne, agrees that there is nothing in the history of Israel and of Jesus Christ himself that would suggest that God intended "to overwhelm us so that we have no options left."[18] Bishop N. T. Wright, a notable biblical scholar, ac-

---

[18] R. Swinburne, *The Resurrection of God Incarnate* (Oxford: Oxford University Press, 2003), 172.

knowledges that even the best historical argument "cannot force anyone to believe that Jesus was raised from the dead."[19] Like Augustine (see above), Alexander Schmemann accepts that "the Lord's glorification does not have the compelling objective evidence of the humiliation on the cross."[20] That Jesus died on a cross is an historically certain fact of human history; only believers hold that he has been raised from the dead and now enjoys a glorified, heavenly life.

Easter faith, while being neither blind nor unreasonable, is always a gift from God. It was because "the Lord opened her heart" that Lydia was enabled to believe and assist Paul in founding the Christian community at Philippi (Acts 16:11–40). The internal word of the Holy Spirit made it possible for her to accept the external word of Paul's preaching.

Freely accepting such Easter faith is undoubtedly a personal matter that has innumerable variations. We might appeal to and adapt the famous remark of Blaise Pascal: "the heart has its reasons."[21] Different hearts have their different reasons, which sustain and nourish their particular beliefs.

Here the case of Malcolm Muggeridge, a leading British journalist, is illuminating. He once toyed with the notion that grave robbers had removed the body of Jesus and so led the disciples into imagining that Jesus had been raised from the dead. But then Muggeridge came to accept that Jesus had truly risen from the grave and lives with us today. What had happened to Muggeridge? It was not that he had studied more assiduously the relevant bibli-

---

[19] Wright, *The Resurrection of the Son of God*, 718.
[20] A. Schmemann, *For the Life of the World: Sacraments and Orthodoxy* (Crestwood, NY: St Vladimir's Seminary Press, 1973), 28.
[21] B. Pascal, *Pensées*, trans. A. J. Krailsheimer (London: Penguin Books, 1966), nr 424.

cal scholarship and examined more closely the historical evidence. Rather he took the step to Easter faith because of various experiences. In the Holy Land he saw Christian pilgrims whose faces "were bright with faith."[22] In India he came to know, admire, and love Mother Teresa of Calcutta. Her personal example, friendship, and prayers helped him find in Easter faith the answer to his fundamental questions about the nature and destiny of human life. The answer, a fresh relationship with the risen Jesus, gave Muggeridge a coherent, deeply satisfying way of living and construing reality.

Believing in the risen Jesus involves entering here and now into a trusting, loving commitment to him. It means recognizing in him, with profound gratitude, God's personal self-communication to us: in other words, the Redeemer who saves us and the Revealer who has shown us what God is like.

Ludwig Wittgenstein expressed a profound truth when he wrote: "it is love that believes the resurrection."[23] We might express this more personally. On the one hand, it is love, our love, that believes in the risen Christ. On the other hand, our final, personal identity is bestowed on us by the love he has for us. The example of Jesus meeting Mary Magdalene (John 20:11–19) remains the paradigm. It is to the risen Lord and his love that we owe our lasting identity.

---

[22] M. Muggeridge, *Jesus: The Man Who Lives* (London: Collins, 1969), 8; see also 16–36.
[23] L. Wittgenstein, *Culture and Value*, trans. P. Winch (Oxford: Basil Blackwell, 1980), 33c.

15

A Cumulative Approach to the Resurrection

When considering the resurrection of Jesus Christ, Thomas Aquinas proposed a "cumulative" approach.[1] "Cumulative" can express the tasks that face those who set themselves to explore a case for faith in Jesus risen from the dead. They deal with issues of at least three major kinds: philosophical; biblical/historical; and theological/spiritual. As we will see, these areas overlap, notably over the nature of God and what is involved in acknowledging God's action in raising Jesus from the dead. This chapter attempts a mapping operation and details major issues to be handled in constructing a case for the resurrection.

Philosophical Issues

Given the epistemological turn of modern philosophy, any apologist who claims to know and accept the resurrection of Jesus must tackle the nature and limits of human knowledge.[2] To believe in his resurrection implies that one has already reasoned about reason, evidence, and knowledge. Serious questions abound. How far, for instance, can reason take us in knowing present and past

---

[1] *Summa theologiae*, Ia.q.55.6 ad 1; see also *Summa contra gentiles*, III.ch. 38.
[2] See Jonathan Daucy, Ernest Sosa, and Matthias Stemp (eds), *A Companion to Epistemology* (Malden, MA: Wiley-Blackwell, 2009); Michael Huemer and Robert Audi (eds), *Epistemology: Contemporary Readings* (Abingdon, Oxon.: Routledge, 2002); George S. Pappas, "Epistemology. History of," *Routledge Encyclopedia of Philosophy*, vol. 3 (London: Routledge, 1998), 371–84.

reality, including the reality of a transcendent God? What counts as appropriate evidence (meaning evidence from the external world) for what we can know and rightly claim to know—specifically, about God acting to raise the dead Jesus to new and glorious life and Jesus appearing to individuals and groups after this resurrection?

Apologists for the resurrection may not ignore contemporary contributions and debates in the area of epistemology. What are the conditions for the possibility of *knowing* the resurrection? What, for example, have philosophers like William P. Alston proposed about validating truth claims and justifying beliefs?[3] Unquestionably, belief in the truth of Jesus' resurrection involves much more than epistemological considerations and is not to be reduced to the conclusion of a philosophical argument. Nevertheless, if believing in the resurrection is to remain an intellectually honest and humanly responsible act, we may not flatly refuse to hear anything from the epistemologists.

At the same time, philosophical reason is both like and unlike historical reason and theological reason. The kind of evidence to which philosophers appeal, for instance, differs somewhat from the evidence typically cited by historians and theologians. While evidence can be expected to come from the external world, their diverse disciplines prompt philosophers, historians, and theologians into seeking and accepting different kinds of evidence. Their disciplines enjoy a certain autonomy, and it would be a mistake to allege in the matter of evidence to maintain that "one size fits all." If we take evidence to be information bearing on the truth or

---

[3] W. P. Alston, *Beyond "Justification": Dimensions of Epistemic Evaluation* (Ithaca, NY: Cornell University Press, 2005); W. P. Alston, *Perceiving God: The Epistemology of Religious Experience* (Ithaca, NY: Cornell University Press, 1993).

falsity of propositions, by comparing debates in philosophy, history, and theology, we will notice the variety in the evidence cited.

In his *Memorial*, written after an intense religious experience during the night of 23/24 November 1654, Blaise Pascal famously contrasted "the God of philosophers and the scholars" with "the God of Abraham, the God of Isaac, and the God of Jacob, and the Father of our Lord Jesus Christ." Pascal had in mind, among others, Thomas Aquinas who held that "to know in a general and confused way that God exists is implanted in us by God".[4] On the basis of an Aristotelian scheme of causality, Aquinas proceeded to clarify matters by developing philosophical arguments for the existence of God, the so-called Five Ways.[5] Aquinas and Pascal present a basic choice for those seeking a philosophical propaedeutic to faith in the resurrection. Should they embrace (a) the reasoned arguments of philosophical theology or (b) the way of direct encounter with the risen Jesus and the God revealed in his resurrection? If they opt for (b), they will need to face the question: how can we justify what is conveyed by allegedly immediate, religious experience?[6]

In modern times the exponential growth and success of sciences and, above all, of the natural sciences lured many towards the epistemological conclusion that science is the only source of genuine knowledge about anything.[7] Such full-blooded scientism

---

[4] *Summa theologiae*, 1a.q.2.1 ad 6.
[5] See John F. Wippel, "The Five Ways," in Brian Davies (ed.), *Thomas Aquinas: Contemporary Philosophical Perspectives* (Oxford: Oxford University Press, 2002), 159–225; Robert J. Spitzer, *New Proofs for the Existence of God: Contributions of Contemporary Physics and Philosophy* (Grand Rapids: Eerdmans, 2010).
[6] See e.g. Phillip H. Wiebe, *Visions of Jesus: Direct Encounters from the New Testament to Today* (New York: Oxford University Press, 1997); P. H. Wiebe, *God and Other Spirits: Intimations of Transcendence in Christian Experience* (Oxford: Oxford University Press, 2002).
7 See Tom Sorell, *Scientism: Philosophy and the Infatuation with Science* (London/New York: Routledge, 1991).

may have waned, but its epistemological progeny in "objectivism" still enjoys numerous supporters. In the name of "objective" and "scientific" knowledge, they expect authentic knowledge to be and remain independent of human interests, perspectives, and commitments. Only pure, uninterpreted "facts" are reliable. Followers of "objectivism" need to read Michael Polanyi and others who have argued that all knowledge, including knowledge in the realm of the sciences, is always personal and affected by human interests, perspectives, and commitments.[8] There is no such thing as knowledge that is purely "objective." We cannot expect to enjoy a "view from nowhere."[9] There are always conditions that should prompt us into recognizing that knowledge is always both objective and subjective, involving interaction between the knower and the known. Diverse ideological outlooks and diverse religious faiths have their impact on what we "know" about the resurrection.

Similarly, pure nuggets of non-interpreted facts do not exist. Personal experiences, choices, and evaluations inevitably affect what are deemed to be "the facts." In the case of Jesus' resurrection, one needs to ask, among other things: did the claims and activity of Jesus make him an appropriate person to be vindicated by God by being raised to a new, transformed life? Here we rely on reaching reliable conclusions on the basis of the gospel records, while recognizing that those records derive from such eyewitnesses as Simon Peter, Mary Magdalene, and other disciples who began interpreting Jesus from their very first meetings with him. Significant convergence characterizes what they reported and proclaimed about Jesus. But there never was a set of non-interpreted

---

[8] M. Polanyi, *Personal Knowledge: Towards a Post-Critical Philosophy*, rev. edn (Chicago: University of Chicago Press, 1962).

[9] Thomas Nagel, *The View from Nowhere* (Oxford: Oxford University Press, 1985).

"facts" about Jesus. The nature of human experience and personal knowledge rules that out.

Philosophical reasoning also affects what we can say about historical conclusions that concern the case for the resurrection: for example, the reliability of the tradition that on the third day Jesus' tomb was found to be open and empty Does this tradition do justice to the evidence in a way that alternate scenarios fail to do? Is it a verdict "beyond reasonable doubt" which a jury might accept? Testimony and doing justice to evidence are matters that philosophers and jurists ponder.[10] Historians also constantly put the question: are *these* conclusions historically reliable? In any case, what is historical reliability? We will hear from historians in the next section.

Philosophy is heavily involved in debates about the status and function of religious statements. These statements may concern, for instance, a reality such as the existence of God and an event such as the resurrection of Jesus. Do such statements assert "facts" and are they informative, or do they merely evoke attitudes?

Before leaving philosophical considerations, we can recall one cautionary tale, which exemplifies an epistemological failure in addressing the question of Jesus' resurrection from the dead. Gerd Lüdemann aimed at a "ruthlessly honest quest for truth," one that would take "an undistorted look" at the evidence and "look in a purely historical and empirical way at the historical testimonies to the resurrection." Inevitably those he disagrees with find themselves charged with "dogmatism," "prejudice," and even with knowing "a priori what needs to be proved".[11]

---

[10] See C. A. J. Coady, *Testimony: A Philosophical Study* (Oxford: Clarendon Press, 1994).

[11] G. Lüdemann, *The Resurrection of Jesus: History, Experience, Theology*, trans. John Bowden (Minneapolis: Fortress Press, 1994), 6, 14–15, 19, 69, 178, 211.

Lüdemann's view of human knowledge provides an instance of that naïve realism criticized by Bernard Lonergan and others for presuming knowledge to be merely a matter of taking an "honest look."[12] The profession of ruthless, undistorted honesty repeats what many philosophers have long ago challenged: namely, the claim to make a purely objective and scientific approach to some controversial issue. The truth of Christ's resurrection, a matter of enormous personal significance, is not a merely "historical" matter to be kept at arm's length, looked at dispassionately, and pronounced upon accordingly. Lüdemann alleges that he is pursuing a totally honest inquiry and doing something that others fail to do: he looks without any bias at the evidence, or rather at the evidence that he allows to count. Any debates with him should begin with his flawed background theories about knowledge in general and historical knowledge in particular. He alleges the impossible, to be personally free of "distortions" and bias. Any honest quest of truth requires an awareness of personal biases, not the pretence of engaging *in* presuppositionless research.[13]

Historical/Biblical Issues

Among the different ways in which historical studies touch arguments about the resurrection are the status of *conclusions*, the role of *analogies*, and the *concern for historical truth* in the first-century Mediterranean world. Let me take up in turn these three topics.

Status of Historical Conclusions

As regards *conclusions*, are there only two categories available: (a)

---

[12] See B. Lonergan, *Insight: A Study of Human Understanding, Collected Works of Bernard Lonergan*. vol. 3 (Toronto: University of Toronto Press, 1992), 344, 449–50; *Method in Theology* (London: Darton, Longman & Todd, 1972), 238.

[13] See Hans-Georg Gadamer, *Truth and Method*, trans. J. Weinsheimer and D. G. Marshall (New York: Crossroad, 1989).

the historically certain (e.g. Napoleon's defeat at Waterloo) or (b) the historically indeterminate? If we endorse this stark choice, we seem to be justified in holding, for instance, the discovery of Jesus' empty tomb to be simply historically indeterminate. But is the scheme of only two categories at fault? Should we acknowledge conclusions based on strong evidence which may be strong but still falls short of conclusive evidence that would rule out for ever all possibility of error? We should recognize innumerable historical conclusions that responsible scholars firmly hold, even if they do not claim to have reached utter certainty. Thus J. N. D. Kelly marshalled evidence to draw the conclusion that what we know as the Nicene-Constantinopolitan Creed (used by all Christians at the Eucharist) does in fact come from the First Council of Constantinople (381 AD).[14] There had been considerable diversity of views on this matter. That did not lead Kelly to conclude that no one really knows where the creed in question came from and how it fell into its final shape. Without claiming historical certainty for his conclusion, he argued for it being solidly probable.

Historical studies teem with such examples of leading scholars reaching firm conclusions that they believe to do better justice to the evidence currently available. Although they cannot pretend to have reached the kind of utter certainty that simply discounts the possibility that further evidence might come to light and seriously qualify or even discount their conclusion, they do not throw up their hands and declare the issue they are interested in to be simply "indeterminate." One needs to recognize the range of possibilities for conclusions to historical research: from the utterly certain, through the highly probable, the solidly probable,

---

[14] J. N. D. Kelly, *Early Christian Creeds*, 3rd edn (London: Longman, 1974).

the probable, and various shades of possibility, right down to the genuinely indeterminate.

In the city where I live, a courier service for parcels advertises itself as "delivering certainty." The firm uses "certainty" in the sense of "may be relied on." They deliver punctually and can be trusted not to lose or misdirect any parcels. The firm does not claim to deliver certainty in the sense of always providing some undisputed fact or conclusion which should command our unqualified assent: that is to say, an utter certainty which allows us to discount the possibility of future evidence ever emerging that would challenge, seriously modify, or even disprove some alleged fact or conclusion which we have accepted. Historical investigation does not regularly "deliver certainty" in that sense, by providing conclusions which are not only undoubted but also can never be doubted. *Delivering probability*, even high probability, describes more accurately the task of competent historians.

Delivering probability applies to areas of human activity that carry serious consequences for those involved: for instance, in trials for murder and other serious crimes. Members of the jury are expected to weigh the evidence and reach a "safe" verdict, that is to say, one which is beyond reasonable doubt but not necessarily one which is utterly certain. Over the years I have attributed this kind of historical status to the conclusion that the tomb of Jesus was discovered to be open and empty. It is not open to reasonable doubt, especially when set over against counter-explanations.[15]

Here it is worth reminding ourselves that in matters deeply affecting our human lives we constantly rely on historical conclu-

---

[15] See G. O'Collins, *Believing in the Resurrection: The Meaning and Promise of the Risen Jesus* (Mahwah, NJ: Paulist Press, 2012), 80–99; G. O'Collins, "Buried by His Enemies? Acts 13:28–31," *Expository Times* 130 (2019), 399–403.

sions for which, at least in theory, we cannot discount the possibility of evidence one day challenging or even disproving these conclusions. Take, for example, the unqualified trust towards spouses and other close relatives that provides the ongoing and unchallenged framework for the existence of many human beings. They live, so to speak, "at the mercy" of other people, but do not spend their days morbidly preoccupied with the possibility of betrayal.[16]

Role of Analogies

In 1898, Ernst Troeltsch identified the basic analogical "postulate of the historical method": it maintains that "agreement with normal, customary, or at least frequently attested happenings and conditions as we have experienced them is the criterion of the probability for all events that historical criticism can recognize as having actually or possibly happened."[17] In the twentieth century Troeltsch's principle of analogy shaped much understanding of history and, for many writers, rendered questionable the historicity of the resurrection and events pointing to the resurrection: for instance, alleged appearances of the risen Christ (e.g. 1 Cor. 15:5–8). These appearances have been explained away as ancient examples of *hallucinations* and *bereavement experiences*, "frequently attested happenings" that historical criticism can acknowledge.

Lüdemann and others have judged the Easter appearances to be the experiences of hallucinated persons who, after Jesus' death and burial, expected to meet him again and, through a kind of

---

[16] See G. O'Collins, *Easter Faith: Believing in the Risen Jesus* (London: Darton, Longman & Todd, 2003), 33–38.

[17] E. Troeltsch, "Historical and Dogmatic Method in Theology," in Troeltsch, *Religion in History*, trans. James Luther Adams and Walter F. Bense (Edinburgh: T. & T. Clark, 1991), 11–32, at 13–14.

chain reaction, mistakenly imagined that they saw him.[18] They mistakenly attributed to an external source what they had produced themselves: the "presence" of the risen Christ. The post-resurrection appearances would then be totally internal, psychological events that took place in the minds and imaginations of the first disciples and were not produced by any external stimulus. In short, these so-called appearances were purely subjective visions, with no external reality corresponding to them.

The evidence that we have from the four Gospels does not, however, support any picture of Jesus' disciples excitedly expecting to meet him risen from the dead. Instead of persuading themselves into thinking that they saw him, they had to be persuaded that he was gloriously alive again (e.g., Matt 28:16–18; Luke 24:36–43; John 20:24–25). What the gospels record seems credible: the crisis of Jesus' arrest and disgraceful death on a cross left the disciples crushed. Only by ignoring the evidence can we picture them as anxiously awaiting his return from the dead and out of their imagination hallucinating his appearances.

The theory of an ecstatic, group hallucination might be more plausible if the New Testament had reported only one appearance, and that to a particular group on a particular day. Instead, it witnesses to appearances taking place over a period of time and to different groups as well as different individuals (e.g.,1 Cor 15:5–8). As regards the groups to whom Jesus appeared, the New Testament presents us with at least six cases: the Twelve (1 Cor 15:5); "all the apostles" (1 Cor 15:7; who seem to be a more extensive group than the Twelve); Simon Peter and six others (John 21:1–14); "more than five hundred believers" (1 Cor 15:6); Cleopas and his companion (Luke 24:13–35); and Mary Magdalene and "the

---

[18] See e.g. Lüdemann, *Resurrection of Jesus*, 79–84 (on Paul as allegedly hallucinated).

other Mary" (Matt 28:9–10). The variety of these traditions makes it quite unconvincing to reduce the six groups to one group, who on a specific occasion and by a kind of chain reaction imagined one after another that they saw Jesus.

A psychiatrist, Joseph W. Bergeron, joined forces with a New Testament scholar, Gary Habermas, to produce a landmark article on the hallucination hypothesis. Bergeron supplied technical, clinical considerations about the "complex and varied psychiatric and neuro-physical milieu required for hallucinations to occur", naively ignored by those who indulge hypotheses about the disciples hallucinating the presence of the risen Jesus. Such hypotheses are "at odds with current medical understanding." In particular, they offer "no acceptable explanation for the simultaneous group encounters of the disciples with the resurrected Jesus", but "prove to be unconvincing and implausible."[19]

The hallucination hypothesis depends on what the disciples already *believed* and *expected* before Jesus died. This hypothesis cannot account for two remarkably new things that the disciples began to proclaim.

First of all, what options were open to the disciples after Jesus was executed as a messianic pretender and blasphemer? Could they have modified their incipient messianic belief in Jesus and claimed him to be another martyred prophet, like John the Baptist? Hardly, it seems to me. To be crucified meant not only to suffer an utterly cruel and humiliating form of execution but also to die under a religious curse (Gal 3:13) and "outside the camp" of God's people (Heb 13:12–13). In other words, crucifixion was

---

[19] J. W. Bergeron and G. Habermas, "The Resurrection of Jesus: A Clinical Review of Psychiatric Hypotheses for the Story of Easter", *Irish Theological Quarterly* 80 (2015), 157–72.

seen as the death of a criminal and godless man who perished away from God's presence and in the place and company of irreligious persons.[20]

In fact, the disciples began preaching the crucified Jesus as the divinely endorsed Messiah risen from the dead to bring salvation to the whole world. The notion of a messiah who failed, suffered, was crucified, and then rose from the grave was simply foreign to pre-Christian Judaism, and hence could not have shaped any alleged hallucinations on the part of the disciples.[21] Since their previous religious beliefs could not have prompted them into making such startling claims about Jesus, what triggered this religious novelty? Where did it come from, if not from the resurrection of Jesus himself, now made known through his appearances and the discovery of his empty tomb?

The second novelty concerned a striking shift in religious expectations. By the time of Jesus, some or even many Jews cherished a hope that a resurrection of all the dead would bring an end to human history. But no one imagined that one individual would be raised to a new, transformed existence *in anticipation of the last day*. But then the followers of Jesus began proclaiming that one individual (Jesus) had already been raised to a glorious life which anticipated the end of all history.[22] What prompted this remarkable change in expectations that had no precedent in Jewish faith and hope, and so could not have fed into alleged hallucinations experienced by the disciples? Once again the plausible cause can

---

[20] On the crucifixion, see G. O'Collins, "Crucifixion," *Anchor Bible Dictionary*, vol. 1 (New York: Doubleday, 1992), 1207–10.

[21] The Servant of Isaiah 53 suffered to atone for the sins of others. But he was neither presented clearly as a messianic figure nor said to have been crucified and raised from the dead.

[22] See N. T. Wright, *The Resurrection of the Son of God* (Minneapolis: Fortress, 2003), 85–128.

only be the actual resurrection of Jesus, followed by his Easter appearances.

Lüdemann, Dale C. Allison,[23] and others have used the analogy of bereaved persons who experience their beloved dead to argue that the Easter appearances may have been nothing more than ancient episodes in the psychobiography of bereaved persons. But these writers persistently ignore decisive differences between the experiences of bereaved persons and those of Jesus' disciples shortly after his death and burial. Undoubtedly, we can make some positive comparisons between (a) the experiences of widows and widows studied by Dewi Rees and others and (b) the experiences of the disciples shortly after the death and burial of Jesus.[24] For instance, in both cases we learn of contact with the beloved dead, and it is contact that is life-giving. In both cases those who remain behind have experienced grief, even shattering grief, then followed by unexpected contact with the dead.

The analogy between (a) and (b), however, turns out to be not that close and illuminating. In *Believing in the Resurrection*, I drew attention to numerous points of dissimilarity.[25] First, the bereaved experienced through visions and in other ways their dead ones who had died, but never claimed that these deceased had risen from the dead. Second, that major Easter witness, St Paul, cannot be credited with a bereavement experience. He never knew Jesus

---

[23] See Lüdemann, *Resurrection of Jesus*, 79–84, 97–100. For details of Allison's position, see Matthew Levering, *Did Jesus Rise from the Dead? Historical and Theological Reflections* (Oxford: Oxford University Press, 2018), 40–47.

[24] See Dewi Rees, "The Hallucinations of Widowhood," *British Medical Journal*, 2 October 1971, 37–41. Later Rees regretted using the term "hallucinations"; it implied that the experiences of the bereaved were merely imaginary and not real. On Rees and his successors in his research, see O'Collins, *Believing in the Resurrection*, 72, 175–91, 214–18.

[25] O'Collins, *Believing in the Resurrection*, 179–89.

during the time of the public ministry, still less became a close and loving disciple. He met the risen Jesus as a hostile persecutor, not as a grief-stricken follower. Third, the manner of death in cases of (a) never included a case of death by public execution, still less a horrible and shameful death on the cross. The 293 widows and widowers studied by Rees lost their beloved ones through accidents or deaths by natural causes. He did not report any suicides or homicides, still less any executions. Fourth, apropos of the place of the spouses' death, 270 died at home (161 cases) or in hospital (109 cases). The places, no less than the manner of death examined by Rees, do not parallel what the Gospels report about the dramatic and terrible death that took Jesus away in the prime of life. A fifth reason for differentiating between the Easter experiences of the disciples and those of Rees's widows and widowers emerges from the New Testament reports of appearances to groups, as well as to individuals. The pioneering study by Rees reported only individuals who saw, heard, spoke to, or even felt touched by their dead spouses. The individual nature of these experiences moved them away from the resurrection witness in the New Testament, for which appearances of the risen Christ to groups are at least as significant as the appearances to individuals. A sixth dissimilarity arises when we notice that 40% of Rees's widows and widowers continued to experience their deceased spouses for many years. But the appearances of the risen Christ to individuals and groups took place over a limited amount of time and did not continue for many years. All this should be enough to illustrate some of the major dissimilarities between (a) and (b). Readers who are interested can consult the full list of dissimilarities in my *Believing in the Resurrection*.

Years ago in his *Theology of Hope: On the Ground and Implications of Christian Eschatology*, Jürgen Moltmann described Troeltsch's principle:

> It is generally acknowledged that historical understanding nowadays is always analogical understanding and must therefore remain within the realm of what is understandable in terms of analogy. The omnipotence thus attaching to analogy implies ... the basic similarity of all historical events. [This] presupposes that there is always a common core of similarity, on the basis of which the differences can be sensed and approved.

Moltmann realized that the "presupposition of a fundamental similarity underlying all events" raised serious difficulties against accepting Christ's resurrection and the Easter appearances, events which are strikingly new and even unique. Moltmann briefly insisted that dissimilarity forms the "the other side of the analogical process." Hence, absolutely speaking, analogical understanding does not exclude the resurrection and subsequent appearances of the risen Christ.[26]

This insight must be developed. When analogies for the resurrection of Christ and his Easter appearances are offered, we deal with things that are both like *and unlike*. We face both similarities *and dissimilarities*. We need to ask: does this analogy enjoy enough similarities to make it a close and illuminating comparison? Or is it characterized by too many dissimilarities, so that it fails to be a useful analogy? Sadly, such a calculus of dissimilarities and dissimilarities is something that rarely, if ever, turns up in studies of Christ's resurrection.

---

[26] Trans. James W. Leitch (London: SCM Press, 1967), 175–78.

Concern for Historical Truth in the First-Century Mediterranean World

Challenges to Jesus' resurrection which turn up every now and then can take the form of alleging that first-century writers and their readers had no firm grip on the difference between unfounded myths and historical events. Writers are supposed to have been free of any scruples about dressing up such myths (read "the miracles, resurrection and Easter appearances of Jesus") as history and selling them to a gullible public. Readers are supposed to have been naïve and incapable of recognizing that they were being deliberately deceived.

There is an unintended irony in such a picture coming from modern authors. Notoriously claims in 2003 about "Weapons of Mass Destruction" in Iraq deceived millions of people but proved to be a false "myth" created by western governments. But this is only one among many examples of unscrupulous fabrications that at least for a time have succeeded in hoodwinking a contemporary, gullible public. Nowadays dressing up myths and other fictions as true "facts" has assumed plague proportions. We live in a disinformation age when truth is persistently manipulated in politics and much popular culture but also, to some extent, in academia.[27]

Furthermore, such a picture of the first-century cultural standards normally disdains to recall the intellectual advances made in Graeco-Roman culture right up to the time of Jesus: by philosophers (e.g., Plato and Aristotle), historians (e.g., Thucydides), and mathematicians (e.g., the Pythagoreans). In their different fields, famous Mediterranean intellectuals and their practical counter-

---

[27] See Michiko Kakutani, *The Death of Truth: Notes on Falsehood in the Age of Trump* (New York: Tim Duggan Books, 2018); Peter Pomerantsev, *This is Not Propaganda* (London: Faber & Faber, 2019).

parts in engineering, architecture (e.g., Vitruvius) and law (e.g., Demosthenes and Cicero) cultivated and encouraged the pursuit of truth. Beyond question, they could be driven to write by propagandistic reasons: for instance, Julius Caesar (100–44 BC) in his *Gallic Wars*. But this work, so far from being a mere tissue of fictions and myths, provides a reasonably reliable guide to the Roman conquest of ancient Gaul.

Let me cite one example of an unsatisfactory approach to the issue of historical truth in the first century: M. David Litwa, *How the Gospels Became History: Jesus and Mediterranean Myths*.[28] For a presentation of this book on 13 August 2019 at the Australian Catholic University (Melbourne), Litwa offered the following summary:

> Did the early Christians believe their myths? Like most ancient and modern people, early Christians made efforts to present their myths in the most believable ways. [This book] explores how and why what became the four canonical gospels took on an historical cast...the evangelists responded to the pressures from Greco-Roman literary culture by using well-known historiographical tropes like the mention of famous rulers and kings, geographical notices, the introduction of eyewitnesses, vivid presentation, alternative reports, and a historical preface highlighting careful research. The evangelists deliberately shaped myths into historical discourse to maximize their plausibility for ancient audiences.

The "well-known historiographical tropes" that make up the heart of this summary enjoy their cross-cultural counterparts in innumerable modern works of history. Such works also men-

---
[28] Newhaven, CT: Yale University Press, 2018.

tion famous rulers, provide geographical detail, cite eyewitnesses, aim at vivid presentation, record alternative reports, and claim to be based on careful research. Does the presence of all of these "tropes" in William Manchester's two volumes on Winston Churchill (1874–1965) and Robert Caro's (still to be completed) life of Lyndon Baines Johnson (1908–73), for instance, mean that these remarkable works of contemporary biography are myths masquerading as history? Just because features of historical writing, either in the past or today, follow existing conventions does not by any means point to their mythical falsity. They are simply styles or ways of writing and do not automatically convict works of untruth. Has Litwa confused methods with content? But let us take point by point Litwa's summary.

First of all, the very title of his book presumes an implausible starting-point: a tissue of myths about Jesus constituted the original material that was then dressed up and presented historically in the four Gospels. A full debate with Litwa would involve confronting his position with major contemporary studies on Jesus (e.g., by James Dunn and Richard Bauckham) and major commentaries on the Gospels (e.g., by François Bovon, Ulrich Luz, and Joel Marcus). Such scholars converge in agreeing that the evangelists, for all their editing, interpreting, and embellishing, drew on historically reliable material recalling what Jesus said, did, and suffered.

We should remember also that many of the ancient myths about heroes either dealt with people who most probably never existed, like the legendary founders of Rome, Romulus and Remus. In some myths, these brothers were credited with being twins born of a vestal virgin raped by the god Mars. Other ancient myths dealt with figures who were genuinely historical but lived centuries earlier: for example, Plato. He was sometimes supposed to have had the god of wisdom, Phoebus Apollo, as his father. In the case of Jesus, however, we face someone whose existence is historically certain and who lived and died only a few decades before the Gospels were written.[29]

Second, Litwa answers his opening question ("Did the early Christians believe their myths?") with a strange picture. Early Christians may have believed in myths about Jesus, but these were myths created by themselves! They knew also that many people would not accept their mythical message unless it appeared to be based in history. Hence "the evangelists deliberately shaped myths about Jesus into historical discourse to maximize their plausibility for ancient audiences." They consciously decided to give their myths an "historical cast." To name this decision in ethical terms, deliberately shaping mere myths into true history is a form of lying. That would seriously denigrate the moral standards of the evangelists and understand Christianity to have originated in a "world of lies." The vast majority of New Testament scholars, not to mention others, would have great difficulty in taking seriously the hypothesis that Christianity began with such dishonesty on the part of the evangelists and their associates. Has a worldwide and vast effect, the history of Christianity, been caused by a huge deceit that concerns its key founding documents, the four Gospels?

Third, Litwa's "admission" that, "like most ancient and modern people, early Christians presented their myths in the most believable ways," may seem a gracious recognition that ancient people were not so different from us modern people. But more is at stake here. What of Litwa himself? As a not so different modern per-

---

[29] See Richard A. Burridge, *What Are the Gospels: A Comparison with Graeco-Roman Biography*, rev. edn (Grand Rapids: Eerdmans, 2004).

son, does he too want to present his "myths in the most believable ways"? Or does he pretend to belong to some privileged minority (among both "ancient and modern people") who refuse to indulge such a practice? Critics may easily think of Litwa's own conclusions as myths which he has himself created and which he dresses up as the true history about the foundation of Christianity.

Fourthly and finally, Litwa dismisses the references in the Gospel to "eyewitnesses" as example of a non-historical trope; the so-called eyewitnesses were merely literary and not true eyewitnesses. Naturally the beloved disciple, an eyewitness in the Fourth Gospel, is written off as a purely literary figure. In recent years, Richard Bauckham has strongly and, for many, persuasively disputed both points. Genuinely historical eye-witness fed into all four Gospels, and the beloved disciple was a truly historical figure.[30]

Theological Issues

Besides philosophical and biblical/historical issues, exploring faith in Jesus risen from the dead also involves various theological issues. Let me attend to two of them: the nature of the divine action at work in the resurrection of Jesus, and the differences that belief in the resurrection has made in human life.

The Divine Activity

The Resurrection of God Incarnate by Richard Swinburne[31] contains much that is relevant and convincing, but I must protest against his reducing Jesus' resurrection to the category of miracle and describing miracles as "violations of natural laws".[32] First, the

---

[30] R. Bauckham, *Jesus and the Eyewitnesses: The Gospels as Eyewitness Testimony*, 2nd edn (Grand Rapids: Eerdmans, 2017).
[31] Oxford: Oxford University Press, 2003.
[32] Swinburne, *Resurrection of God Incarnate*, 186, 190.

resurrection should not be called a "miracle" or even a "super-miracle". Jesus' miracles are, to be sure, signs of what he wishes to do for us in the final kingdom (in the perfect bodily "healing" of the resurrection). Nevertheless, they happened and happen within our historical world of space and time, even while they point to what is to come. The resurrection of Jesus goes well beyond any such miracles: it was and is the real beginning of the world to come, the event which initiates a sequence of final events that will fulfil and complete his personal rising from the dead (1 Cor 15:20–28). Second, *violate* has four meanings, all of them negative and even ugly: (1) disregard or fail to comply with; (2) treat with disrespect; (3) disturb or break in upon; (4) assault sexually. Presumably Swinburne wants to use *violate* in sense (1). But when working miracles occasionally and for good reasons, God is surely better described as suspending or overriding the normal working of the laws of nature. Since it was God who first created the precise shape and functions of the laws of nature, it seems odd to speak of God "disregarding" or "failing to comply with" them. *Suspending* or *overriding* seems more appropriate language to describe the divine causality at work in the resurrection.

What might we say about this causality?[33] Three principles may help to clarify matters a little. First, it is easier to grasp and talk about effects than about causes. Effects can often be obvious; causes and their precise nature can remain shadowy and mysterious. Creation itself offers a basic example. We see and in other ways experience a vast sample of created reality every day. But we never directly observe the cause of this effect: God's activity in creation and conservation. At best we glimpse God's creative action

---

[33] See Paul Gwynne, *Special Divine Action: Key Issues in the Contemporary Debate (1965–1995)* (Rome: Gregorian University Press, 1996); R. J. Read and K. A. Richman (eds), *The New Hume Debate* (London: Routledge, 2000).

only in and through its effects. In its mythical way, the Book of Genesis symbolizes this point by picturing Adam being plunged into "a deep sleep", so that he could not observe the creation of Eve (Gen 2:21–22).

Second, a traditional adage about "every agent bringing about something similar to itself (*omne agens agit sibi simile*)" reminds us that efficient causes are also exemplary causes. Effects reflect the "form" of their causes. Children resemble their parents, not only through their common humanity but also genetically and in other ways. In their color, shape, and scent, new roses will take after the bushes from which they have been grown. Causes leave their impression on their effects. They are present in their effects, which participate in them. Hence all effects, albeit in varying ways and degrees, participate in God and share the divine life.

Israelite history illustrates a third principle or characteristic of divine activity. God's different acts on behalf of the chosen people took place in view of a future completion. Together they formed a dramatic movement towards a final goal, a progressive assimilation to God that aimed at full participation in the divine life and presence. Admittedly, God often had to write straight with crooked lines. Human freedom and human dissidents saw to that. Nevertheless, God's acts are never disconnected, still less arbitrary. Paul can reckon on a final divine unity in God's ceaseless activity for the salvation of Jews and Gentiles (Rom 9–11), even if the apostle must admit a deep mystery in the unfolding story (Rom 11:33–35). Israel's special history wrote large what many spiritually sensitive people continue to experience: God's providential activity for each one moves progressively towards its final goal: the fullest possible assimilation to God and participation in the divine presence.[34]

If these reflections are acceptable, how do they fare when applied to the resurrection of the crucified Jesus? Here the first principle stated above is dramatically exemplified. Mary Magdalene, Peter, Paul, and the other Easter witnesses saw the primary and immediate effect of the resurrection manifested to them, the living Jesus himself. They gave their causal explanation: "he has been raised from the dead." But they never claimed either to have witnessed the divine cause in action (the very resurrection itself) or to understand how it worked. In faith, they knew the cause, the resurrecting power of God, but, unlike its effect, that cause remained shrouded in the deepest mystery.

Second, in the resurrection, the divine agent brought about something *sibi simile*. God's resurrecting power left its impression on the effect, Jesus's raised and glorified humanity. In his transformed human existence, Jesus became even more like unto God, as the Son in whom one can recognize even more fully the image of his Father (Rom 1:3–4). Christ's risen humanity reflects and resembles to the ultimate extent possible its divine cause. In the highest degree possible, through his risen life he also participates in God (Rom 6:10).

Finally, the third principle we detected in divine activity towards human beings is realized par excellence in the case of Jesus' resurrection. The divine activity at work, from the incarnation on, formed a dynamic movement towards its future completion: Christ's full participation in the divine presence when he "sits at

---

[34] See William Hasker, "Providence". *Routledge Encyclopedia of Philosophy*, vol 7 (1998), 797–802.

God's right hand" (Rom 8:34) after he has "subjected all things" to God (1 Cor 15:20–28).

The Resurrection and Human Lives

Apologetical theology raises questions about the differences which belief in Jesus' resurrection has made in human lives. Levering, while finding my arguments for the resurrection "quite powerful," believes a "major problem" remains: "if Jesus truly rose from the dead, the world would surely be now a much better place than it is. Why should anyone pay attention to arguments about Jesus' resurrection nearly 2000 years after the event was supposed to have taken place, given that in many ways the world has only gone from bad to worse?"[35]

In *Jesus Risen: An Historical, Fundamental and Systematic Examination of Christ's Resurrection*,[36] I did raise this question: "what testable and valuable differences has belief in the resurrection made to human lives?" The question was then filled out: "have the lives of those who accepted Christ's resurrection proved (i) deeply satisfying and worthwhile to them, and (ii) productive, even heroically productive, to others?" By way of an answer I cited signs of the presence of the risen Lord "in recognizable examples of saintliness". Then I added other "testable and valuable effects" of the living Christ working through his Holy Spirit: "the personal witness of Christians and their various movements concerned with education, medical care, and work for refugees, drug addicts, prisoners and the powerless poor." In many ways there have been signs of the world becoming a better place through faith in the risen Christ.

---

[35] Levering, *Did Jesus Rise from the Dead?*, 27.
[36] (New York: Paulist Press, 1987), 144–45.

Questioning the effects of faith in the resurrection to be recognized in the last two thousand years calls for a book-length response. In part such a response has been provided by a work published by Mario Farrugia and myself.[37] But I say "in part," since our work focused on past and present Catholic life and would need to be supplemented to achieve a truly global vision of Christian history and the signs it displays of the risen Christ's presence and activity. Such signs come, above all, from the lives of such saintly men and women as Dietrich Bonhoeffer, Chiara Lubich, Dorothy Day, Pope John XXIII, Oscar Romero, Mother Teresa of Calcutta, Nguyen Van Thuan, and Thérèse Vanier.

As is obvious above, biblical and philosophical considerations converge with theological insights for those who wish to reflect on the uniquely special activity of God that effected the resurrection of Jesus and on the valuable differences belief in the resurrection has made in human lives. These are closing examples for a chapter that has aimed to map some of the major, cumulative tasks facing scholars who explore Jesus' resurrection. They need to possess considerable gifts in philosophy, historical/biblical studies, and theology.

---

[37] *Catholicism: The Story of Catholic Christianity*, 2nd edn (Oxford: Oxford University Press, 2015).

Epilogue

This collection of New Testament essays comes divided into three sections: questions arising from the Gospels of Matthew, Mark, Luke, and John; (2) topics concerned with the Pauline Letters (understood in a wider sense that includes the Letter to the Hebrews); and (3) perspectives on Jesus' preaching and resurrection. But, one way or another, all the chapters examine the person and work of Jesus.

Chapter 5 reflects on his virginal conception and its significance; chapters 1, 2, 3, and 13 centre on the manner and content of his unique preaching; chapter 11 interprets his whole life as being lived with perfect faith, from start to finish; chapters 4, 7, 8, 9, 14, and 15 face issues emerging from his death on a cross and glorious resurrection from the dead; chapter 6 presents a dynamic view of believing in the incarnate and risen Jesus developed by John's Gospel; chapter 10 proposes lessons to be drawn from Paul, the great apostle of Jesus, to guide the spiritual reform of the Vatican Curia; finally, chapter 12 takes up the task of translating the Letter to the Hebrews, a NT text unique for its exposition of Jesus' high priesthood.

In its variety and unity I hope that this volume might satisfy the personal interests which different readers bring to reflections about Jesus nourished by the New Testament. From the outset, Christians found in him a unique answer to life's questions. To cite an evangelical refrain, "Jesus is Lord. Jesus is King. Jesus is our everything."

Do these fifteen chapters convey fresh insights? I leave it to the readers to reply.

Index of Names

Adams, J. L. 223 n.

Alexander the Great 55–56

Allison, D. C. 5, 6 n., 7, 8 n., 10, 12 n., 13 n., 14 n., 15 n., 16 n., 17, 19–20, 21 n., 196, 203, 207, 227 n.

Alston, W. P. 216

Angelico, Beato 61

Aquinas, St Thomas x, 152, 157, 215, 217

Archer, J. vi, 49–62

Aristotle 182, 230

Arndt, W. F. 3 n., 28 n., 29 n., 63 n., 89 n., 103 n., 162 n.

Attridge, H. W. 154–55, 161 n., 170 n.

Audi, R. 215 n.

Augustine of Hippo, St 12 n., 59–60, 197, 212

Augustus Caesar, Emperor 56

Badham, L. 198

Badham, P. 198

Balentine, S. B. 34 n.

Balthasar, H. U. von 12, 24

Baltzer, K. 104 n., 117

Barrett, C. K. 67, 70, 80 n., 89

Barton, J. 159, 160 n.

Basil the Great, St 12

Bauckham, R. 52 n., 110, 126 n., 186 n., 199–200, 232, 234

Bauer, W. 3 n., 28 n., 29 n., 63 n., 89 n., 103 n., 162 n.

Beasley-Murray, G. R. 65 n.

Bennett-Hunter, Guy x

Bense, W. F. 223 n.

Bergeron, J. W. 205, 225 n.

Bertram of Minden, Master 60–61

Betz, H. D. 114

Bockmuehl, M. 110, 126 n.

Bodrov, A. xi

Boer, M. C. De 77 n.

Bonfiglio, R. P. 34

Bonhoeffer, D. 239

Boring, M. E. 44

Bourke, M. 153 n.

Bovon, F. 13 n., 22 n., 123, 186 n., 232

Bowden, J. 204 n., 219 n.

Brettler, M. Z. 151

Bromiley, G. 65 n.

Brown, Raymond E. 23, 50 n., 56, 69–70, 79, 85 n., 86 n., 88, 91–92, 95. 98. 126 n., 153 n., 186n.

Bruce, F. F. 127 n.

Bultmann, R. 20 n., 64–66, 70–71

Burridge, R. A. 233 n.

Byrne, B. 74, 79, 128 n., 138 n.

Calvin, J. 152 n.

Capizzi, N. 101 n., 122–23

Caro, R. 232

Carson, D. A. 85 n., 99

Carter, W. 26 n.

Celsus 195–96, 203

Chadwick, Henry 50 n., 56 n., 196 n.

Challoner, R. 147

Churchill, W. 232
Cicero, Marcus Tullius 231
Claudius, Emperor 139
Coady, C. A. J. 219 n.
Coogan, M. D. 115 n., 151
Cook, J. G. 102 n.
Costa. T. 80 n.
Coverdale, M. 146 n., 149
Crouch, J. E. 14 n., 31 n., 120 n.
Culpepper, R. A. 71–72
Cyril of Alexandria, St 50
Cyril of Jerusalem, St 12, 59

Dante Alighieri 181–82, 193
Danker, F. W. 3 n., 29 n., 63 n., 89 n., 103 n., 162 n.
Daucy, J. 215 n.
Dautzenberg, E. 165 n.
Davies, B. xi, 217 n.
Davies, W. D. 5, 6 n., 7, 8 n., 10, 12 n., 14 n., 15 n., 16 n., 17, 19–20, 21 n.
Day, D. 239
Deer, D. S. 13 n., 121 n.
Delling, G. 3 n.
De May, P. 12 n.
Demosthenes 231
Denzinger, Heinrich 59 n.
Descartes, R. 182
DeSilva, D. A. 151, 156
Deventer, C. Van 76–77
Diodorus Siculus 54–55
Dionysus of Halicarnassus 55
Dodd, C. H. 66, 70, 148
Donfried, K. P. 126 n,
Dunn, J. D. G. 102–103, 232
Dwyer, Timothy 44–45

Eliot, T. S. 182
Ellingworth, P. 156
Evans, C. A. 12 n., 14 n., 19
Eych, Hubert van 161
Eych, Jan van 161

Faggioli, M. viii, 125, 143
Farrugia, M. 239
Fee, G. D. 103 n., 110, 117, 130 n., 131 n.,
Fitzmyer, J. A. 107 n., 117–18, 128 n., 130 n., 138–40, 153 n., 186
Foçant, C. 25 n., 30, 46–47
Francis, Pope 143
Freedman, D. N. 33 n., 127 n.
Funk, R. W. 146 n.

Gadamer, H.-G. xi, 181, 185, 192, 220
Gill, R. xi
Gillman, F. M. 127 n., 138 n., 140 n.
Gillman, J. 127 n.
Gingrich, W. 3 n., 28 n., 29 n., 63 n., 89 n., 103 n., 162 n.
Grässer, E. 165 n.
Gregersen, N. xi
Grobel, K. 65 n.
Grosvenor, M. 97 n.
Gupta, N. K. 109–10
Gwynne, P. 235

Habermas, G. 205. 225 n.
Hamm, D. 155–56
Harvey, J. W. 39 n.
Hasker, W. 237 n.
Hawthorne, G. F. 110

INDEX OF NAMES

Heidegger, M. 181
Hengel, M. 126 n.
Herod the Great, King 191
Hoare, R. W. N. 65
Hofius, O. 103 n.
Holloway, P. A. viii, 100–24
Homer 190
Hooker, M. D. 27, 37, 41–42, 117
Hoover, R. 109
Hoy, P. xi
Huemer, M. 215 n.
Hughes, G. 154–56
Hünermann, Peter 59 n.
Hunsinger, George 101 n.
Hurtado, L. 103 n., 110

Ignatius of Antioch, St 138 n.
Irenaeus, St 7, 52, 59
Iscariot, Judas vi–vii, 16, 40–41, 49–62, 89

Jewett, R. 128 n.
John Chrysostom, St 12, 15 n.
John XXIII, Pope St 239
Johnson, W. B. 232
Josephus, Flavius 200
Joubert, S. J. 135 n.
Julius Caesar 191, 231
Justin Martyr, St 52–54

Kakutani, M. 230 n.
Kant, I. 182, 184
Käsemann, E. 110
Keener, C. S. 72–73, 88 n.
Kelly, J. N. D. 221
Keylock, L. R. 25 n., 47 n.
King, N. 150, 152, 170

Kittel, G. 65 n.
Kittredge, C. B. 151, 156
Klink, E. W. 84–86
Knox, R. A. 147–50, 169
Koestenberger, A. J. 63 n., 73, 88 n., 89
Koester, C. R. 155–56, 161–63, 165 n., 167 n.
Kohl, M. 117 n.
Kon, G. A. 87 n.
Krailsheimer, A. J. 212 n.

Lampe, P. 126 n., 139 n.
Laynesmith, M. 3, 10
Lee, D. E. xi
Légasse, S. 26 n.
Leitch, J. 210 n., 229 n.
Leo the Great, St 59
Levering, M. 196 n., 199 n., 227 n., 238
Lieu, J. M. 76 n.
Lightfoot, R. H. vi, 37–39
Lincoln, A. T. 73, 87–88
Lindemann, A. 118
Lindsay, D. R. 65 n.
Lippi, Fra Lippo 61
Litwa, M. D. 231–34
Livy 55
Loader, W. 63–65
Lonergan, B. 220
Louth, A. 164 n.
Lubich, C. 239
Lüdemann, G. 204, 207, 219–20, 223–27
Luther, M. 152 n., 168
Luz, Ulrich 6, 13 n., 14–15, 17, 19–20, 30, 31 n., 32, 120, 186 n., 232

Madwig, D. H. 28 n.
Magness, J. L. 45 n., 46–47
Manchester, W. 232
Marcus, J. vi, 25–33, 37, 43–44, 199, 232
Marmion, D. xi
Marsh. J. 20 n.
Marshall, D. G. 220 n.
Martin, M. 109
Martin, R. 11–12
Martin, R. P. 110
Martyn, J. L. 114–15, 133 n.
Marxsen, W. 197–98
McMurray, P. xi
Meier, J. P. 186 n.
Merrigan, T. xi, 12
Metzger, B. M. 151
Meyer, B. F. 14
Michel, O. 153–56
Moffatt, J. 147–50, 170
Moller, P. xi
Moloney, F. J. 25 n., 33 n., 37, 42–43, 49–62, 87–88
Moltmann, J. 209–10, 229
Montgomery, W. 121 n.
Moo, D. J. 93, 128 n.
Morgan, T. 74–76, 78
Moule, C. F. D. 197 n.
Muggeridge, M. 195, 212–13
Murphy, R. E. 151, 153 n.

Nagel, T. 218 n.
Nero, Emperor 139
Nickle, K. F. 135 n.
Nida, E. A. 160 n., 162 n.
Nineham, Dennis 30, 37–39, 46–47
Nolland, J. 31

O'Brien, P. T. 110
Ollrog, W.-H. 127 n.
Origen 25, 123, 196 n.
Otto, R. 39–40

Pappas, G. S. 215 n.
Pascal, B. 212, 217
Perkins, P. 151
Perrin, N. 37, 40–41
Pesch, R. 37, 39–40, 46–47
Peterman, G. W. 110
Phillips, J. B. 148 n., 149–50, 169
Pilate, Pontius 191, 201
Plato 52, 55, 181–82, 230, 232
Plutarch 56
Polanyi, M. 218
Pomerantsev, P. 230 n.
Pompey 190
Pythagoras 230

Rahner, K., 12, 24, 34
Read, R. J. 235 n.
Rees, D. 203 n., 208–09, 227–28
Reumann, J. 126 n., 132 n., 136 n., 140 n.
Richardson, C. A. 152., 156
Riches, J. K. 65 n.
Richman, K. A. 235 n.
Rogers, J. 35 n.
Romero, St Oscar 239

Sakenfeld, K. D. 135 n.
Schmemann, A. 212
Schnackenburg, R. 63 n., 68–69, 87, 91, 94, 186
Schrage, W. 118 n.

INDEX OF NAMES

Schweitzer, A. 121
Schweizer, E. 28 n.
Scullion, J. J. 33 n.
Silva, M. 110
Smith, D. 87 n.
Smyth, K. 63 n.
Socrates 181, 184, 183
Sorell, T. 217 n.
Sosa, E. 215 n.
Spadaro, A. xi
Spicq, C. 152–53, 156–57
Spitzer, R. J. 217 n.
Steinhauser, M. 126 n.
Stemp, M. 215 n.
Stibbe, M. W. G. 85 n.
Suetonius 56
Swartley, W. M. 86 n., 90
Swinburne, R. 211, 234

Talbert, C. H. 85 n.
Teresa of Calcutta, Mother St 213, 239
Tertullian 195
Thiselton, A. C. 107 n., 118 n.
Thuan, Nguyen Van 239
Thucydides 230
Thyen, H. 86, 90
Trapp, T. H. 126 n.
Troeltsch, E. 209–10, 223, 229
Tyndale, W. passim

Vanhoye, A. 153, 155–57

Vanier, T. 239
Virgil 190
Vitruvius 231

Wahle, U. C. von 30, 88
Wansbrough, H. 148
Wallace, D. B. 77–78, 84, 97 n.
Walsh, B. xi
Weber, H. R. 26 n.
Weinsheimer, J. 220 n.
Wengst, K. 86–87, 89
Wenzel, D. H. 11 n.
Westcott, B. F. 88–89, 152–53, 155–56
Whitacre, R. A. 87, 90
Wicks, J. xi
Wiebe, P. H. 217 n.
Wilkins, J. 161 n.
Winch, P. 213 n.
Wippel, J. F. 217 n.
Witherington, B. 86 n., 110
Witherup, R. xi
Williams, C. H. 76 n., 79 n.
Wittgenstein, L. 182–84, 213
Wordsworth, W. 182
Wright, N. T. 107 n., 110, 207 n., 211–12, 226 n.
Wycliffe, J. 146 n.

Yarbro Collins, A. 26 n.

Zerwick, M. 97 n.

BIBLICAL INDEX

Old Testament

Genesis
1:26–27 102, 103
2:21–22 236
3:15 62
6:1–4 50
6:11 50
15:12 43
18:2–15 27
19:1–14 27

Exodus
3:14 33

Leviticus
11:44 5
11:45 5
19:2 5, 7
20:7 5

Numbers
13:33 50

Deuteronomy
2:10–11 50
6:4 118
6:4–5 107
16:9–12 210
18:13 5

1 Samuel
2:1–10 57

2 Esdras
8:3 14
9:15 14

Isaiah
7:14 57
7:14–16 34
9:1–7 34
11:1–2 58
42:14 32
45:23 104, 106, 111, 115, 116, 117, 123
49:15–16 32
53 206, 226
66:13 32

Hosea
2:19 24
11:1–11 34

Jonah
3:4 21

Daniel
7:15 39
7:28 39
8:17 39
8:27 39
10:7 39
10:15 43

Tobit
12:1–20 27

New Testament

Matthew
1:18–25 vii
1:21 6
1:23 6
4:1–11 6

5:1–2 3
5:3 10
5:3–12 6
5:20 4
5:21–22 182
5:21–48 7
5:44 7
5:45 6, 183
5:48 3, 4, 5, 10
7:13–14 22
7:21–23 22
8:11–12 15
9:10–11 24
9:11–12 11
11:4 185
11:7 184
11:25–30 10
11:29 10
12:7 5
12:13–17 191
12:36–37 184
13:24–30 16
13:33 31
13:36–43 16
13:44 32
13:47–50 16, 18
16:6 32
19:16 8
19:16–21 7
19:16–30 10, 19
19:18–21 4, 6
19:21 4, 8
19:23–24 9
19:26 9
19:27 9
21:28–32 19, 23
21:33–45 24

21:33–46 15, 19
22:1 22
22:1–7 15
22:1–14 v, 10, 12, 23, 24
22:3–7 20
22:4 12
22:6 12, 13
22:7 12, 13
22:8–9 12
22:8–14 17
22:9–13 20
22:11–13 12, 16
22:13 13
22:14 11, 12, 21
24:45–51 19
25:1–13 19, 22
25:31–46 19, 22, 28, 35
25:35 28
25:40 28
25:43 28
25:45 28
26:29 12
27:45 7
27:51–54 7
27:57–61 202
28:1 16
28:1–8 198
28:2 7
28:7 16
28:9–10 205, 225
28:10 16
28:11–15 15
28:16 16
28:16–18 204, 224
28:16–20 16
28:19 53

BIBLICAL INDEX

Mark
1:1–3 29
1:3 47
1:11 105
1:29–31 42
1:44 45
2:7 29
2:10 29
2:21 187
2:22 187
4:35–41 38
4:41 38
5:19–20 29
5:34 42
6:52 40
7:29 42
8:14–21 41
9:2 25
9:2–8 32
9:33–37 31
9:35 25
9:36–37 vi, 25
9:37 26, 27, 28
10:17–31 8
10:21 8, 182
12:26–27 35
12:41–44 42
13:17 188
13:32 23
14:3–9 40
14:5–9 42
14:36 35
14:50 42
14:51–52 41
14:52 42
15:33 45
15:40 40, 200
15:40–41 40, 42, 200
15:42–47 40, 201
15:47 40, 42
16:1 40
16:1–8 37, 40, 43, 45–47, 197–98, 202
16:2 45
16:5–8 38
16:6 43
16:7 46, 199, 200
16:8 38, 40, 41, 43, 47

Luke
1:5–17 58
1:20 39
1:26–38 vii, 54
1:31–32 60
1:46–55 57
1:58 58
3:23–37 57
4:23 192
5:34 188
5:39 192
6:9 184
6:36 5
7:22–23 58
10:29–37 192
11:5–8 189
11:11–12 188
12:16–21 187
12:24 190
12:27 190
12:54–55 187
13:1–2 191
13:34 190
14:15–24 10, 12
14:18–20 13

14:21–23 13
14:24 14
15:8–9 188
15:11–32 188
16:18 187
16:21 184
18:22 8
19:12 191
23:34 7
23:50–56 201
24:1–10 197
24:10 200
24:13–35 205, 224
24:34 195
24:36–43 204, 224

John
1:1–12 65
1:4 80
1:4–5 79
1:5 80
1:7 64, 78, 79
1:12 75, 78, 79
1:14 73
1:37 79
1:40–42 72
1:43 65
2:11 72, 75, 79, 80
2:19–22 94
2:22 90, 91
2:23 79
2:23–24 80
4:42 65, 79
5:1–18 72
5:8 96
5:21 95
5:24 65

5:25 95
5:26 95
5:28–29 95
5:29 96
5:40 65
6:29 67
6:35 65, 80
6:39 96
6:39–40 96
6:40 96
6:44 71, 76, 79, 96
6:54 96
6:65 76
6:66 72, 79, 89
6:67 89
6:69 63, 65, 66, 67
6:70 89
6:71 89
7:29 67
7:37 65
8:29 80
8:43 66
8:45–47 66
8:55 67
9:1–41 72
10:5 66
10:11 95
10:15 67, 95
10:16 66
10:17–18 95
10:18 86
10:27 66
10:30 95
10:37–38 95
11:9 80
11:23 96
11:24 96

BIBLICAL INDEX

11:25 86, 96, 98
11:26 78, 79
11:31 96
12:9 91
12:17 91
13–17 97
13:16 89
14:1 78
14:3 96
14:6 96
14:8–14 76
14:18 96
14:23 96
15:4–7 65
16:16 96
17:26 96
18:15–18 90
18:25–27 90
19:31 94
19:38–42 202
19:41–42 195
20 88, 89
20:1–2 199
20:2 203
20:8–9 76
20:9 96
20:11–18 88, 89, 195
20:11–19 213
20:13–15 203
20:19–23 88, 90
20:24 89
20:24–25 204, 224
20:24–29 90
20:26–29 88
20:31 63, 78, 79
21:1 84, 85
21:1–14 97, 205, 225
21:4–14 88
21:14 vii, 84– 89, 91–92, 97–98

Acts
3:1–10 58
4–15 134
5:14–16 58
8:4–8 58
8:14–25 126
9:32–43 58, 126
10:23 127
10:24 126
10:45 127
11:12 127
12:19 126
13 201
13:16–41 201
13:27–31 201
13:28–31 202, 222
14:8–10 58
15 126
15:22–18:5 128
16 132
16:2–3 141
16:3 129
16:11–40 212
18:2 139
18:3 139
18:5 130
19:22 130
19:23 140
28:26 139

Romans
1:3–4 237
4:24–25 93
5:5–10 105

5:8–10 124
5:12–21 103
6:4 93
6:9 93
6:10 237
7:4 93
8:3 124
8:11 93
8:32 105, 124
8:34 238
8:38 104
9–11 236
11:33–35 236
12:1 173
14:10–11 116, 117
15:20 126
15:25–27 135
16 128
16:1–2 127, 138
16:2 138
16:3 139
16:3–15 128
16:4 139
16:9 140
16:16 128
16:17–20 128
16:20 128
16:21–23 128

1 Corinthians
1:12 126
2:9 168
3:9 140
4:2 131
4:15–17 130
4:17 129, 130
6:14 92
8:3 104
8:6 102, 107, 117, 118
9:6 134
11:1 130
15:3–8 203
15:4 93
15:5 195, 224
15:5–8 205, 224
15:6 205, 224
15:7 205, 224
15:12 93
15:15 94
15:20 210
15:20–22 93
15:20–28 235, 238
15:23 210
15:32 140
16:1–4 135
16:10 129
16:10–11 129, 130
16:19 139

2 Corinthians
1:1 129, 130, 134
1:8–9 140
1:19 128, 130, 134
2:3–4 134
2:7–8 134
2:13 134
4:6 35
4:14 93
7:6–7 134
7:13–15 135
8:6 135
8:16–17 135
8:18 136
8:22–23 136

BIBLICAL INDEX

8:23 135
9:5 136
11:14 104
11:28 132
12:4 39
12:14–18 135
12:18 136
13:13 53

Galatians
1:1 92
1:8 104, 115
2:1 134
2:1–10 133
2:11–21 126
2:9 134
2:13 134
3:13 206, 225
3:19 104
4:4 124
4:14 114, 115
4:16 75
5:9 31

Ephesians
4:15 76

Philippians
1:1 129, 140
1:12–26 129
1:27–30 141
2 116, 124
2:6 102
2:6–7 103
2:6–8 111
2:6–11 viii, 101, 103–05, 111, 113–14, 117, 122–23
2:7 103
2:9–11 106
2:10–11 viii, 115, 116, 123
2:9 v
2:11 106, 109
2:17 173
2:19–24 131
2:25 137
2:25–30 136
2:26–30 137
4:2–3 140
4:3 141
4:18 136, 137, 173–74

Colossians
1:1 129
2:18 105
4:10–14 141

1 Thessalonians
1:1 128
1:6 130
1:10 93
2:7 128
3:2 128
2:19 130
3:2 130

2 Thessalonians
2:1 129

1 Timothy
1:3 129

2 Timothy
1:1–3:22 129, n, 11

Titus
1:4 136
1:5 136

Philemon
1:1–3 129
24 141

Hebrews
1:3 167
1:3a 175
2:10 6
2:17 155
2:17–18 155
3:1–6 156
3:2 155
4:15 155, 156
5:7–8 155
5:9 5
10:5–10 155
11 166
11:1 165, 176, 177
11:1–40 155
11:1–12:1 152
11:1–12:2 145
11:1–12:3 156, 165
11:1–12:23
11:1–40 155
11:4 145
11:11 145
12:1 145
12:1–2 155
12:2 176
12:2a ix, 145–58, 169–70, 177
13:2 27
13:12–13 206, 225
13:15 173
13:16 171, 174–76
13:23 129

1 Peter
1:1 126
2:5 173, 174
5:12–13 127
5:13 126

www.ingramcontent.com/pod-product-compliance
Lightning Source LLC
Chambersburg PA
CBHW070321240426
43671CB00013BA/2327